AF344458

THE "Q" MODEL
For the Effective Management of
PERSONAL STRESS

THE "Q" MODEL

FOR THE EFFECTIVE MANAGEMENT OF PERSONAL STRESS

Edward Zerin, Ph.D.
and Marjory Zerin, Ph.D.

Foreword by Virginia M. Satir

GARDNER PRESS, INC.
New York   London

GARDNER PRESS, INC.
19 Union Square West
New York 10003

All foreign orders except Canada and South America to:
Afterhurst Limited
Chancery House
319 City Road
London N1, United Kingdom

Library of Congress Cataloging-in-Publication Data

Zerin, Edward.
   The "Q" model for the effective management of personal
stress.

   Bibliography: p.
   Includes index.
   1. Stress (Psychology) I. Zerin, Marjory. II. Title.
BF575.S75Z46 1985   158′.1   85-15856
ISBN 0-89876-107-7

Printed in the United States of America

Diagrams by Aldo Pellini
Book design by Sidney Solomon

To our grandson

Joshua Stephen

and our children

Jonathan

Wendy

Michael

Ruth

TABLE OF CONTENTS

ILLUSTRATIONS

TABLES

FOREWORD

Fifty years ago, this book would not and could not have been written. It would not even have been conceived of. I make a point of this, because this book, with its unique "Q" Model diagram, represents an important evolutionary link in human beings' management of themselves.

Most of the information on which this book is based has surfaced since 1946. Perhaps as much as 80 percent of our current medical knowledge has been discovered since that time, and, technologically, we have made Buck Rogers, including "the impossible journey" to the moon, a living reality.

Two spectacular and gruesome events occurred just prior to 1946, however, which make the contents and contributions of this book especially welcome—even imperative. The first was World War II, initiated by Adolph Hitler and perpetuated by other Nazis, which resulted in the deaths of tens of millions of people and included the deliberate and systematic, cold-blooded murder of millions of innocents, including six million Jews. This gross and almost unthinkable activity was carried out by human beings, by persons who, like you and me, had names; by people who, like you and me, were sons and daughters, mothers and fathers to someone.

The nagging question is, what has to happen for human beings to behave in this way toward their fellow human beings? The answer lies within the province of this book. Those people were profoundly distressed, and I use "distress" as defined by the authors. The Nazis' behavior showed the ultimate in what distress can do. Distressed people act out of fear, defensiveness and blind protectiveness. The specter of Hitler—and the physical, psychological, and spiritual upheaval that resulted universally—still haunts us today. It is a sobering thought to know that such events could happen again—to any and all persons who negate their life energies, and to their victims.

The other earth-shaking event closed the war in the Pacific. The United States dropped an atom bomb on Hiroshima and Nagasaki in Japan, killing tens of thousands of innocent people. That we had the technology to accomplish this and willingly chose to rain such a destruction upon others in the name of peace also shook the world.

I believe that the responses to these two events led inevitably to the emergence of the next evolution in humankind. With the resounding defeat of Hitler, Tojo and Mussolini, there was an air of attention to justice and freedom. All the "sacred cows" of the past were challenged. The United Nations was born of this optimism. A review of the legal changes since 1946, with respect to human beings, is impressive. The changes in divorce laws, the new place of women and of minorities in society and the new attitudes toward sex are all indications of the beginning of a new respect for human rights. All the hungers and the longings that had been voiceless now began to be voiced. Society was waking up to new possibilities for being and becoming. Much of this was embraced in something called the Human Potential Movement. Peering around the corner was the notion that human beings could understand themselves;

indeed, they could actively take charge of their own lives. This book is a manifestation of what one needs to know—and how one can use that knowledge—to live a happier, more creative life.

Actually, most of the information contained in this book is known on some level by almost all human beings. In the past, it was regarded as private, so it was not shared. Individuals would conclude that they were the only ones and alone. Well, the secret is out, and the authors present the material in a way that makes it possible for everyone to identify with it. I can hear the "aha's" as people read, study and use this book.

Up until recently, most "ordinary" people believed that all things psychological were of the provinces of psychology and psychologists and basically of use only to people who had "problems." This point of view was also shared by many professionals. Now, the same professionals have come to believe that people need, in their own hands, the tools for personal change and growth. This book provides good ways to put these tools into the hands of laypeople.

The "Q" Model is simple without being simplistic, wonderfully human and engaging. The authors, both of whom are active professionals, have done a fine service in writing this book.

Virginia M. Satir

PREFACE AND ACKNOWLEDGMENTS

Distress, not Stress, is the enemy. Stress is natural, a human birthright. Stress is the life energy to think, to feel and to act—seeking to express itself.

Distress is the misuse of the human birthright. It is the abuse of Stress.

Borrowing the term Eustress from Dr. Hans Selye, the father of stress research, we urge our readers to Eustress themselves—to examine themselves and to use their natural life energies creatively and appropriately.

In parts I to V of the book, we use the "Q" Model to describe Six Personality Types that imprison themselves behind locked-in feelings, thoughts and behaviors and push Stress-Buttons wherever they can find them. We examine the origins of Distress, probing gently into the unfinished business which grownups bring with them from childhood into the adult world.

In Part VI we ask readers to become playwrights and to note the themes, characters, scenarios and outcomes of their own Distress life dramas—whether they be Fairy Tales without happy endings, Adventure Stories without success, Melodramas without laughter or Case Studies without resolution. We invite readers to turn from Distress to Eustress and rewrite their life dramas, to free themselves from their prisons of locked-in patterns and to opt for the celebration of "That I Am," "How I Am," "Who I Am," and "What I am."

We have built the book around Chicken and/or Egg situations, which represent universal predicaments and make this book useful for people in all walks of life. At the same time we want this book to be a personal book and invite the imaginative reader to fill in the details according to his/her own needs—personal, marital/family, social, or professional/business.

In the Bibliography we have listed resources which we have integrated into The "Q" Model. Much of the material used for this book represents an integration of literature from the various schools of Transactional Analysis.

For example, Kahler's Counterscript Drivers are integrated into the chapter on Distress Authorities; the Goulding's Injunctions in Distress Don'ts; Berne's Life-Positions in Distress Life Attitudes; James's Self-Reparenting in Eustress Autonomy; Erskine and Zalcman's Racket System in Distress Feelings; Steiner's Stroke Economy in Eustress Behaviors; Levin's Cycle of Development in Permissions and Protections; Crossman's Permission and Protection in Permissions and Protections; Berne's Scripts in Distress Themes; Karpman's Drama Triangle in Distress Players; English's Racketeering in Switching Distress Roles, Kahler's Tone of Voice, Postures, Gestures and Facial Expressions in Distress Signals; Berne's Uses of Time in Distress Scenarios; Berne's Games in Distress Games; Schiff and Mellor's Discounting in Distress Make Believe; Schiff's Passivity Behaviors, Holloway's Escape Hatches and Ernst's OK-Corral in Distress Escapes.

While this book primarily constitutes an effort to integrate the literature of Transactional Analysis within the framework of other psychological, sociological, epistemological and physiological disciplines through the use of the one "Q" diagram, discerning readers will note an indebtedness to the writings of Erik Erikson, Anna Freud, Melanie Klein, Margaret Mahler, Jean Piaget and others as well. They also will recognize the integration of skills from Gestalt and communication theories and from assertive training. We are indeed grateful to each of our colleagues who have enriched our resources, and acknowledge in the References and in the Bibliography their respective contributions to The "Q" Model.

While developing The "Q" Model, we received the encouragement and support of many friends, colleagues and clients—from all parts of the United States, some even from other continents. They offered us opportunities to experiment with and to test our theory and its application, and read and critiqued the manuscript. Their numbers are many, and we owe them a great debt of gratitude.

At the same time, we do want to acknowledge a special few. Denton W. Roberts, for more than a decade since we presented the first inklings of our theory in one of his training seminars, has cast a watchful eye on "Q" and its progress; Lois Johnson demonstrated, from the very outset, confidence in "Q," conducting the first pilot project and continuing over the years to provide sustaining professional support and personal friendship; Major Henry (Hank) Vader, USAF, discovered "Q" and believed in us and in what we were doing; and Mary Goulding's perceptive talents enriched the manuscript.

Our gratitude is also extended to Fran Newby, the late Liladee Bellinger, Peggy Kucorek, J. Gail Perry and Lt. Col. Larry T. Higbie; to our students at the Yuma Marine Corps Air Station and the Yuma Army Proving Grounds: Mary Newell, Michael Driscoll, Edward Pachilla, Loren Hajdur, Lt. Barbara A. Krzewinski, Chaplain (Lt.) Gary Dallman and Lt. Commander Forrest Sherman; to the students in our Human Relations classes at the UCLA School of Dentistry; and to the many clients in our own training groups who helped bring "Q" to reality.
January 1985

Edward Zerin
Marjory Zerin
Westlake Village, California

INTRODUCTION

This book talks about a Chicken or an Egg. Really, though, it's not about a Chicken or an Egg. It's about YOU and the ways in which you can effectively manage your personal Stress.

The Chicken or the Egg is just a symbol of a situation—any situation—in your life. The situation doesn't even have to be a problem situation. It just has to be a situation where there is a difference of opinion and the issue is important enough for you to take a stand—to make a choice. It could be a personal situation—something going on inside of you—or an interpersonal situation—something going on between you and other people. The Chicken or Egg could relate, for example, to your personal social life—to something going on between you and your friends or a very special partner; or, to your marriage and family life—to something going on between you and your spouse and children; or, to your business life—to something going on between you and your boss, your colleagues, your employees or your customers.

There are so many situations in which Stress is involved that this book could go on and on just listing them. The emphasis in this volume, therefore, is not upon how many situations you have; rather, the primary focus is on how you use your Stress, whatever the Chicken or Egg situation may be.

The goal of this book is to enable you to function without Distress and to effectively manage your personal Stress—whether the Egg is soft, medium or hard-boiled, or whether the chicken is a rooster or a hen.

DEFINITIONS

Stress is energy. Stress is normal. Stress means that there are energies inside of you that are waiting to be used. Without Stress there is no life. Stress is the natural "taking" and "giving"—the *push* and the *pull* of the life energies. Inhaling and exhaling as well as eating and eliminating are two examples of stressful activities taken for granted by most people.

Stress is your gift of life. It is the genetic inheritance of the past with which you enter the world. It is also the raw material and the energy of the present with which you fashion the future.

You can abuse your gift of life, or you can learn to use it. You, too, can enjoy and get the satisfaction that you want for yourself and that you deserve to have because you are you—a human being.

STRESS IS YOUR LIFE ENERGY TO FEEL, THINK AND ACT—SEEKING TO EXPRESS ITSELF.

Distress is the inappropriate use and, therefore, the misuse of your life energy. Hans Selye refers to Distress as "damaging or unpleasant stress." You can "distress" yourself by: 1) what you let others do to you, 2) what you do to others, and 3) what you do to yourself.

Eustress (pronounced you-stress) is the appropriate and, therefore, constructive use of your life energies. You can "eustress" yourself by: 1) what you choose to let others do with you, 2) what you choose to do with others, and 3) what you choose to do with yourself.

II:
INTRODUCING "Q"

 1 THE "Q" MODEL

ABOUT THE MODEL

Drawing upon our experience as human relations specialists we created the "Q" [Quadrant] Model and applied its originality, usefulness and universality to one of society's major human problems—the Abuse of Stress.

The "Q" Model is an original model, wedding the Medical Model with its emphasis upon disease, alienation, rehabilitation and treatment to the Holistic Model with its concerns for health, well-being, prevention and education.

The "Q" Model is an elegantly useful model, bringing many of the contemporary sources of physiological, philosophical, sociological and psychological information into one discrete simplified diagram and transforming what often appears to be chaos into an efficient management tool.

The "Q" Model is a universal model, appropriate to people in all fields of human endeavor. It presents business executives and personnel with a cost-effective method for stimulating success, maximizing motivation, increasing productivity and boosting morale. It provides mental health and health-care professionals with an instrument for promoting well-being and health. Its benefits are applicable to the teaching profession, to the social service field and to all those disciplines, whether in civilian or military life, where personal esteem and social concern are at issue. It offers lay people, no matter what their economic, social or educational status, a map to explore the human birthright. No human being is excluded. Everyone is included.

The "Q" Model is based upon the story of the proverbial elephant exemplified in the fable of the six blind men, each of whom described the total elephant in terms of the part he touched.

Many years ago when we began our formal study of psychology we were overwhelmed with and, at times, even distressed by the number of theories, each with its own jargon and each with its own claim to truth. How to make sense out of what appeared to us, all too frequently, to make no sense seemed an almost insurmountable task. Each course was a potential intellectual quagmire.

We recognized, of course, that there are differences between disciplines and that, even where similarities predominate, not all disciplines place their emphasis upon the same part of the "elephant." There are, to be sure, "tail" personality theories and "tusk" theories; some emphasize the "trunk," while others define themselves in terms of the "ears." However, what at first seemed to us like separate disciplines soon blended into one larger discipline. As we delved deeper, the parts of the elephant began to merge, and the elephant itself, to emerge.

First, we recognized that we could break through the morass if we concentrated upon "function," or how things work, rather than upon "structure," or parts. Second, we recognized that many of the psychological disciplines, though using different methods and terminology, seemed to follow a similar theme-pattern based upon the phases of early childhood development, which were recycled with each successive developmental level. Four well-being themes were discernable. Translated into the language of the "life energies," they are:

1. becoming aware of the life energies,
2. exploring and developing the life energies,
3. integrating the life energies, and
4. committing the life energies to relationships.

The alienation counterparts to these well-being themes were also apparent:

1. self-estrangement
2. normlessness
3. meaninglessness
4. powerlessness

Third, by using the "Q" Model Diagram and assigning one of the developmental themes to each Quadrant (beginning in Q1 and proceeding clockwise to Q2, Q4 and Q3) (see diagrams 1.2 and 1.4) we recognized that we could demonstrate how the functional aspects of the psychological discipline were interrelated. The well-being themes were assigned to the Quadrants of the inner Eustress Ellipse, and the alienation themes, to the outer Distress Ellipse. We followed a five-fold procedure:

1. We made a separate set of Distress and Eustress Ellipses for each discipline.
2. We assigned to each Quadrant one of the themes derived from our studies.
3. We made a separate ellipse for each developmental level.
4. We inserted into the respective Quadrants the alienation and the well-

being contents corresponding with the themes and with each developmental phase.

5. We placed the "Q" Model Diagrams for each psychological discipline one upon the other so that the Quadrants, in accordance with their themes and their developmental levels, overlaid each other.

By following this five-fold procedure, we were able to integrate a vast storehouse of content-resources for personal growth, marital happiness, family satisfaction, business success and professional proficiency. We now are better prepared to ask appropriate questions of ourselves and of others. We are better tuned in to what others are saying to us and to what we are hearing. We are better equipped to diagnose problem areas within ourselves and within others, and we are more resourceful in managing our own stress and the stress produced by others. Further studies in philosophy and physiology also have added to our growing storehouse of resources.

In a way, the "Q" Model is somewhat analagous to the Periodic Table in Chemistry. Once the parameters of the Table were established, chemists sought and discovered missing elements, and scientists began to open new frontiers by challenging the Periodic boundaries. The "Q" Model performs a similar function. By bringing together the different disciplines, each with its own emphasis, theoreticians can fill in the gaps on the continuum from well-being to alienation and investigate what is missing. Also, the integration invites those who are interested in opening new frontiers by challenging The "Q" Model boundaries.

"Q"—THE POTENTIAL FOR LIVING

"Q" is a map, an imaginative diagram, a paradigm of the human potential for living. It begins with the *central core* where all forms of human energy for living come together—the potential energy for experiencing

THAT YOU ARE . . .
HOW YOU ARE . . .
WHO YOU ARE . . .
WHAT YOU ARE . . .

The central core represents the enfolded potential to which each newborn is heir. It is the source from which the energy of your being unfolds in the same sense that DNA in the nucleus of a cell harbors potential life and directs the nature of the cell's unfolding.

THE "Q" DIAGRAM

"Q" is an ellipse drawn around this central core with a horizontal line through the middle, so that half of the unfolding of the human potential is mapped above the line and half of the unfolding is diagrammed below the line (see Diagram 1.1). The part above the line refers to how you use your potential energy to have an impact on other people. The part below the line refers to how you use your potential energy so that other people have an impact on you. How you impact on yourself is reflected both above and below the center line.

The upper and the lower segments of the ellipse are divided again, this time by two diagonal lines which cross at the central life core. "Q" now becomes Four Quadrants, called Q1, Q2, Q3, and Q4 (see Diagram 1.2).

Q1 falls entirely below the horizontal line and is a primary Quadrant. Q4 also is a primary Quadrant diagrammed entirely above the horizontal line. Q2 and Q3 are transitional Quadrants, each having a part above the line and a part below the horizontal line. In Q2 the part below the line is called Q2A, and the part above the line is called Q2B. In Q3 the part above the line is called Q3A, and the part below the line is called Q3B.

The Quadrants map patterns of thoughts, feelings and behaviors through which the *en*folded potential *un*folds:

Q1 maps the unfolding thoughts, feelings and behaviors of the human potential to experience and be aware THAT YOU ARE;
Q2 explores the unfolding thoughts, feelings and behaviors of the human potential to develop HOW YOU ARE;
Q4 integrates the unfolding thoughts, feelings and behaviors of the human potential into WHO YOU ARE;

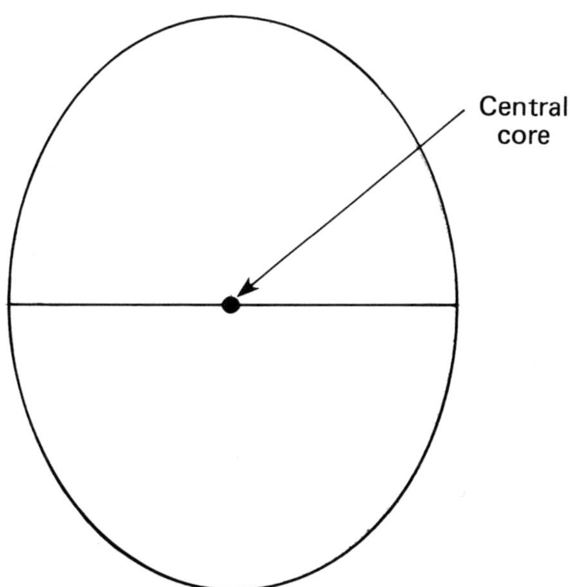

Diagram 1.1
"Q": AN ELLIPSE DIVIDED IN HALF

Diagram 1.2
FOUR QUADRANTS

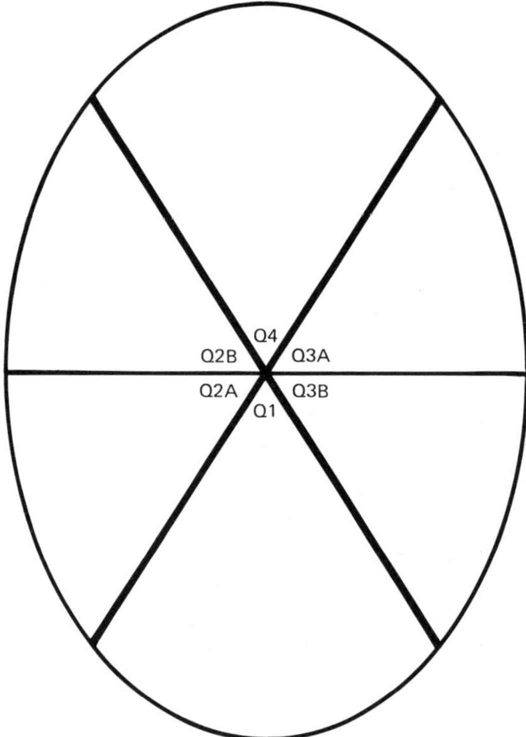

Q3 commits the unfolding thoughts, feelings and behaviors of the human potential to WHAT YOU ARE.

A second vertical line is drawn through the middle of the ellipse so that half of the unfolding of the human potential is mapped to the left of the line and half of the unfolding is diagrammed to the right of the line (see Diagram 1.3). One side of the ellipse is called the *ascending* half and refers to how you shift the use of your human potential from yourself to other people. The other side of the ellipse is called the *descending* half and refers to how you shift the use of your human potential from others to yourself. In this book only the horizontal line will be indicated in the "Q" diagrams. While the vertical line will not be drawn, you will learn in a later chapter that the unfolding of the human potential proceeds through a series of developmental stages, each of which contains an ascending and a descending phase.

THE TWO ELLIPSES

The "Q" Model Diagram consists of an ellipse within an ellipse: 1) the Distress Ellipse and 2) the Eustress Ellipse. Both ellipses start from the central core, with the Eustress Ellipse forming an inner ellipse and the Distress Ellipse forming the outer one (see Diagram 1.4).

When you are aware and use your life energy appropriately, your feelings, thoughts and behaviors are diagrammed in the inner Eustress Ellipse. When you are unaware of your life energies and/or misuse them, your feelings, thoughts and behavior patterns are diagrammed in the outer Distress Ellipse. The further a pattern is diagrammed from the central core, the greater the Distress or the alienation quality of life (neurotic disorders, personality or character disorders, and psychotic disorders, respectively). The closer to the central core, the greater is the Eustress or well-being of life.

In this book the two ellipses will be treated separately—i.e., one at a time—and not together.

The Outer Distress Ellipse

You will use the Distress Ellipse and its Four Quadrants to become acquainted with your most frequently used patterns of feelings, thoughts and behaviors when you are under pressure in a Chicken or Egg situation. These patterns, you will discover, are locked-in techniques, which put you into a psychological straitjacket. They are inappropriate patterns for you, for the other

Diagram 1.3
THE UNFOLDING HUMAN POTENTIAL

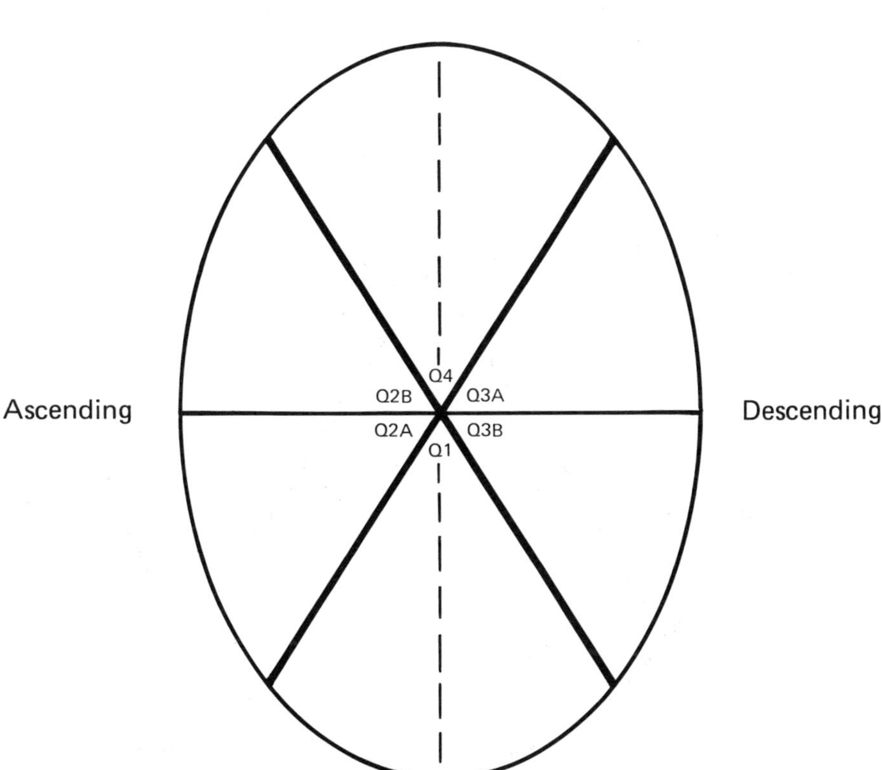

person or for the situation in which you find yourself. They utilize substitute feelings instead of authentic feelings, contaminated thoughts instead of clear thoughts, and non-relation-building or alienation behaviors instead of relation-building behaviors. Once you have locked yourself into a straitjacket, you automatically follow these patterns whenever and wherever you Distress yourself in a Chicken or Egg situation.

Everything *above* the center line suggests that you consider yourself to be *one-up* ("top-dog") to the other person. (↑ ↓). Everything *below* the center line suggests that you consider yourself to be *one-down* ("bottom-dog") to the other person (↓ ↑) (see Diagram 1.5). The Distress Ellipse is an *either-or* ellipse.

**Diagram 1.4
THE TWO ELLIPSES**

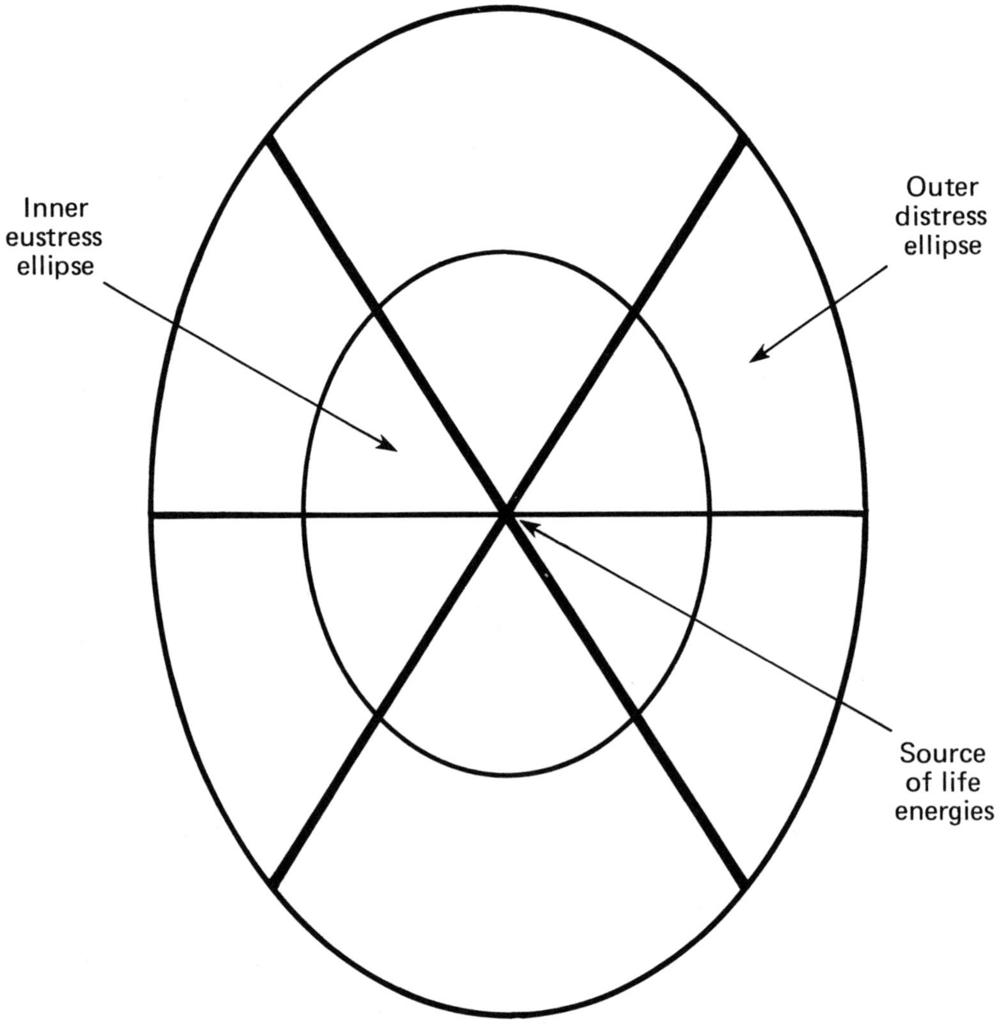

Diagram 1.5
THE OUTER DISTRESS ELLIPSE

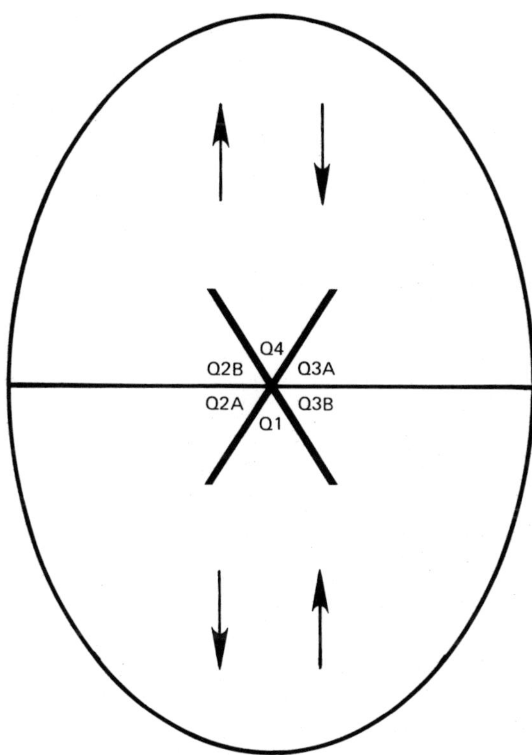

The Inner Eustress Ellipse

The Eustress Ellipse is used exactly as you would use the Distress Ellipse, with one major exception. The Eustress Ellipse is a *both/and* and not an *either-or* Ellipse (see Diagram 1.6). There are no locked-in inappropriate patterns in the Eustress Ellipse. Eustress patterns are appropriate patterns and utilize authentic instead of substitute feelings, uncontaminated instead of contaminated thoughts and relation-building behaviors instead of alienation or non-relation-building behaviors. In addition, whether you are above or below the center line, in the Eustress Ellipse you consider yourself and the other person to be neither one-up ("top-Dog") nor one-down ("bottom-dog") to each other. You are "up" with yourself, and the other person is "up" with you, too. Another way to say it is "I'm OK—You're OK" with me, too.

Diagram 1.6
THE INNER EUSTRESS ELLIPSE

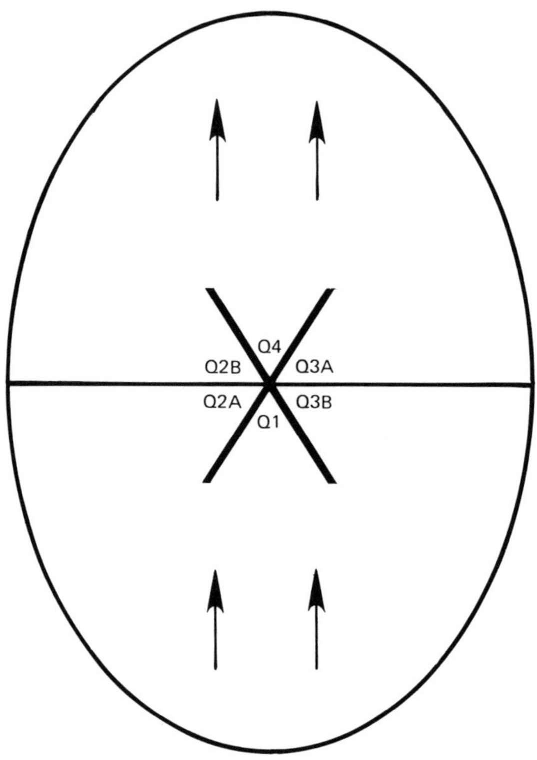

III:
ENTERING THE PROCESS

A BIT OF DISTRESS THEORY

When you were young you learned from your parents, whom you regarded as authority figures, what was and what was not acceptable to them. The parental message, in effect, implied: "You are okay with us if...," that is, if you feel the way we want you to feel, think the way we want you to think and behave the way we want you to behave, then and only then are you acceptable to us. Keenly aware of the parental imperatives, you then decided how you would feel, think and behave as a member of the family in a Chicken or Egg situation.

Lacking in adult experience you forced yourself to fall back on survival patterns known to your limited experience and unschooled intellectual resources. You were, so to speak, on your own, dependent on whatever had worked for you in the past or however your young impulses may have pushed you to react at that moment. If a maneuver worked, you locked in on it, repeating it over and over, assuming that what worked once would work again and again. You now had a pattern on which you believed you could rely.

Your pattern soon became automatic and habitual. Even when you no longer lived at home with its ever-present impactful parental messages, you continued throughout your life to repeat the locked-in pattern—now, however, without awareness. Only as you recalled the old decisions you had made and only as you opted for new feeling, thought and behavior choices were you able to free yourself from your old pattern. In the meantime, you undertook to replace your parents by finding new authority figures with whom you could unwittingly continue to replay the old locked-in patterns.

When you made your decision in childhood under high pressure and distressful conditions, you thought that you had two alternatives available to you.

You believed that you were in an either-or situation: Either you could give in or you could defy your authority figures. You could become Compliant and agree with your parents or Defiant and disagree with your parents. As you locked yourself into one of these alternatives, you also could have proceeded in a routine between compliance and defiance, as though you were caught up in a "Vicious Ellipse." You could go around and around the ellipse, sometimes appearing Compliant-Defiant and at other times Defiant-Compliant as you sought to find strength in your defiance and to take comfort in your compliance. You also could move from one Quadrant to another in the ellipse as you dealt with your Distressful situation. In fact, you may have developed numerous response patterns, utilizing a different one for each of the many kinds of Chicken or Egg situations in which you experienced Distress. Distress patterns, however are patterns of feelings, thoughts and behaviors that are inappropriate to the here and now. They are locked-in ways of dealing with authority.

DISTRESS MESSAGES FROM YOUR PARENTS

When you were young, you received two kinds of Conditional messages from your parents. One kind consisted of Positive messages, which told you what kind of a person you were to be and how to become that person. The other kind consisted of Negative messages, which told you what kind of a person not to be and how not to be that person. Both the Positive and the Negative messages, however, were Conditional messages. One told you that "you were okay *if...*," and the other told you that "you were not okay *if...*". The Positive messages were verbal messages and said "Do..." or "Be...". The Negative messages most frequently were nonverbal messages and said "Don't...". Sometimes the Negative messages were even more powerful than the Positive messages because they seemed to speak to the deepest parts of your psyche.

Both kinds of messages were important to you, and you based your decisions on how to live as a member of the family on the Positive and Negative messages you received—or thought you received—from your parental authority figures. You either accepted or rejected their messages. When you locked yourself into a compliance or into a defiance of their messages, you distressed yourself.

DISTRESS AUTHORITIES

Conditional Positive Messages: Distress Do's

There are six different Conditional Positive Distress Messages which you may have received from your parents in Chicken or Egg situations. They are called Distress Do's (see Diagram 2.1).

Q1. *BE STRONG:* When things go wrong, square your shoulders. Grin and bear it. Keep your feelings to yourself. Boys never cry. Girls cry only in private.

Q2A.   *TRY HARD:* When there is a task to be done, put your shoulder to the wheel and stay with the job.

Q2B.   *HURRY UP-IMPULSIVE:* When an impulse comes suddenly, act on it right away. There is no mañana.

Q4.   *BE PERFECT:* When standards or values are involved, like getting all A's at school, settle only for the best. Pride is important.

Q3A.   *HURRY UP-COMPULSIVE:* If there is a task to be done, especially if it is a long-standing and repetitive one, be on time. There is no mañana.

Diagram 2.1
DISTRESS AUTHORITIES
Conditional Positive Messages (Do's)

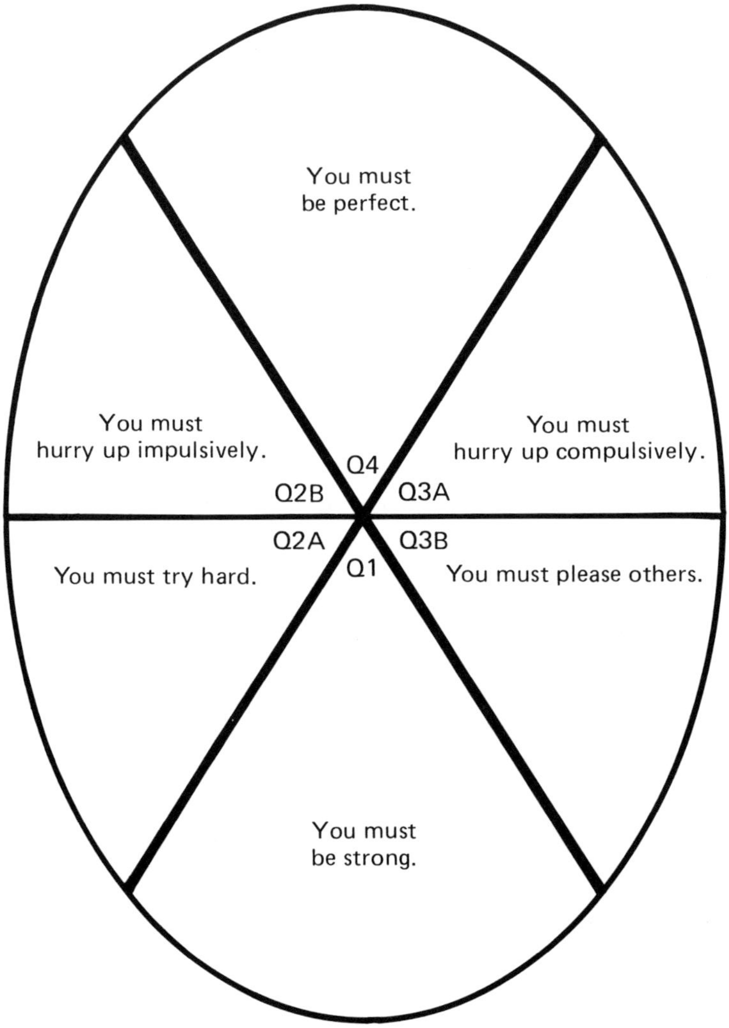

Q3B.   *PLEASE OTHERS:* Where other people are involved, make sure that they like you. Watch your *p*'s and *q*'s.

Conditional Negative Messages: Distress Don'ts

There are 14 different Conditional Negative Distress Messages which you may have received from your parents in Chicken or Egg situations. They are called Distress Don'ts (see Diagram 2.2).

Q1.   *DON'T BE:* because you weren't wanted in the first place.
DON'T FEEL: because if you want to get along in an unfair and tough world, it is necessary for you not to feel your feelings, or at least, not to show your feelings.
DON'T BE YOU: because you are not the person and/or the sex your parents wanted.
DON'T BELONG: because when all is said and done, you are not going to be trusted or accepted anyway.
DON'T BE CLOSE: because your parents don't trust you (or themselves) and are not comfortable hugging, kissing or showing other open expressions of affection.
DON'T WANT: because no matter what you want to feel, think or do, you are not supposed to want.
Q2.   *DON'T SUCCEED:* because you are not really adequate, and, moreover, you can't be better than your parents.
A. *DON'T BE SICK (INSANE):* because the only way you will get attention is to go away (or, to go A.W.O.L.).
B. *DON'T BE A CHILD—GROW UP:* because you are to be responsible and not have fun until your chores are done.
Q4.   *DON'T:* because no matter what you do, you are not supposed to do it.
DON'T THINK: because your parents know all the answers and will do your thinking for you.
Q3.   *DON'T BE IMPORTANT:* because your parents are boss, and children are to be seen and not heard.
A. *DON'T GROW UP—BE A CHILD:* because afterwards, your parents won't have anyone around to take care of them.
B. *DON'T BE WELL (SANE):* because the only way to get attention is to be sick (or, to go crazy).

DISTRESS DECISION-RESPONSES TO YOUR PARENTS

The decisions that you made about how you would live as a member of the family were chosen from the same Conditional Positive and Negative Messages which your parents gave you. You may or may not have chosen the same messages as your parents did, or, even if you had, you may not have put them in the same order as they did.

Diagram 2.2
DISTRESS AUTHORITIES
Conditional Negative Messages (Don'ts)

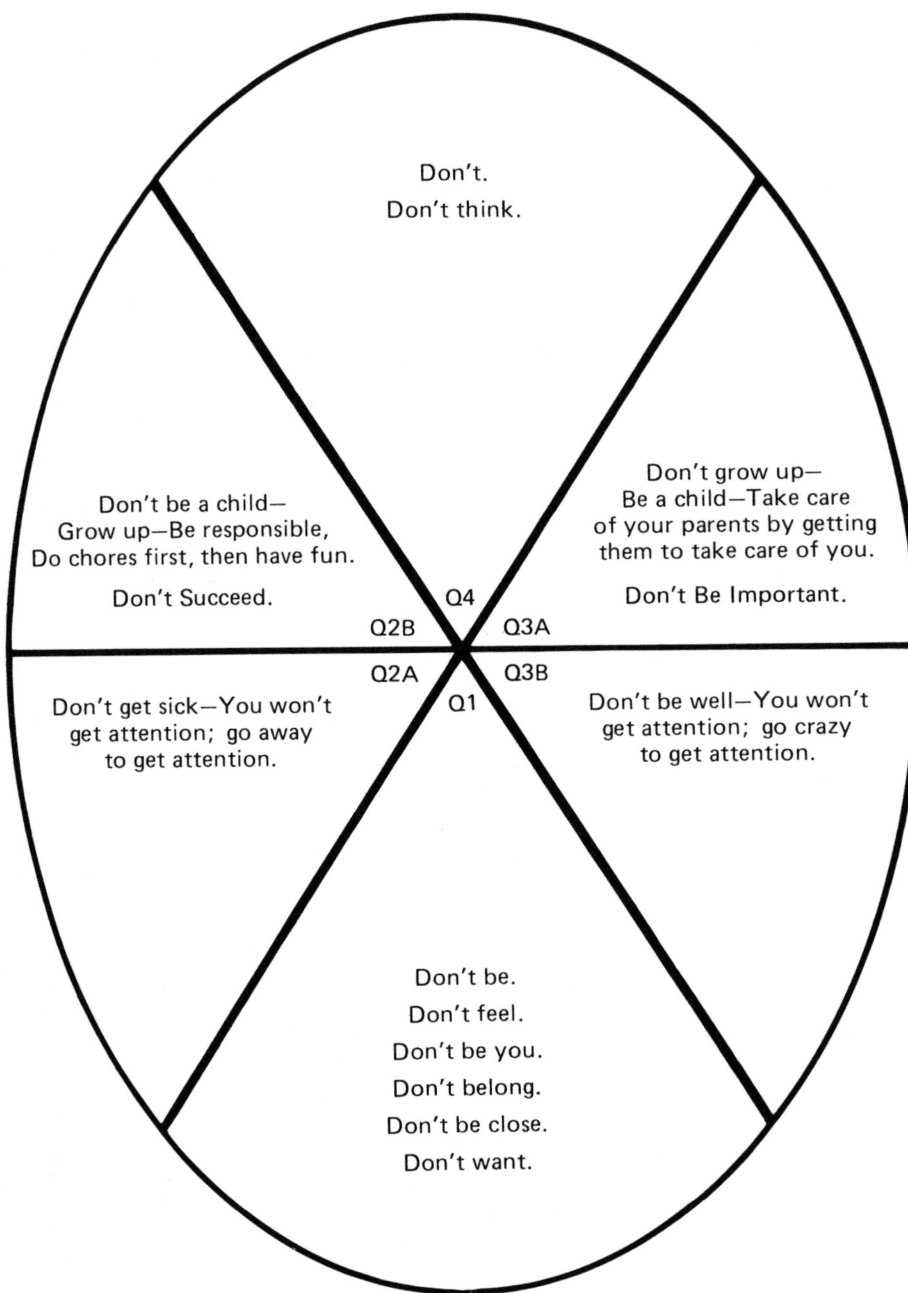

Sometimes parents do not give complete messages. Sometimes they do not tell you what kind of a person to be and how to be that person. Sometimes they tell you what kind of a person to be but do not tell you how to achieve that goal. In those circumstances you were forced to turn to other people for guidance. If you were unable to find them, you were thrown completely on your own resources. You had to decide for yourself what kind of a person you wanted to be and/or how to become that person. These patterns were appropriate for you when you were little since they helped to reduce your level of Distress. You were small and inexperienced, and you figured out the best ways you could devise under those conditions. However, if you are still employing these childhood patterns today to deal with your Distress, you have locked yourself into inappropriate techniques. Deprived of flexibility, you are misusing your life energies.

As a child, when you locked yourself into a Defiance or Compliance pattern, you began to misuse your life energies and invited several consequences (see Diagram 2.3). In a Chicken or Egg situation, for example, if you locked yourself into a:

Diagram 2.3
COMPLIANT-DEFIANT DECISION-RESPONSES

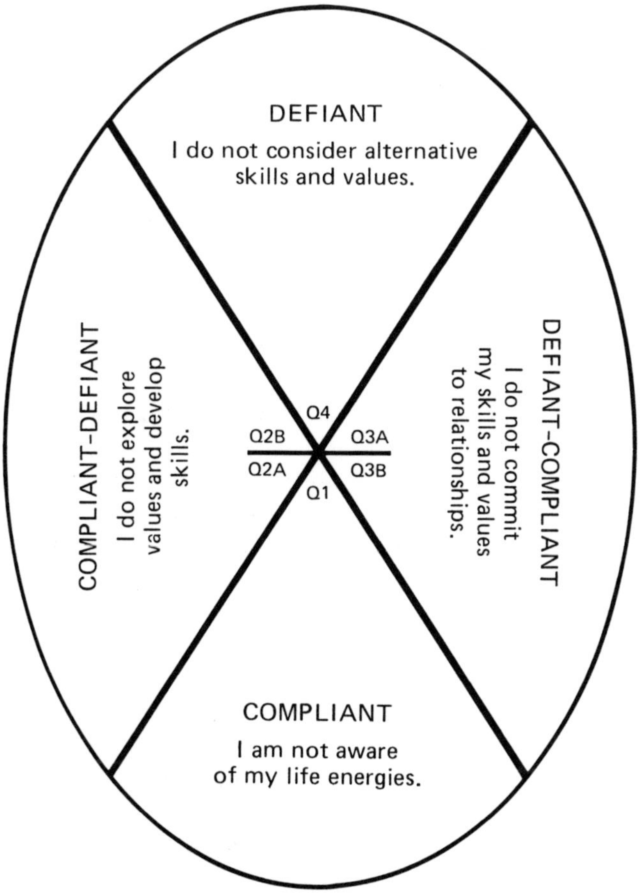

Q1.   Compliant pattern, you gave up on yourself—you sacrificed your sense of self-worth whenever you refused to be aware of your birthright—your life energies. The more you estranged yourself from yourself, the more you increased your Distress.

Q2.   Compliant-Defiant pattern, you made yourself inadequate whenever you refused to explore values and develop skills necessary for your success. The more you made yourself incompetent, the more you increased your Distress.

Q4.   Defiant pattern, you made yourself into a "bull in a china shop" or you became stubborn and refused to consider alternative skills and values whenever your Chicken or Egg situation didn't work out for you. The more rigid you became, the more increased your Distress.

Q3.   Defiant-Compliant pattern, you became powerless whenever you hesitated to commit your skills and values to relationships. The more powerless you became, the more you increased your Distress.

DISTRESS CONSEQUENCES

Positive

There are six different Conditional Positive Decision-responses (see Diagram 2.4) that you may have made when you received your Conditional Positive Messages from your parents in a Chicken or Egg situation.

Q1.   *I MUST BE STRONG:* When things go wrong, I must square my shoulders, grin and bear it and keep my feelings to myself. If I am a boy, I must never cry. If I am a girl and I cry, I must cry in private.

Q2A.   *I MUST TRY HARD:* When there is a task to be done, I must put my shoulder to the wheel and stay with the job.

Q2B.   *I MUST HURRY UP IMPULSIVELY:* When the impulse comes suddenly, I must do the task right away.

Q4.   *I MUST BE PERFECT:* When standards or values are involved, I must settle only for the best. My pride is important.

Q3A.   *I MUST HURRY UP COMPULSIVELY:* When the urge to do a task is long-standing and repetitive, I must do the task right away.

Q3B.   *I MUST PLEASE OTHERS:* When other people are involved, I must make sure that they like me. I must watch my *p*'s and *q*'s.

Negative

There are 14 kinds of Conditional Negative Decision-responses (see Diagram 2.5) that you may have made to the Conditional Negative Messages which your parents gave you in a Chicken or Egg situation.

Q1.   *I MUST NOT BE:* because I wasn't wanted in the first place.
I MUST NOT FEEL: because it is necessary for me not to show my feelings in an unfair and tough world.

I MUST NOT BE ME: because I am not the person and/or the sex my parents wanted.
I MUST NOT BELONG: because I won't be trusted or accepted anyway.
I MUST NOT BE CLOSE: because I don't trust myself (or my parents) enough to kiss, hug, or show open affection to them.
I MUST NOT WANT: because no matter what I want to feel, think or do, I'm not supposed to want.

   Q2.   *I MUST NOT SUCCEED:* because I am not really adequate, and, moreover, I am not supposed to be better than my parents.
A. I MUST NOT BE SICK (INSANE): because the only way I can get attention is to go away.

Diagram 2.4
DISTRESS CONSEQUENCES
Conditional Positive Decision–Responses

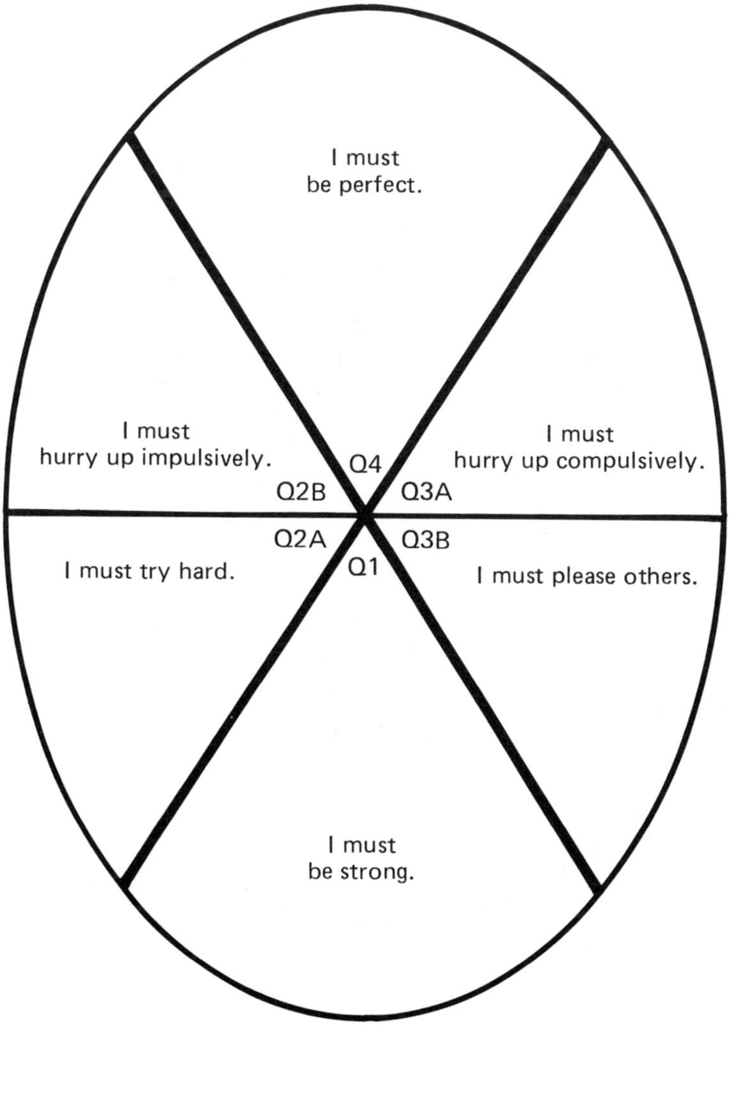

Diagram 2.5
DISTRESS CONSEQUENCES
Conditional Negative Decision-Responses

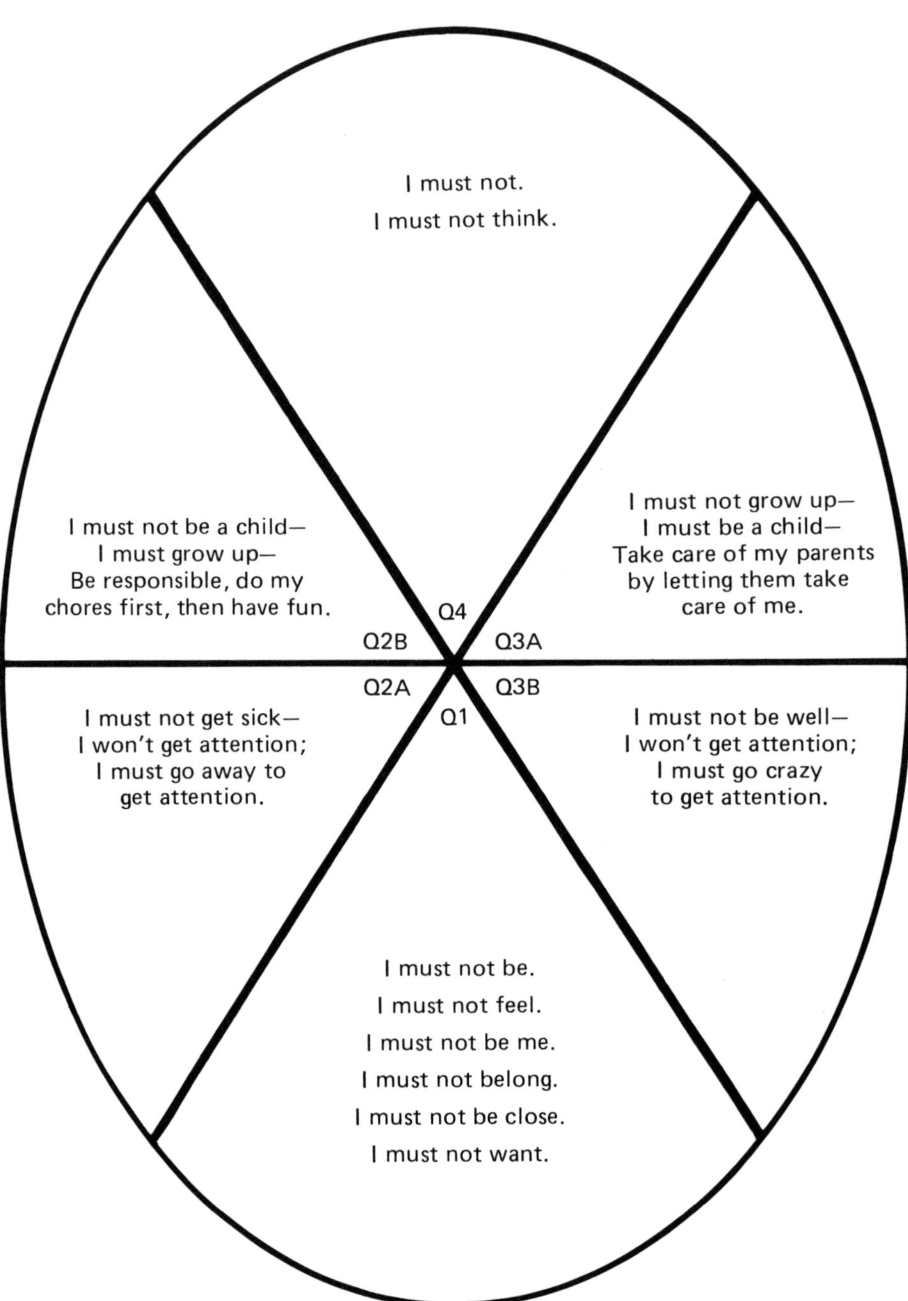

B. I MUST NOT BE A CHILD—I MUST GROW UP: because I am to be responsible and not have fun until my chores are done.

Q4.   *I MUST NOT THINK:* because my parents know all the answers and will do my thinking for me.

I MUST NOT DO ANYTHING: because no matter what I do, I am not supposed to do it.

Q3.   *I MUST NOT BE IMPORTANT:* because my parents are the boss, and I am to be seen and not heard.

A. I MUST NOT GROW UP—I MUST BE A CHILD: because afterwards I must take care of my parents.

B. I MUST NOT BE WELL (SANE): because the only way for me to get attention is to get sick (or, go crazy).

DISTRESS LIFE ATTITUDES

When your parents gave you their Conditional Distress Messages—whether Positive or Negative—unwittingly they were setting you up for a Chicken or Egg situation. Their Positive and Negative Messages implied: "If you feel, think and behave as though the Chicken came first, you are okay with us." Or, "If you feel, think and behave as though the Egg came first, you are okay with us." Conditional Distress Messages create an *either-or* situation. *Either* you are for us, *or* you are against us.

Being small and dependent upon your parents, you quickly figured out what your position is. There were two patterns from which to choose:

1. A *one-down* ("bottom dog") position (↓)
2. A *one-up* ("top dog") position (↑)

Your preference for one of these patterns may have existed prior to your final Decision-response to your parents, going back to the first moments of your existence. Now, however, you have an excuse to justify, support and lock yourself into a rigid position. You can blame it on your parents and on the Conditional Distress Messages they gave you. You can decide that your position in life from this time on—that is, forever—will be one of the following:

I'm *one-down,* and my parents are *one-up.* (↓ ↑)

I'm *one-down,* and my parents are *one-down,* too. (↓ ↓)

I'm *one-up,* and my parents are *one-down.* (↑ ↓)

When you lock yourself into a rigid Life Attitude, not only your Decision-responses but also your feelings, thoughts and behaviors are inappropriate. You are stuck!

In all the Quadrants below the center line (see Diagram 2.6), you say to yourself: "I'm one-down, but you are one-up to me." In Q1 you also say: "All of us are one-down. I'm bottom dog, but you're bottom dog, too. I don't count myself, but I don't count you either."

In all the Quadrants above the center line you say to yourself: "I'm one-up,

Diagram 2.6
DISTRESS LIFE ATTITUDES

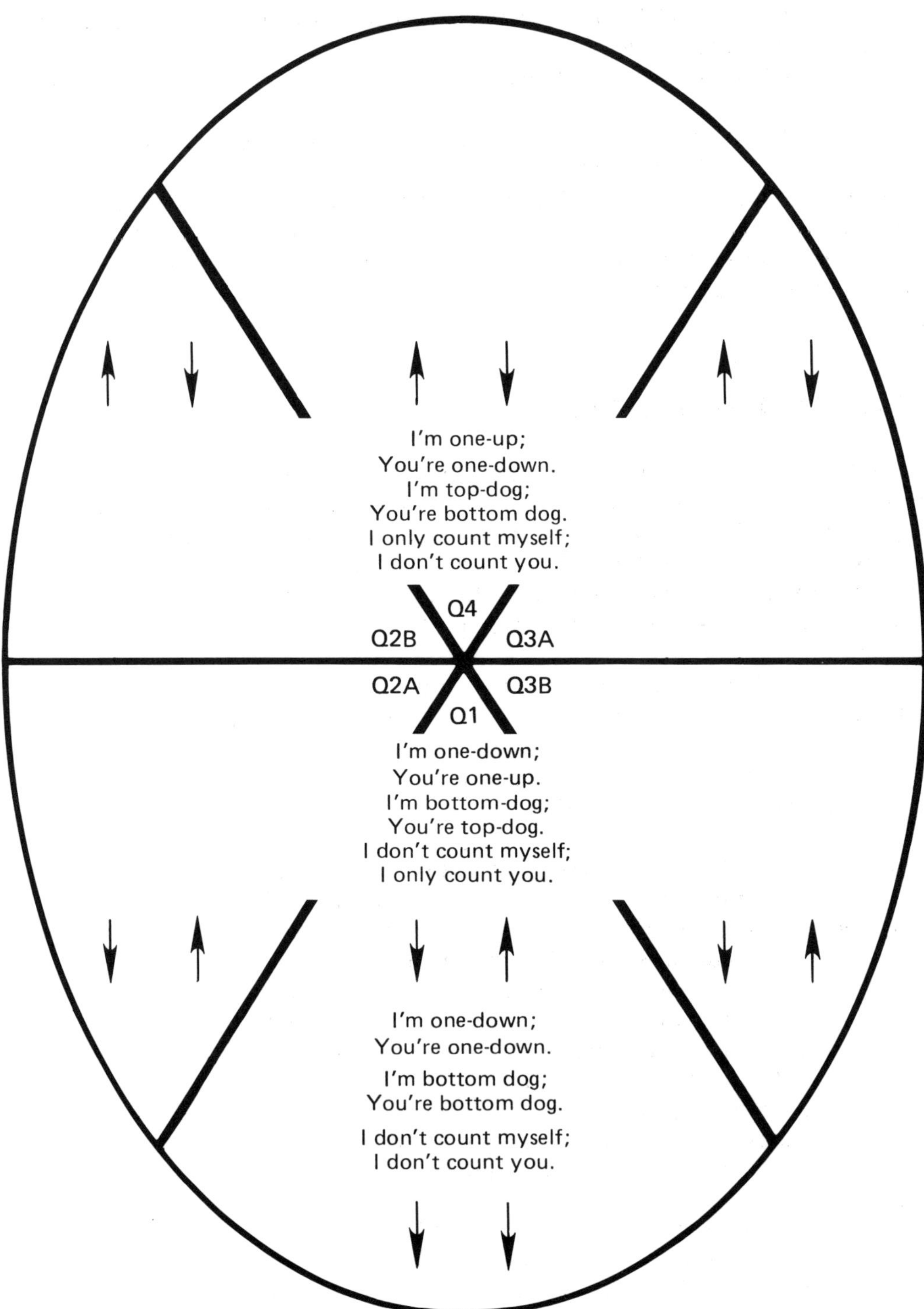

but you're one-down. I'm top dog, but you're bottom dog. I count myself, but I don't count you."

In Q2 you say to yourself: "I'm one-down, but I don't like it. I'll figure out a way to make myself one-up by putting you down."

In Q3 you say to yourself: "I'm one-up, but I'm worried. It's better that I make myself one-down by putting you one-up."

DISTRESS WORDS

Words are important. There is a difference between the positive words "must," "should" and "could." These words often are used interchangeably even though the speaker intends differently. "Must," for example, refers to an external authority which prescribes what you are to feel, think and behave. "Should," on the other hand, refers to an authority which you have internalized and which you now hear as your own conscience telling you what you are to feel, think and behave in certain ways. "Could" refers to the physical ability to carry out the directives authorized by the external and the internal authorities. In many instances, for example, you do have the physical capability but you don't want to use it. Instead of saying I "won't" or I "don't want to,"

Table 2.1
DISTRESS WORDS

YOU ARE OKAY IF . . .

"You must . . ."   "You must not . . ."

TRANSLATES INTO

"I must . . ."   "I must not . . ."

TRANSLATES INTO

"I should . . ."   "I should not . . ."

TRANSLATES INTO

"I could . . ."   "I can't . . ."

TRANSLATES INTO

I'm one-down, but others are one-up.
I'm one-down, but others are one-down, too.
I'm one-up, but others are one-down.

TRANSLATES INTO

Q1: I'm not aware of my life energies.
Q2: I do not explore values and develop skills.
Q4: I do not consider alternative skills and values.
Q3: I refuse to commit my skills and values to relationships.

you admit that you "could," knowing deep down that you "won't." "Could" means that you will try to get away with whatever you can.

The same holds true for the negative words "must not," "should not" and "can't." "Must not" refers to an external authority which gives you a Prohibition concerning what not to feel, think and behave. "Should not" refers to an authority which you have internalized and which you now hear as your own conscience saying that you are not to feel, think and behave in certain ways. "Can't" implies a supposed physical inability. When you don't want to defy either your external or your internal authorities, you say I "can't" when you really mean "won't." The word "can't" takes you off the hook, so to speak.

The words you use, therefore, have an impact on many aspects of your life (see Table 2.1). They reveal the level of your awareness, your willingness to explore and grow, your flexibility to seek out meaningful alternatives in the face of opposition and your capacity to commit yourself responsibly to an interdependent network of human relationships. Words betray your life attitude and tell others where you are with them and where you are with yourself.

STOP!

Before you begin to feel sorry for yourself or begin to attack your parents for what they did, consider the many appropriate and constructive ways in which you are aware, develop, give meaning to and creatively utilize your life energies. . . .

A BIT OF EUSTRESS THEORY

When you were newborn, you were a very important, though only a potential, source of life energy. Many of your neural connections were as yet unconnected, and, to put it mildly, you were socially inexperienced and psychologically unsophisticated. Conditional Messages—both Positive and Negative—were your parents' way of short-circuiting your learning process so that you didn't have to spend your life energy rediscovering fire and reinventing the wheel.

Let's do a little experiment. The experiment involves finding out what you might have done as your nerve endings became more connected and your capacity to feel, to think and to behave developed. As you made the transitions from infancy to childhood to young adulthood, suppose that your parents had transformed the Chicken *or* Egg situation into a Chicken *and* Egg situation and had said to you at each transitional point: "In this Chicken *and* Egg situation we would/would not feel, think and do the following. However, you are growing up, and it is appropriate for you to accept responsibility for making your own decisions and for taking the consequences of those decisions. We love you. You decide what you want/do not want to feel, think and do in this situation."

If your parents were like most people, they didn't change their methods of dealing with you as you grew up. They continued to do the best they knew how. They continued to give you Do's and Don'ts, stopping only out of necessity either when you left home or got too big to control. If you were like most children, you locked yourself in. Either you gave in and to this day continue to conform to your parents, or else you broke away and to this day continue to defy your parents.

Another possibility is that you accepted the opportunity and challenged yourself in four different ways (see Diagram 3.1):

Q1. You asserted your awareness of your life energies and established your self-worth and esteem.

Q2. You explored and acquired skills and values necessary for your success.

Q4. You considered alternative skills and values and integrated your alternatives into a meaningful plan.

Q3. You committed and negotiated your integrated values and skills in relationships.

In brief, you Eustressed yourself. You made constructive use of your life energies. With each new transitional stage of your development, as you faced new Chicken or Egg situations, you learned to be more socially experienced and psychologically sophisticated. You still dealt with Positive and Negative Messages; however, now they were your own, i.e., you took responsibility for your feelings, thoughts and behaviors in your situations. Instead of being either Compliant or Defiant, you were Assertive.

EUSTRESS AUTONOMY

The same kinds of Conditional Positive Distress Messages which you received from your parents also can be Eustress Messages. The difference between

Diagram 3.1
ASSERTIVE DECISION-RESPONSES

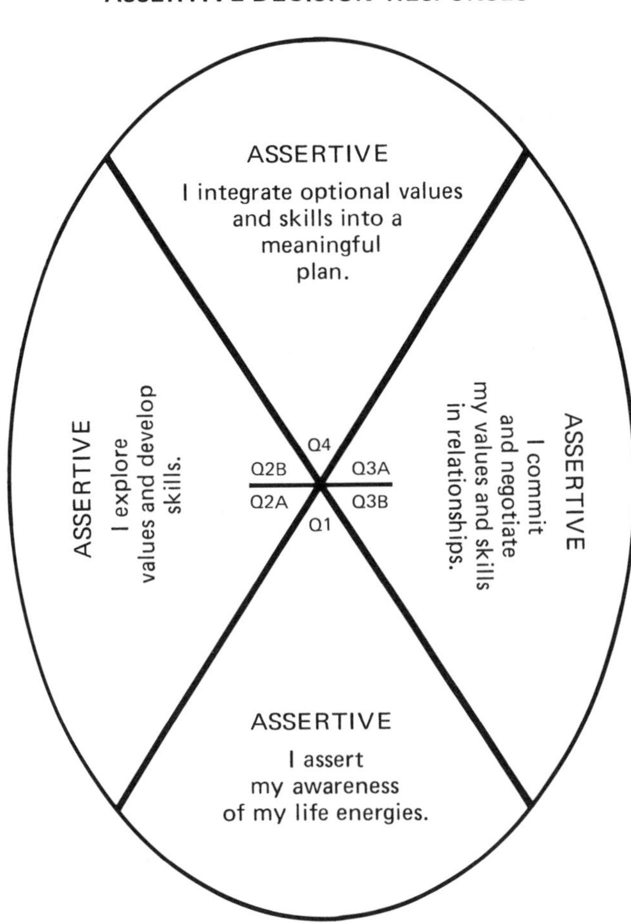

Distress and Eustress Messages has nothing to do with whether the messages are positive or negative. Eustress Messages can be both positive and negative. Nor does the difference reside in the content of the messages. Eustress Messages can have the same content as Distress Messages.

Eustress Messages are Unconditional Messages and have *both* a Positive *and* a Negative aspect. There is an appropriate time for each. Distress Messages are Conditional Messages and have *either* a Positive *or* a Negative aspect to them. "Appropriate to what?" you may ask. The term "appropriate" refers to two things:

1. whether the message is in keeping with your developmental stage, especially as you are growing through infancy, childhood and adolescence. In each developmental stage there are certain essential tasks to be achieved if growth to the next stage is to be maximized. Appropriate messages from your parents can help you in your growth. Inappropriate Messages can hinder you.

2. whether the message is associated with a Chicken *and* Egg rather than a Chicken *or* Egg situation. When you were young it was appropriate for your parents to make the transition from the Chicken *or* Egg situations to Chicken *and* Egg situations as you developed from one stage to the next. Appropriate messages from your parents help you in your Chicken *and* Egg situations.

When you were growing up, it was appropriate for your parents to tell you to be what kind of person they wanted you to be and to tell you how to be that kind of a person. When you are grown up it is appropriate for you to tell yourself what kind of person you want to be and to tell yourself how to be that kind of person. When you make the transition from "being told" to "telling yourself," you exercise your autonomy.

Unconditional Positive Messages

There are six optional Unconditional Positive Messages which you may have received from your parents (see Diagram 3.2).

Q1. *BE HUMAN.* There is a time to Be Strong—to suck it in and keep your feelings to yourself—and a time *not* to Be Strong—to cry and let others know how you feel. Choose what is appropriate for you in the immediate context.

Q2A. *BE SUCCESSFUL.* There is a time to Try Hard—to put your shoulder to the wheel and explore values and learn skills—and a time *not* to Try Hard—to accept limitations and be satisfied with your achievements. Choose what is appropriate for you in the immediate context.

Q2B. *BE FLEXIBLE.* There is a time to Hurry Up impulsively and allow time for spontaneity—and a time *not* to Hurry Up impulsively and to do the necessary routines. Choose what is appropriate for you in the immediate context.

Q4. *BE HUMBLE.* There is a time to Be Perfect—to insist on what you think is right—and a time *not* to be Perfect—to consider alternatives. Choose what is appropriate for you in the immediate context.

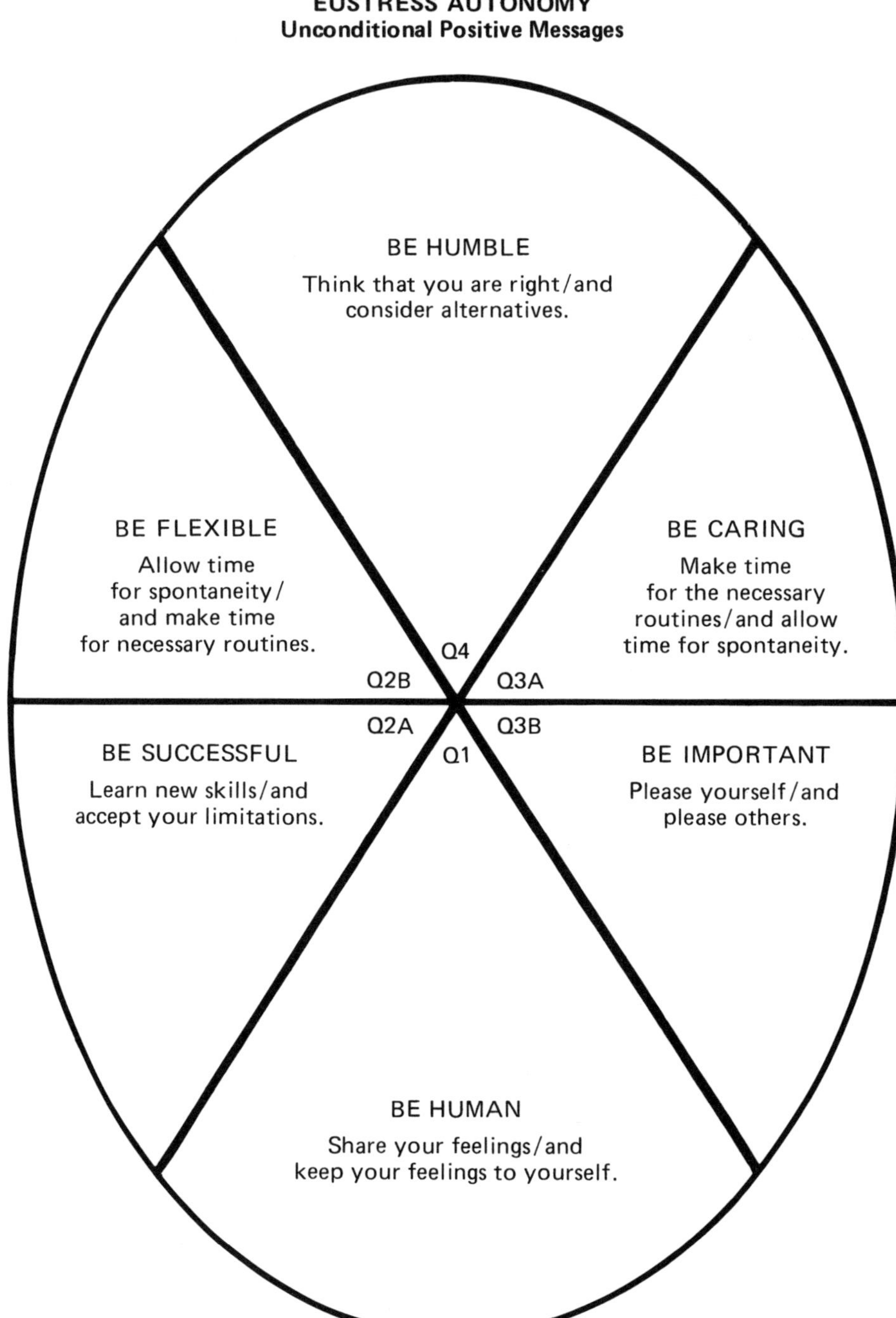

Diagram 3.2
EUSTRESS AUTONOMY
Unconditional Positive Messages
BE HUMBLE
Think that you are right/and
consider alternatives.
BE FLEXIBLE
Allow time
for spontaneity/
and make time
for necessary routines.
BE CARING
Make time
for the necessary
routines/and allow
time for spontaneity.
Q4
Q2B
Q3A
Q2A
Q3B
Q1
BE SUCCESSFUL
Learn new skills/and
accept your limitations.
BE IMPORTANT
Please yourself/and
please others.
BE HUMAN
Share your feelings/and
keep your feelings to yourself.

Q3A. *Be CARING.* There is a time to Hurry Up compulsively and to do the necessary routines—and a time *not* to Hurry Up compulsively and to allow time for spontaneity. Choose what is appropriate for you in the immediate context.

Q3B. *BE IMPORTANT.* There is a time to Please Others—to make others important by watching your *p's* and *q's*—and a time *not* to Please Others—to make yourself important by pleasing yourself. Choose what is appropriate for you in the immediate context.

Unconditional Negative Messages

There are 14 optional Unconditional Negative Messages that you may have received from your parents (see Diagram 3.3).

Q1. *DON'T BE / BE.* There is an appropriate time to withdraw and an appropriate time to be present. Choose what is appropriate for you in the immediate context.

DON'T FEEL / FEEL. There is an appropriate time not to express your feelings and an appropriate time to express your feelings. Choose what is appropriate for you in the immediate context.

DON'T BE YOU / BE YOU. There is an appropriate time not to express your individuality and an appropriate time to express your individuality. Choose what is appropriate for you in the immediate context.

DON'T BELONG / BELONG. There is an appropriate time to be a loner and an appropriate time to be a joiner. Choose what is appropriate for you in the immediate context.

DON'T BE CLOSE / BE CLOSE. There is an appropriate time to question and mistrust, and an appropriate time to trust and be affectionate. Choose what is appropriate for you in the immediate context.

Q2. *DON'T SUCCEED / SUCCEED.* There is an appropriate time to meet your parents' expectations and an appropriate time to fulfill your own wants. Choose what is appropriate for you in the immediate context.

A. *DON'T GO AWAY / GO AWAY.* There is an appropriate time to stay at home and succeed and an appropriate time to go away from home and succeed. Choose what is appropriate for you in the immediate context.

DON'T BE SICK / BE SICK. There is an appropriate time to succeed without getting sick and an appropriate time to succeed even though you *are* sick. Choose what is appropriate for you in the immediate context.

B. *DON'T BE A CHILD / BE A CHILD.* There is an appropriate time not to have fun and do your chores, and an appropriate time to have fun and not do your chores. Choose what is appropriate for you in the immediate context.

Q4. *DON'T / DO.* There is an appropriate time not to do your own thing and an appropriate time to do your own thing. Choose what is appropriate for you in the immediate context.

DON'T THINK / THINK. There is an appropriate time to accept the other person's opinion and an appropriate time to think for yourself. Choose what is appropriate for you in the immediate context.

Diagram 3.3
EUSTRESS AUTONOMY
Unconditional Negative Messages

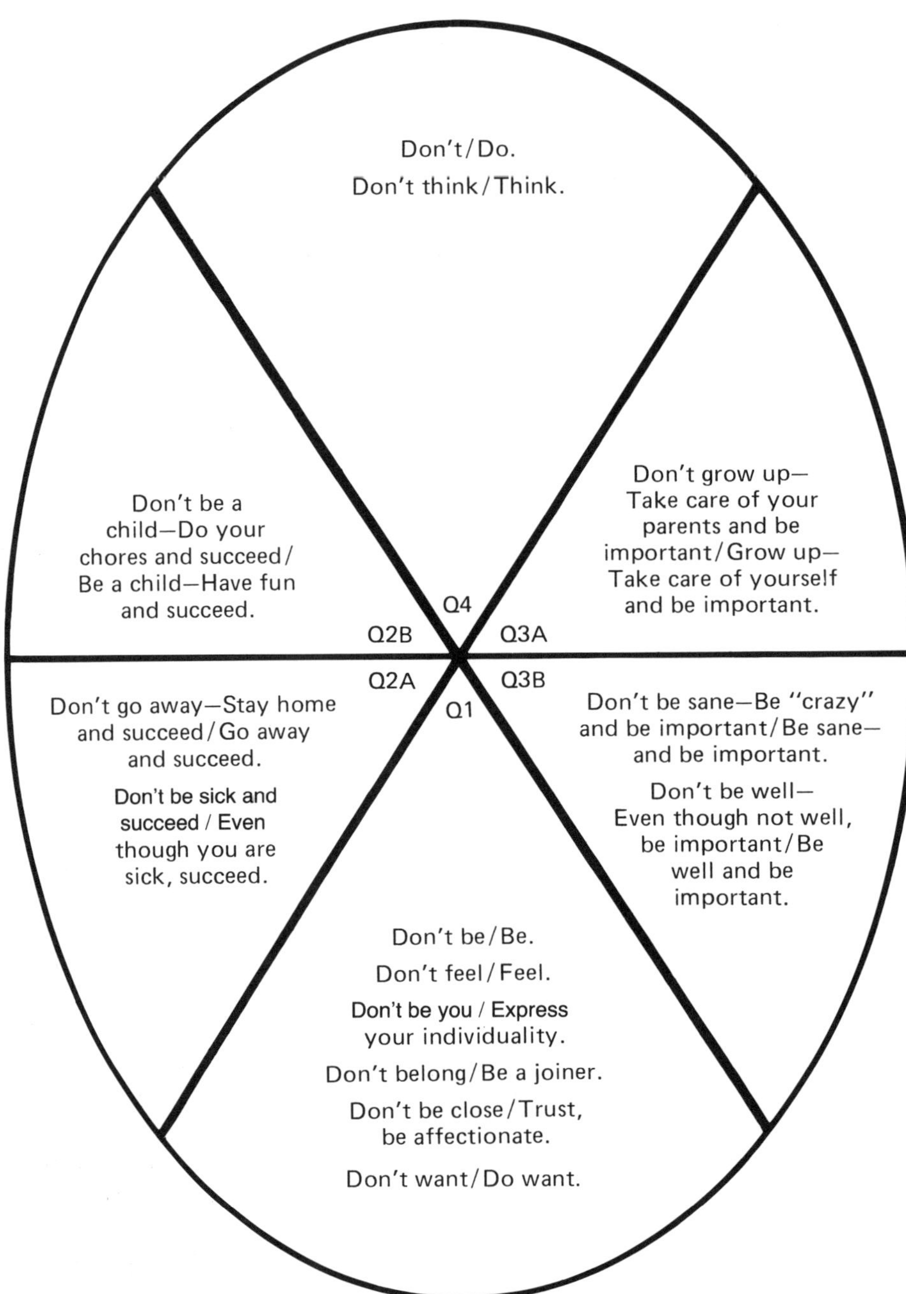

Q3. *DON'T BE IMPORTANT / BE IMPORTANT.* There is an appropriate time to be on the sidelines and an appropriate time to be in the center of the action. Choose what is appropriate for you in the immediate context.

A. *DON'T GROW UP / GROW UP.* There is an appropriate time to take care of your parents and be important and an appropriate time to take care of yourself and be important. Choose what is appropriate for you in the immediate context.

B. *DON'T BE SANE / BE SANE.* There is an appropriate time to be "crazy" and be important and an appropriate time to be sane and important. Choose what is appropriate for you in the immediate context.

DON'T BE WELL / BE WELL. There is an appropriate time to be important even though you are not well and an appropriate time to be well and important. Choose what is appropriate for you in the immediate context.

EUSTRESS RESPONSIBILITY

An Unconditional Eustress Decision-response is an expression of your authentic life energy—it is one of the two ways that you exercise Responsibility.

Responsibility represents the use of your life energies to choose, to make decisions and to act on those decisions. When you exercise your Responsibility, you allow yourself to feel, think and behave in a way that is comfortable and that you believe will bring you the joy and satisfaction that is your birthright. To exercise your Responsibility is to Eustress yourself.

When you lock yourself into a Decision-response inappropriate to your situation, you abdicate Responsibility, and you feel, think and behave in a way that is uncomfortable and that brings you unhappiness and disappointment. When you distress yourself, you surrender your Responsibility and destroy your birthright.

Make believe! Suppose your parents had given you Eustress messages instead of Distress messages. How would you have exercised your Responsibility? What kind of Decision-responses would you have given? You don't know the answer. Neither do we. If we did, we would be talking about what might have been. However, the odds are that you would have based your Decision-responses about what kind of a person you want to be and how to be that person upon the very same Unconditional Positive and Negative Eustress Messages your parents gave you. You may have changed the order or even picked different messages, but your answer would have come from the same messages.

Unconditional Positive Decision-responses

There are six optional Unconditional Positive Decision-responses which you may have made when you received the Unconditional Positive Messages from your parents (see Diagram 3.4).

Q1. I WILL BE HUMAN. I will decide when it is appropriate for me to Be

Diagram 3.4
EUSTRESS RESPONSIBILITY
Unconditional Positive Decision-Responses

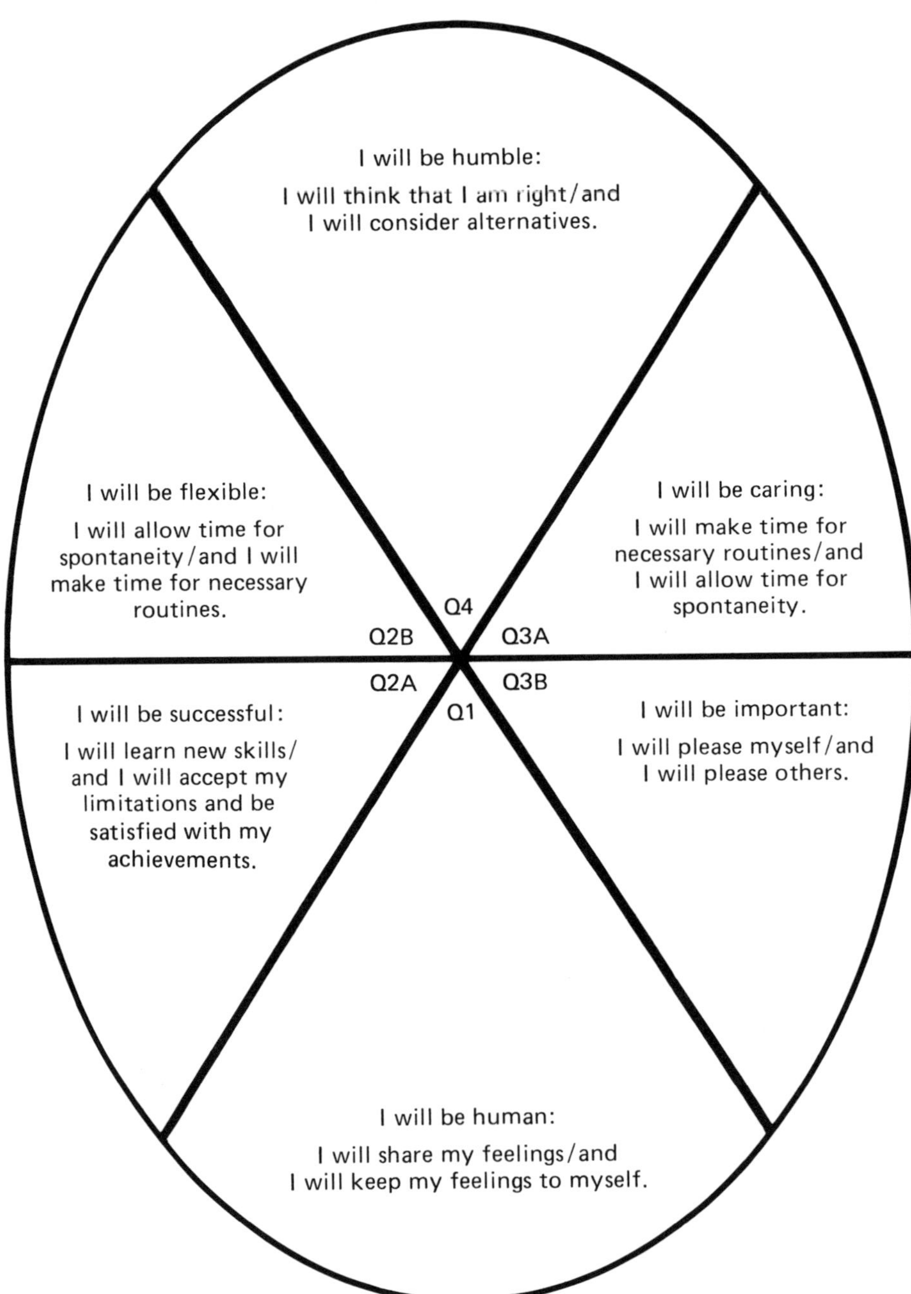

Strong—to suck it in and keep my feelings to myself—and when it is appropriate for me *not* to Be Strong—to cry and let others know how I feel.

Q2A.   I WILL BE SUCCESSFUL. I will decide when it is appropriate for me to Try Hard—to put my shoulder to the wheel and explore new values and learn new skills—and when it is appropriate for me *not* to Try Hard—to accept my limitations and be satisfied with my achievements.

Q2B.   I WILL BE FLEXIBLE. I will decide when it is appropriate for me to Hurry Up—impulsively and be spontaneous—and when it is appropriate for me *not* to Hurry Up impulsively and do the necessary routines.

Q4.   I WILL BE HUMBLE. I will decide when it is appropriate for me to Be Perfect—to think that I am right—and when it is appropriate for me *not* to Be Perfect—to consider alternatives.

Q3A.   I WILL BE CARING. I will decide when it is appropriate for me to Hurry Up—compulsively and do the necessary routines—and when it is appropriate for me *not* to Hurry Up compulsively and allow time for spontaneity.

Q3B.   I WILL BE IMPORTANT. I will decide when it is appropriate for me to Please Others—to make others important by watching my *p*'s and *q*'s—and when it is appropriate for me *not* to Please Others—to make myself important and please myself.

Unconditional Negative Decision-responses

There are 14 optional Unconditional Negative Decision-responses that you may have made when you received the Unconditional Negative Messages from your parents (see Diagram 3.5).

Q1.   I WON'T BE / I WILL BE. There is an appropriate time for me to withdraw and an appropriate time for me to be present. I will choose what is appropriate for me in the immediate context.

I WON'T FEEL / I WILL FEEL. There is an appropriate time for me not to express my feelings and an appropriate time for me to express my feelings. I will choose what is appropriate for me in the immediate context.

I WON'T BE ME / I WILL BE ME. There is an appropriate time for me not to express my individuality and an appropriate time for me to express my individuality. I will choose what is appropriate for me in the immediate context.

I WON'T BELONG / I WILL BELONG. There is an appropriate time for me to be a loner and an appropriate time for me to be a joiner. I will choose what is appropriate for me in the immediate context.

I WON'T BE CLOSE / I WILL BE CLOSE. There is an appropriate time for me to question and mistrust and an appropriate time for me to trust and be affectionate. I will choose what is appropriate for me in the immediate context.

I WON'T WANT / I WILL WANT. There is an appropriate time for me to deny my wants and an appropriate time for me to express my wants. I will choose what is appropriate for me in the immediate context.

Q2.   I WON'T SUCCEED / I WILL SUCCEED. There is an appropriate time for me to meet my parents' expectations and an appropriate time for me to fulfill my own wants. I will choose what is appropriate for me in the immediate context.

Diagram 3.5
EUSTRESS RESPONSIBILITY
Unconditional Negative Decision-Responses

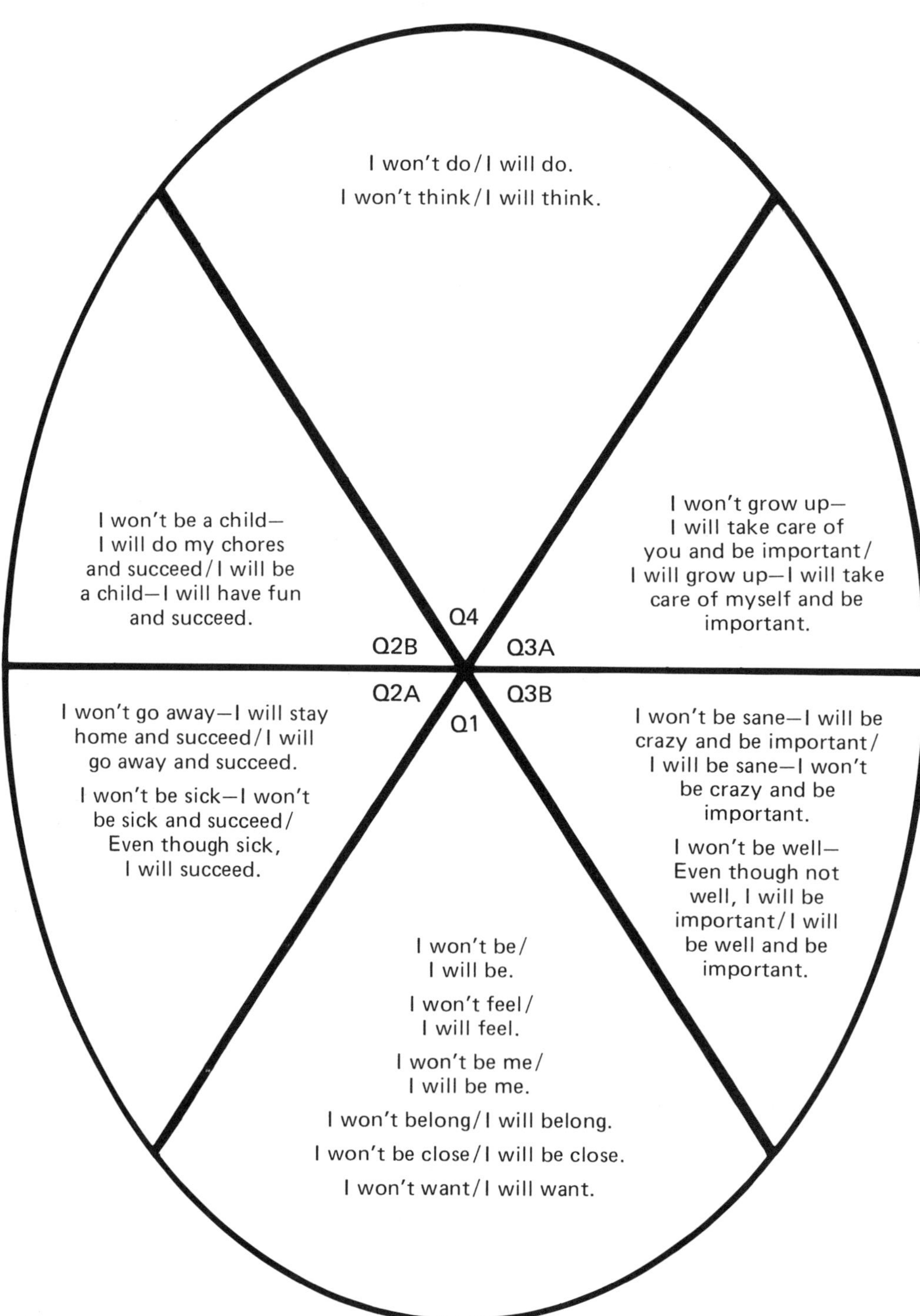

A. I WON'T GO AWAY / I WILL GO AWAY. There is an appropriate time for me to stay at home and succeed and an appropriate time for me to go away from home and succeed. I will choose what is appropriate for me in the immediate context.

B. I WON'T BE SICK / I WILL BE SICK. There is an appropriate time for me to succeed without getting sick and an appropriate time for me to be sick and still succeed. I will choose what is appropriate for me in the immediate context.

I WON'T BE A CHILD / I WILL BE A CHILD. There is an appropriate time for me not to have fun and do my chores and an appropriate time for me to have fun and not do my chores. I will choose what is appropriate for me in the immediate context.

Q4.   I WON'T / I WILL. There is an appropriate time for me not to do my own thing and an appropriate time for me to do my own thing. I will choose what is appropriate for me in the immediate context.

I WON'T THINK / I WILL THINK. There is an appropriate time for me to accept another person's opinion and an appropriate time for me to think for myself. I will choose what is appropriate for me in the immediate context.

Q3.   I WON'T BE IMPORTANT / I WILL BE IMPORTANT. There is an appropriate time for me to be on the sidelines and an appropriate time for me to be in the center of the action. I will choose what is appropriate for me in the immediate context.

A. I WON'T GROW UP / I WILL GROW UP. There is an appropriate time for me to take care of others and be important, and an appropriate time for me to take care of myself and be important. I will choose what is appropriate for me in the immediate context.

B. I WON'T BE SANE / I WILL BE SANE. There is an appropriate time for me to be "crazy" and still be important and an appropriate time for me to be "mentally healthy" and be important. I will choose what is appropriate for me in the immediate context.

I WON'T BE WELL / I WILL BE WELL. There is an appropriate time for me not to be well and still be important and an appropriate time for me to be well and be important. I will choose what is appropriate for me in the immediate context.

THE EUSTRESS LIFE ATTITUDE

You can be both for your parents and against your parents. You can be flexible. Unconditional Eustress Messages create a *both/and* situation. Every Positive Eustress Message has a Negative built into it, and every Negative Eustress Message has a Positive built into it.

Even when you are small and dependent upon your parents, this is possible. Much depends on the kinds of Permission and Protection your parents give you as you grow through infancy, childhood and adolescence. Most parents are well-intentioned. They provide you with what they believe is the best information available, and they probably received this information from their own parents. Their messages are intended both for their own reassurance and for your safety.

As used in this book, the term *Protection* refers to a perception of basic safety, which parents give you and which you develop for yourself when you become responsible and choose a strategy for coping with life. Protection becomes *Prohibition,* however, when the messages that parents give you are designed for *their* reassurance and not for *your* sense of safety. The term Prohibition, therefore, will be used in connection with the Don'ts of Distress Negative Messages and the term Protection will be reserved for use with Eustress Negative Messages.

A similar distinction is made in this book between the terms Permission and Prescription. *Permission* is used with reference to Eustress Positive Messages and Prescriptions with reference to the Do's of Distress Positive Messages. *Prescriptions* are demands and imply limitations. Permissions suggest opportunities and invite the testing of options.

The Permissions and the Protections of Eustress Messages promote autonomy and maximize responsibility. The Prescriptions and Prohibitions of Distress Messages impose authority and minimize responsibility.

When your parents send you Distress Messages, their Positive Messages give you Prescriptions and their Negative Messages provide you with Prohibitions. The Prescriptions and Prohibitions, though addressed to you, are intended primarily for your parents' reassurance and comfort. They think that they themselves are a success and that you will be a success, too. They can show you off and be proud. They also can tell themselves that you will be safe in a difficult world.

When you are Compliant, you accept their Prescriptions and Prohibitions. When you are Defiant, you reject them. In neither case, however, do you have authentic Protection. You believe that you are safe only as long as you follow their directives. You remain dependent and vulnerable to your parents' disapproval. When you comply with your parents, you see yourself as one-down and your parents as one-up. When you defy their directives, you see yourself as one-up. In both instances, however, your responses still are controlled by them. You are afraid to be autonomous.

Eustress Messages, on the other hand, offer you *both* Permission *and* Protection. Parents who send Eustress Messages don't need their children to "protect" them. They take responsibility for their own Protection. In addition, because you are small and they are big, they accept two other responsibilities:

1. to provide you with Protection while you are small, and
2. to give you Permission to protect yourself as you grow big.

Of course, you have to seize this opportunity. You have to be responsible. You know the old statement: "You can lead a horse to water, but you can't make it drink." If you don't seize the opportunity, you lock yourself into inappropriate Compliance-Defiance patterns.

If you do give yourself both Permission and Protection, you become responsible and you no longer remain in a Life Attitude where you are either one-down or one-up. Now you are able to be *up* with yourself, and your parents, too, are *up* with you (↑ ↑) (see Diagram 3.6). You give yourself

Permission to agree with your parents, and you give yourself Permission to disagree with your parents. Whether you agree or disagree, however, you also know—both from the example of your parents and from your own experience (trials and errors)—what is appropriate and what is not appropriate for you to feel, think and do. You distinguish between an inappropriate Decision-response and an appropriate Decision-response. You give yourself Protection.

EUSTRESS WORDS

Just as there are Distress words (*must, should, could* and their negative equivalents *must not, should not* and *can't*), so there are Eustress words. These words also give you Permission and Protection; however, they enable you to give yourself your own Permission and Protection. Instead of receiving Permission from an external source or from an external source which you have internalized, as in the case of Distress words, you now are the source of your own Permission. Similarly, the Protection you now have is for your own good as well as for the welfare of someone else. The result, of course, is that you have Power. You no longer are Powerless, because through the words that you

Diagram 3.6
THE EUSTRESS LIFE ATTITUDE

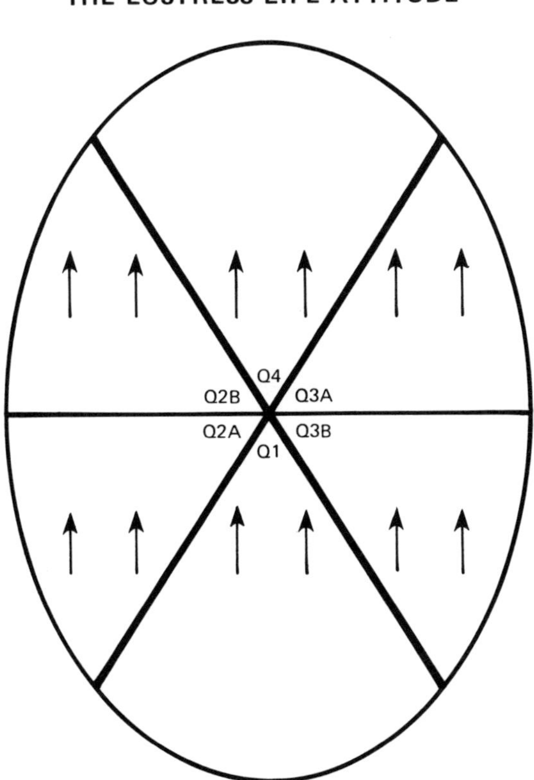

use you become autonomous and take responsibility for your own Permission and Protection (see Table 3.1).

May is a Eustress word concerned with Permission, both external and internal. *May not* is its Eustress Protection counterpart.

In addition to Permission words, Protection words, and Power words, however, there are two necessary sets of Eustress words: 1) Intention words and 2) Capability words. *Want* and *don't want* are Intention words. They are very important Eustress words because they indicate your preferences—what you *want* and what you *don't want;* however, they are not the same as, nor are they to be confused with, Action or Power words. The old adage "there is many a slip between the cup and the lip" is very apropos when connecting Intention words with Power or action words. *Can* and *cannot (can't)* are Capability words, referring to your physical, intellectual and emotional capability to fulfill your *wants* and *don't wants.*

The ultimate in Power words, however, are those words which indicate your *doing* and *not doing* after 1) you give yourself Permission and Protection, 2) declare your preferences and 3) are aware of your capabilities. There are two sets of such Power words: *will (do)* and *won't (do)*, and *am (doing)* and *am not (doing)*. Power words are Action words.

Table 3.1
EUSTRESS WORDS

YOU ARE OKAY.

"You may . . ."   "You may not . . ."

TRANSLATES INTO

"I may . . ."   "I may not . . ."

TRANSLATES INTO

"I want . . ."   "I don't want . . ."

TRANSLATES INTO

"I will . . ."   "I won't . . ."

TRANSLATES INTO

I'm UP and others are UP with me, too.

TRANSLATES INTO

Q1 OPTION: I am aware of my life energies.
Q2 OPTION: I explore my values and develop my skills.
Q4 OPTION: I consider my alternative skills and values and
                      integrate them into a meaningful plan.
Q3 OPTION: I commit my integrated skills and values to
                      relationships.

A CHICKEN AND/OR EGG STORY

It is not within your Power to control whether your parents or other people confront you with a Chicken *or* Egg situation or a Chicken *and* Egg situation. People are the way they are, and they will continue either to be locked into inappropriate ways of feeling, thinking and behaving or they will use their life energies in appropriate ways. Sometimes they will do both, using inappropriate ways in one particular situation and appropriate ways in another situation.

How you respond to other people, however, *is* within your Power. Whether you are presented with a Chicken *or* Egg situation or a Chicken *and* Egg situation, you can decide to deal with the situation from an *up* Life Position—you are *up* and the other person is *up* with you, too. The choice is yours.

You Distress yourself when you choose an *either-or* response—in which either you are one-up and the other person is one-down, or you are one-down and the other person is one-up. You Eustress yourself when you choose an up Life Attitude both for yourself and for the other person. The Eustress Life Attitude is a *both/and* Attitude. Therefore, from now on in this book, situations no longer will be presented as Chicken *or* Egg situations or as Chicken *and* Egg situations. They will be presented as Chicken *and/or* Egg situations.

While it is preferable that other people deal with you in terms of *both/and* rather than *either-or,* what is more important is how you deal with them. How they deal with you is their choice, often made for reasons that have little or nothing to do with you. How you choose and decide to respond, however, has very much to do with you. It is within your Power to decide.

PUTTING IT ALL TOGETHER

For purposes of this book, it is preferable that you use the Distress Ellipse and the Eustress Ellipse as two separate diagrams. However, to give you a glimpse of how the two work together, picture again the Eustress Ellipse inside the Distress Ellipse, as presented in Chapter One and illustrated in Diagram 3.7.

The Eustress Ellipse is closer to the center or source of your life energy and indicates how you Eustress yourself when you use your feeling, thought and behavior life-energies appropriately. The Distress Ellipse is further from the center or *source* of your life energy and indicates how you Distress yourself when you use your feeling, thought and behavior life-energies inappropriately.

All the Messages and Decision-responses, both Positive and Negative, in the Eustress Ellipse emphasize an appropriate and constructive use of the life energies. All the Messages and Decision-responses, both Positive and Negative, in the Distress Ellipse emphasize an inappropriate and destructive use of the life energies.

By looking from the Distress Ellipse inward to the Eustress Ellipse you find in each Eustress Quadrant ways to enrich yourself and to grow with others.

The Eustress Quadrants are the well-being Quadrants and provide you with information about how to manage your stress and to use your life energies more effectively.

At the end of each section of this book, you will find this reminder to put the Eustress Ellipse inside the Distress Ellipse and to recall how the two work together.

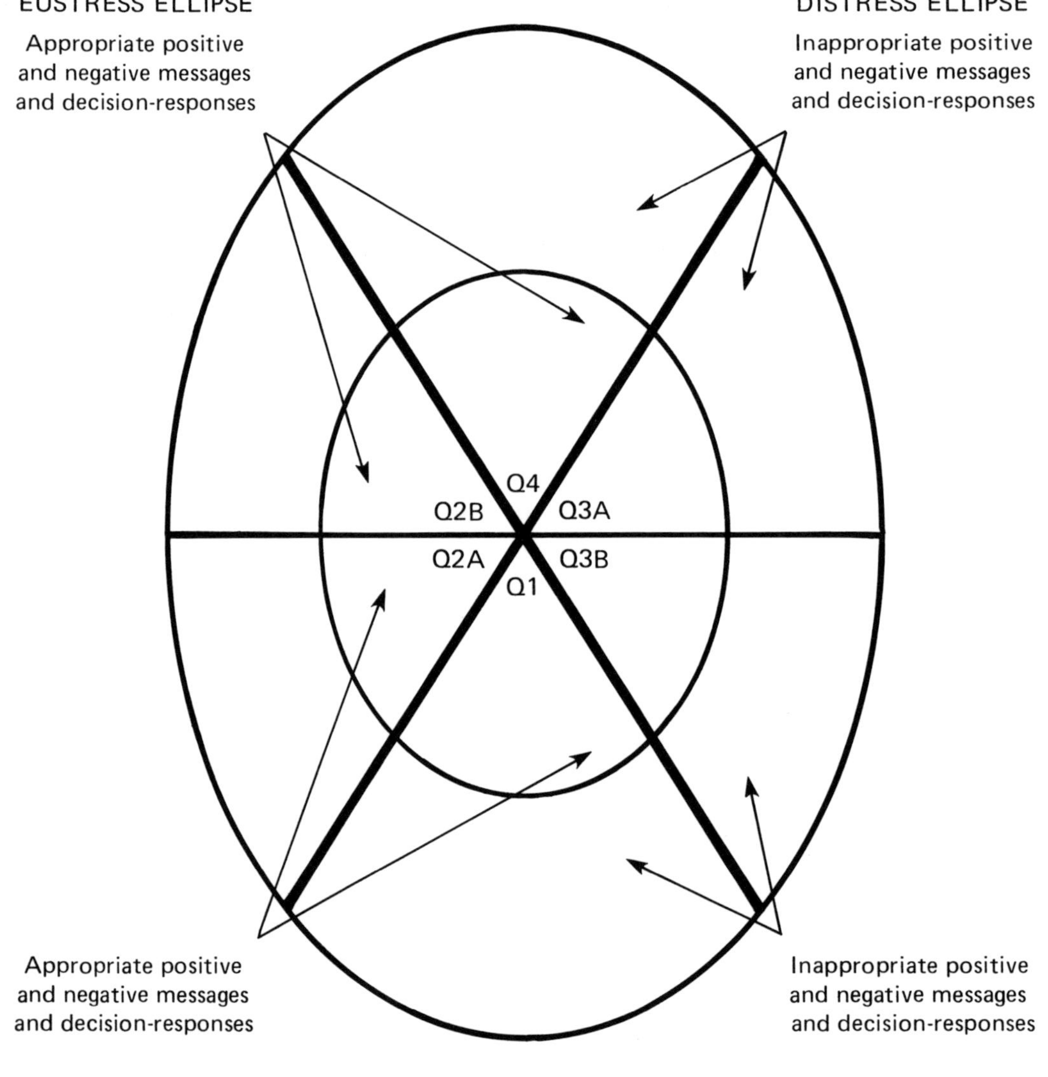

Diagram 3.7

IV:
FROM PROCESS TO CONTENT

CHAPTER 4 FEELINGS, THOUGHTS, BEHAVIORS

Human relationships constitute on-going patterns of stimuli and responses that involve feelings, thoughts and behaviors. The patterns can be Distressful, or they can be Eustressful.

In this section you will learn about *content* (and not *process* as you did in the previous sections). You will learn about the feelings, thoughts and behaviors that occur when you distress yourself, and the feelings, thoughts and behaviors that occur when you eustress yourself.

Since it is impossible to cover the content of every Chicken and/or Egg situation, the contents in this section will be *generic* contents; that is, they will indicate contents characteristic of Distress patterns and contents characteristic of Eustress patterns. For example, when you Distress yourself, while you may not use the identical words used in this book to describe your feelings, thoughts and behaviors, nonetheless the content of your responses characteristically will fit into one of the Distress Quadrants. The same thing holds true when you Eustress yourself. Whatever your words or actions, your response will be drawn from a range of generic Eustress alternatives.

When you distress yourself, you lock yourself into a generic Distress content. When you eustress yourself you choose from a variety of generic Eustress alternatives. It is important, therefore, that you learn the generic contents. In this way, whatever the Chicken and/or Egg situation, you will be able to recognize the signposts of your Distress and avail yourself of Eustress directions to enjoy your life energies.

FEELINGS ARE IMPORTANT

Feelings are emotions. Feelings are the names given to sensations going on inside of you. Feelings can operate without your awareness and even against your will. Feelings are the physiological responses which your body gives to stimuli or messages that you receive from someone else or that you send to yourself.

A feeling without a name we call a mood. A *mood* is a vague sensation of something going on inside your body. It is not shared with other people. When you describe the mood and give it a name you bring the mood into the world. Now you can deal with your feelings and share them with other people.

Feelings are defined or labeled with one word. You may have many feelings; however, each feeling is expressed in *only one word*. If you use more than one word to express a feeling, undoubtedly you are expressing your thoughts and not your feelings.

It is important to separate feelings from thoughts because thoughts are arguable. They are your opinions or beliefs, and someone can disagree with them. Feelings, on the other hand, are not arguable. They are physiological responses. The adrenalin either flows or does not flow. The blood pressure either rises or falls or remains the same.

A feeling is either comfortable or uncomfortable for you. Freud said that feelings are either pleasurable or painful. There are many labels used to describe both comfortable and uncomfortable feelings. In dealing with your Chicken and/or Egg situation, however, you will use 12 feeling labels. Six of the labels will be used to describe uncomfortable or painful feelings, and six will describe comfortable or pleasurable feelings. There are, of course, many other feeling labels that can be used for both comfortable and uncomfortable feelings; however, in our opinion, most feeling labels can be subsumed under the 12 labels.

Distress Feelings (Either-Or)

In the Distress Ellipse there is only one kind of feeling—substitute feelings. Distress feelings, moreover, are uncomfortable feelings. They are never comfortable. (See Diagram 4.1.)

Very often when you Distress yourself in a Chicken and/or Egg situation, you will convince yourself that you are feeling a comfortable feeling instead of an uncomfortable feeling. What you are feeling, however, is *glee* and not joy. Glee is substitute joy. Glee implies settling for half a loaf; joy signifies the whole loaf. The term glee, used in this book, does not refer to mirth or merriment but rather to a perverse form of exultation or satisfaction stemming from the conviction that one's strategy for coping with life is the right one. Glee has to do with what was going on in your life in the past. It means that you are still fighting old battles and attempting to finish the unfinished business of long ago with people in the here and now. If you had finished your business of the past in the past, at that time you would have felt authentic joy and you would have freed yourself to be able to feel authentic joy in the present. Instead, you locked yourself in and are still willing to settle for momentary glee, for getting comfort from winding up with uncomfortable feelings in your current Chicken and/or Egg situations.

Sad, frustrated and *guilty* are Compliant substitute feelings. They are below the center line. Although you end up with uncomfortable feelings, you are inappropriately deriving momentary gratification (glee) from these feelings by being influenced by the other person's feelings, thoughts and behaviors.

Resentful, angry and *worried* are Defiant substitute feelings. They are above the center line. Although you end up with uncomfortable feelings, you are inappropriately deriving momentary gratification (glee) from these feelings by resisting the influence of the other person's feelings, thoughts and behaviors.

Eustress Feelings (Both/And)

Eustress feelings are both comfortable and uncomfortable feelings, and always authentic. Eustress feelings usually come in pairs (see Diagram 4.2). Sometimes there may be three or more authentic Eustress feelings. All of these feelings are in dialogue with each other.

Most often the two Eustress feelings in dialogue with each other are opposite kinds of feelings, one a comfortable feeling and the other an uncom-

Diagram 4.1
DISTRESS FEELINGS (EITHER-OR)
Substitute Painful Feelings

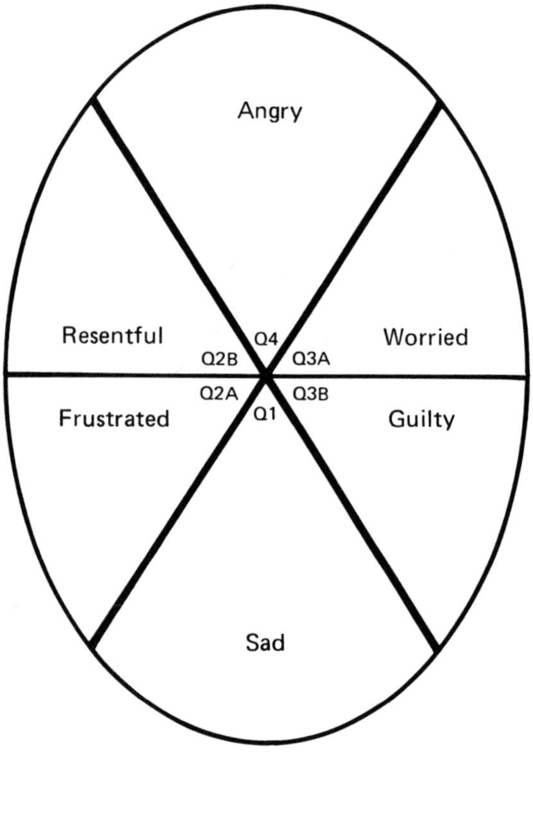

fortable feeling. In their conversation these two feelings are saying to you that you are feeling multiple feelings in your Chicken and/or Egg situation and that it is important for you to recognize that even when you feel appropriately comfortable feelings you may be feeling some appropriately uncomfortable feelings of which you should be aware. Or, vice versa: when you feel appropriately uncomfortable in a situation you also may be feeling some appropriately comfortable feelings of which you should be aware. In other words, the glass can be *both* more or less full *and* more or less empty at the same time.

The six inappropriate substitute gleeful Distress feelings also can be the same appropriate authentic painful Eustress feelings. SAD (Q1), FRUSTRATED (Q2A) and GUILTY (Q3B) are authentic Passive Eustress feelings and are

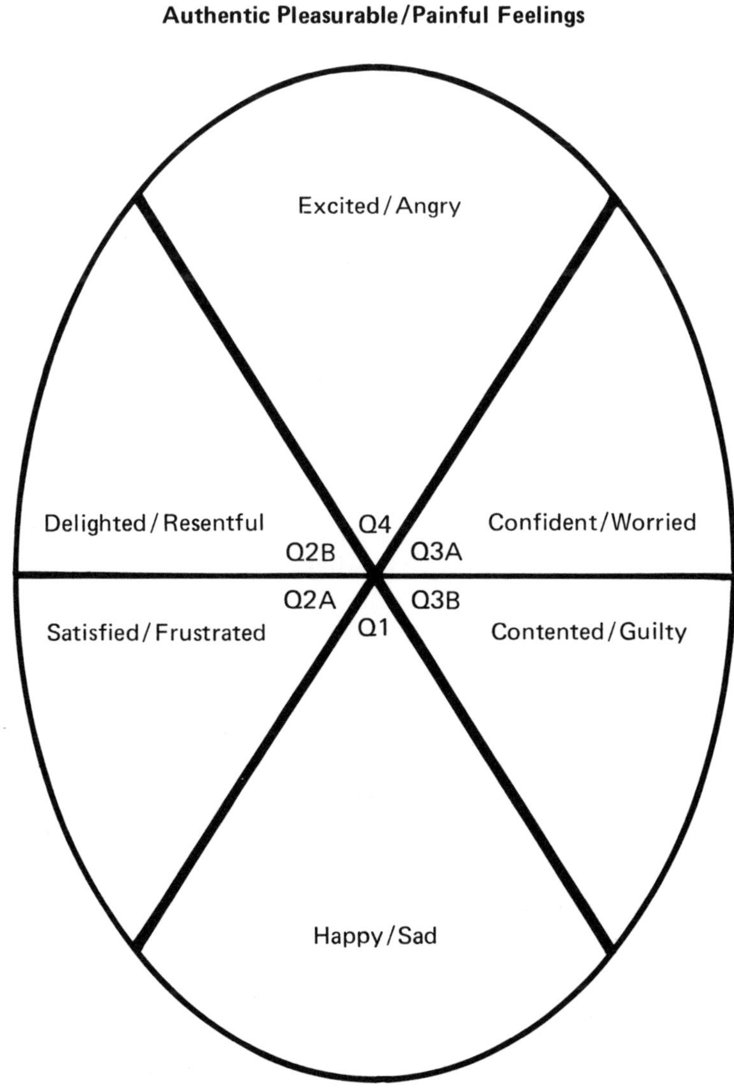

Diagram 4.2
EUSTRESS FEELINGS (BOTH/AND)
Authentic Pleasurable/Painful Feelings

diagrammed below the center line. RESENTFUL (Q2B) ANGRY (Q4) and WOR-RIED (Q3A) are authentic Active Eustress feelings and are diagrammed above the center line.

There also are appropriate authentic pleasurable Eustress feelings. HAPPY (Q1), SATISFIED (Q2A) and CONTENTED (Q3B) are authentic pleasurable Passive Eustress feelings and are diagrammed below the center line. DE-LIGHTED (Q2B), EXCITED (Q4) and CONFIDENT (Q3A) are authentic plea-surable Active Eustress feelings and are diagrammed above the center line.

There are many human emotions, and there are many names for feelings. Our six authentic pleasurable and six authentic painful feelings are some of the most frequently expressed Eustress feelings. You may be more familiar with other feelings that may or may not be related to the feelings used in this book. You might think of what other Eustress feelings you would have included and in what Quadrant you would have put each of them.

THOUGHTS ARE IMPORTANT

Thoughts, like feelings, also are important. You were born with a capacity or energy to think. The energy with which you do your thinking generates inescapable stress. It is a given of your life. You can misuse your thoughts and Distress yourself, or you can use your thoughts constructively and Eustress yourself.

Thoughts give shape and meaning to your existence. They form the inter-pretations of what you notice with your five senses—what you hear, see, smell, taste and touch. Thoughts are your opinions about what you believe—your intentions for yourself, for others and for your relationships with them. Thoughts represent your belief system. They are the values upon which you premise your life.

Thoughts are very useful. Usefulness, however, is not the same as truth-fulness. Someday someone may show you that your interpretation and/or belief is not true. This happened with the theory that the sun turns around the earth and that the earth is flat. Believing alone may make a thought useful, but it cannot make it truthful. You Distress yourself when you equate usefulness with truthfulness. It may be useful for you to believe that the Chicken or the Egg came first, but that doesn't make your belief true. You lock yourself into a contaminated way of thinking when you convert a belief or an opinion into a truth. What is even more significant is that you may not even be aware that you are turning your beliefs into truths.

Distress Thoughts (Either-Or)

Distress thoughts are locked-in thoughts that are inappropriate to your Chicken and/or Egg situation. They are contaminated ways of thinking.

There are six contaminated ways of thinking, which are diagrammed in the Distress Ellipse (see Diagram 4.3). As long as you are locked into the belief that either the Chicken or the Egg must come first, the chances are that you will think in one of these six contaminated thought patterns. You may not use the same language, but your thinking will be characteristic of one of the patterns. Which one you will use, of course, will depend on the Quadrant in which you most often invest your energy.

Contaminated thoughts can arise in almost any situation, no matter how complicated or simple. All that needs to occur, for example, is for someone to ask, "What is your opinion about...?" If you are locked into Q1, you probably will think to yourself: "It's best to be silent and say nothing," or "It's best to be irrelevant and give some off-the-wall kind of answer." If you are locked into Q2A, you probably will think to yourself: "I believe that I'm con-

Diagram 4.3
DISTRESS THOUGHTS (EITHER-OR)
Contaminated Thoughts

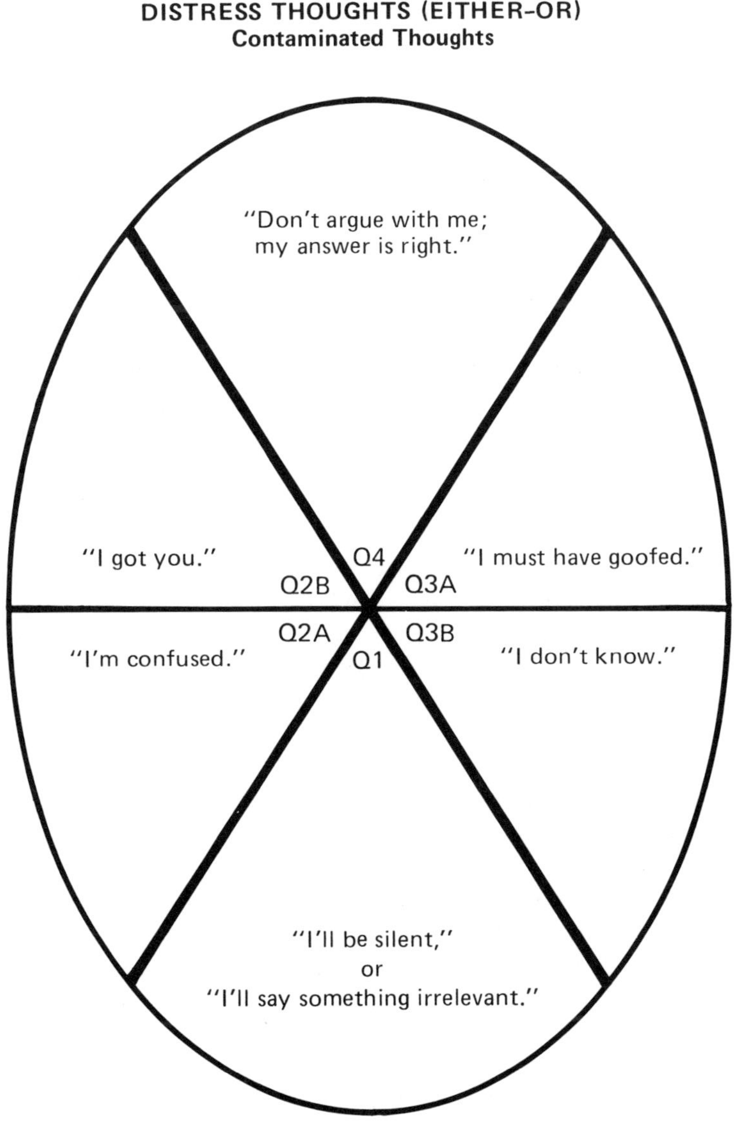

fused." If you are locked into Q2B, you probably will think to yourself: "I really got you now." If you are locked into Q4, you probably will think to yourself: "They better not argue with me. I know what's right." If you are locked into Q3A, you probably will think to yourself: "If they're asking me, I must have goofed." If you are locked into Q3B, you probably will think to yourself: "If I tell them what I think, they won't believe me. If I keep quiet, they won't like it. So, I guess it's better just to say, 'I don't know'."

Eustress Thoughts (Both/And)

Eustress thoughts are thoughts whose usefulness is accepted until there is sufficient evidence to the contrary. Eustress thoughts are uncontaminated thoughts (see Diagram 4.4). They are checked out regularly against evidence. In your lifetime, however, you may never know what is true because in your lifetime all the evidence about the Chicken and about the Egg might not be discovered.

Eustress thoughts, therefore, are useful thoughts, and they are thoughts that are held tentatively. Eustress thoughts are significant and meaningful thoughts, and they are not to be taken lightly. They are to be accepted, and, at the same time, they are to be tested. They are to be used until they are refuted by more significant and meaningful thoughts.

To doubt and question, to acknowledge mistakes, even to admit ignorance and to say that you do not know and, simultaneously to theorize and to affirm tentatively the beliefs that you do hold are all part of the process of Eustress thinking. Eustress thinking seeks to maximize the possibilities for the joyful use of your life energies. Eustress thoughts are appropriate to your here-and-now Chicken and/or Egg situation. They are not locked-in beliefs from the past that you are continuing to use in the present for every Chicken and/or Egg situation.

Eustress thoughts, like Eustress feelings, are thoughts in Dialogue. The Dialogue may be between two Eustress thoughts. When Eustress thoughts talk with each other, they agree that it is possible for both the Chicken and the Egg to have come first. Sometimes the evidence seems to be stronger for the Chicken and sometimes for the Egg. There is no way of proving, however, which did come first, and conclusions drawn from the Dialogue are based on individual preferences.

Sometimes, however, the Dialogue is between a Eustress thought and a Distress thought. When these two thoughts dialogue together, there is the danger that they will not talk *with* each other but *at* each other. There may be a clash between Eustress thoughts based on current evidence and Distress thoughts rooted in past Chicken or Egg situations. The conversation may be about apples and oranges and not about apples and apples. Whether the conclusion or decision drawn from this debate may be regarded as rational will depend on the individual's ability to separate the Eustress thoughts from the Distress thoughts. If the person is sufficiently aware and adequately skilled to do so, there will be no contamination of the two; if not, the outcome will be colored by past Chicken or Egg situations, and the thought will be contaminated and unclear.

Diagram 4.4
EUSTRESS THOUGHTS (BOTH/AND)
Uncontaminated Thoughts

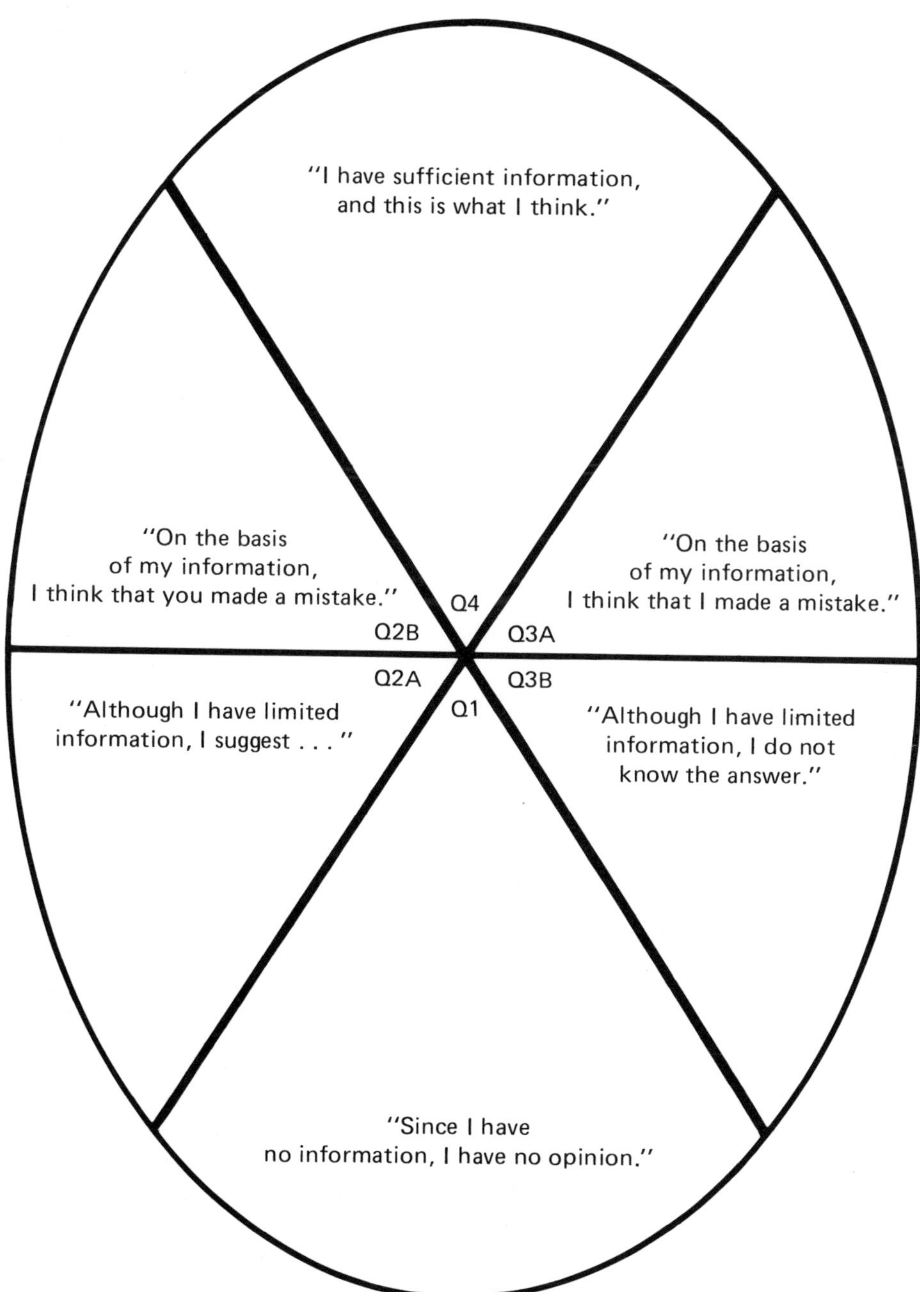

Like Distress thoughts, Eustress thoughts can arise in almost any Chicken and/or Egg situation no matter how complicated or simple. All that needs to occur, again, is for someone to ask, "What is your opinion about . . . ?" In Q1 you think to yourself: "Since I don't have any information, it's best to have no opinion." In Q2A you think to yourself: "Although I have some information, I am not sure what to say; however, I suggest." In Q2B you think to yourself: "On the basis of the information I have, I think that you made a mistake." In Q4 you think to yourself: "I have sufficient information, and this is what I think." In Q3A you think to yourself: "On the basis of the information I have, I think that I made a mistake." In Q3B you think to yourself: "Although I have some information, I do not know the answer."

BEHAVIORS ARE IMPORTANT

Behaviors, like feelings and thoughts, also are important. Your behavior can be appropriate and, therefore, a constructive use of your life energies. Your behavior also can be inappropriate and, therefore, a destructive use of your life energies. You Eustress yourself when your behavior is appropriate. You Distress yourself when your behavior is inappropriate.

There is, however, a very big difference between your behaviors and your feelings and thoughts. Your feelings and thoughts are inside of you, and unless you tell other people what you feel and think the others will not know. When you tell others what you are feeling and what you are thinking, you are translating your feelings and thoughts into behaviors. Of course, when you don't tell them what you feel and think, they can second-guess you, and many times they will be right. However, only you know whether they are right or not. You are the final authority on what you feel and think.

This is not so with behaviors. Unlike your feelings and your thoughts, your behaviors can be seen, heard, smelled, tasted and touched by other people. They still may not know the feelings and thoughts behind your behaviors; however, they will be affected by your behaviors. Your behaviors are measurable stimuli which evoke a response in other people.

Behavior reflects a series of muscle movements. Your particular behavior is the muscle movement or the physical expression of your feelings and thoughts in action and can take many forms. There is *verbal* behavior in which you express your feelings and thoughts. You say to another person, for example, "I feel sad because I believe that . . ." Or you say, "I am resentful because I think that . . ." There also is *non-verbal* behavior, in which you act out your feelings and thoughts without telling anyone what they are. Your behavior takes on certain postures, gestures and facial expressions. Your tone of voice also may change. Most often, when you express yourself non-verbally, other people begin to second-guess you.

When your verbal and non-verbal behaviors send two different messages, most likely one of your messages is appropriate and the other inappropriate to your Chicken and/or Egg situation. While you may gain momentary satisfaction (glee), in the long run you probably are alienating yourself from others and experiencing Distress. When your verbal and non-verbal behaviors send the same appropriate message, you most likely are building relationships and Eustressing yourself.

Distress Behaviors (Either-Or)

Distress Behavior is Alienation and non-relation-building behavior (see Diagram 4.5). It is the behavior you use when you set out to prove that the Chicken or the Egg came first. It is win-lose behavior. Either you win and the other people lose, or you lose and the other people win. Either you get what you want, or the other people get what they want. Both of you cannot be winners at the same time.

Distress behavior is based upon the belief that there are not enough reinforcements to go around. A reinforcement is a way of giving recognition to other people and of receiving recognition from them. You acknowledge the other people for who they are and for what they do, and they acknowledge you for who you are and for what you do. It is also a way of giving recognition to yourself. You acknowledge yourself for who you are and for what you do, and the other people also acknowledge themselves for who they are and for what they do.

In Distress behavior, however, the recognition goes only one way. Either you give recognition to yourself or you give recognition to the other person. Moreover, there is no reciprocal relationship. Neither you nor the other people are concerned with acknowledging each other. There is no mutual reinforcement.

Distress behavior is either Passive behavior or Aggressive behavior or a combination of the two. You are Passive, Aggressive, Passive-Aggressive or Aggressive-Passive. Passive behavior is equivalent to Compliant behavior, and Aggressive behavior is equivalent to Defiant behavior. Therefore, when you distress yourself, you are either Compliant, Defiant, Compliant-Defiant or Defiant-Compliant.

To determine what kind of behavior you or the other person is acting out, complete the following sentence: "I want what I want. If you don't give me what I want . . ."

In the following illustration (see Diagram 4.6), assume that you believe that the Egg came first.

Q1. You become TIMID. You give in. You don't insist that the Egg came first. You accept the other person's opinion that the Chicken came first, hoping that eventually the other person will change and that, at last, you will get what you want. In the meantime, you do without whatever it is you want and become PASSIVE. You are Compliant.

Q2. You become SNEAKY-SLY like a fox. At first, in Q2A, you are PASSIVE and Compliant. You pretend that the Chicken came first. You walk softly. Then you switch. In Q2B, you become AGGRESSIVE and Defiant. You no longer pretend, but now carry a big stick and figure out a way to convince the other

Diagram 4.5
DISTRESS BEHAVIOR (EITHER–OR)
Alienation

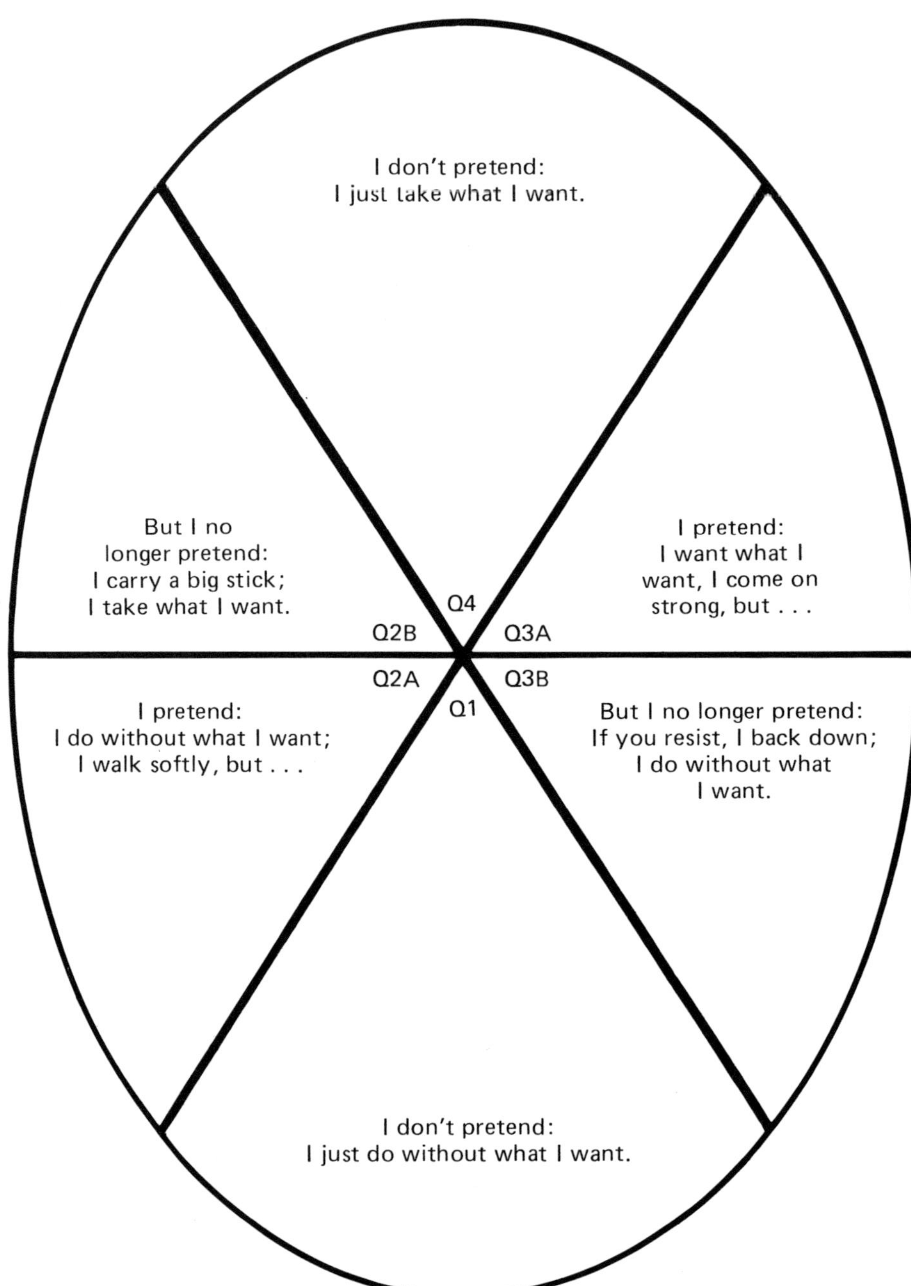

person that the Egg came first. In Q2, your behavior is PASSIVE-AGGRESSIVE. You are Compliant-Defiant.

Q4. You become PUSHY. You insist that the Egg came first, and you force the other person to accept your view. You take what you want and become AGGRESSIVE and Defiant.

3. You become SNEAKY, only this time you are not SLY but SORRY. At first, in Q3A, you are AGGRESSIVE and Defiant. You pretend that the Egg came first. You come on strong. When the other person also comes on strong you switch. In Q3B you become PASSIVE and Compliant. You no longer pretend but give in, under pressure, and accept the position that the Chicken came first. In Q3 your behavior is AGGRESSIVE-PASSIVE. You are Defiant-Compliant.

Eustress Behaviors (Both/And)

Eustress behavior is relationship-building behavior. It is the behavior you use when you believe that there are many useful ways to deal with a Chicken and/or Egg situation. You are not locked into one and only one way.

Eustress behavior, moreover, is Assertive behavior, and you are concerned with enhancing your self-esteem. You take care of yourself. Unless you enhance

Diagram 4.6
DISTRESS BEHAVIOR (EITHER–OR)
Passive-Aggressive

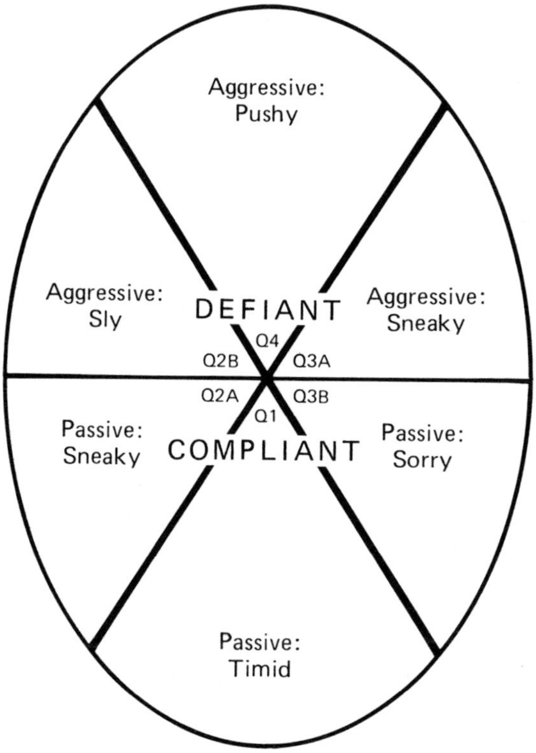

your self-esteem, there is little likelihood of your building a Eustress relationship.

Assertive behavior, however, is not the same as Aggressive behavior. The hallmark of Aggressive behavior is: "I want what I want. If you don't give it to me, I take it anyway." In Aggressive behavior what the other person wants is unimportant to the aggressor. When you are Assertive, on the other hand, you are very much concerned with what the other person wants. You care; moreover, you take into consideration and, if necessary, negotiate with the other person so that both of you get what you want. First, however, you assert yourself. Your self-esteem is important.

Though you are Assertive, you still may not get what you want. There are no guaranteed Eustress behavioral outcomes. Eustress behavior is the result of a Dialogue between two people, both of whom are Assertive. You are Assertive and want what you want, and the other person is also Assertive and wants what s/he wants. Both of you are decision-making human beings, deciding how much to give and how much to receive in a given context.

Being Assertive, therefore, does not mean that you automatically get what you want. Being Assertive means that you stand up for your rights in a way that preserves your self-esteem. When you have self-esteem, you maintain your energy and use it constructively. You explore new alternatives. You plan new strategies. You commit to new relationships. An Assertive person is a winner and, like the proverbial cat, continues to land "on all fours." The worst thing that can happen when you are Assertive is that you may not get what you want and have to come up with new alternatives. The best thing that can happen is that you will be creative, continue to land on all fours and enhance your self-respect as you get more and more of what you want.

Eustress behavior is based upon the belief that there are enough reinforcements available for everyone and that there are many appropriate ways to give and receive these reinforcements. You can win, and the other person can win, too.

Like feelings and thoughts, there are many Eustress Assertive behavior options from which to choose. In this book six options are used (see Diagram 4.7), and they serve only as guidelines (there may be others which you prefer):

Q1. If you don't give me what I want, I give it to myself.	Q4. If you don't give me what I want, I consider alternatives, integrate skills and values and plan new strategies.
Q2A. If you give me what I want, I accept it and say "thank you."	Q3A. If you give me what I don't want, I refuse and say "No, thank you."
Q2B. If you ask for what you want, I give it to you.	Q3B. If you don't give me what I want, I ask for it.

Let us summarize Distress and Eustress characteristics (see Table 4.1).

Distress is the misuse of your life energies. Distress calls for techniques that bind you to an either-or mentality. You are caught up in a Chicken or Egg

Diagram 4.7
EUSTRESS BEHAVIOR (BOTH/AND)
Relationship–Building

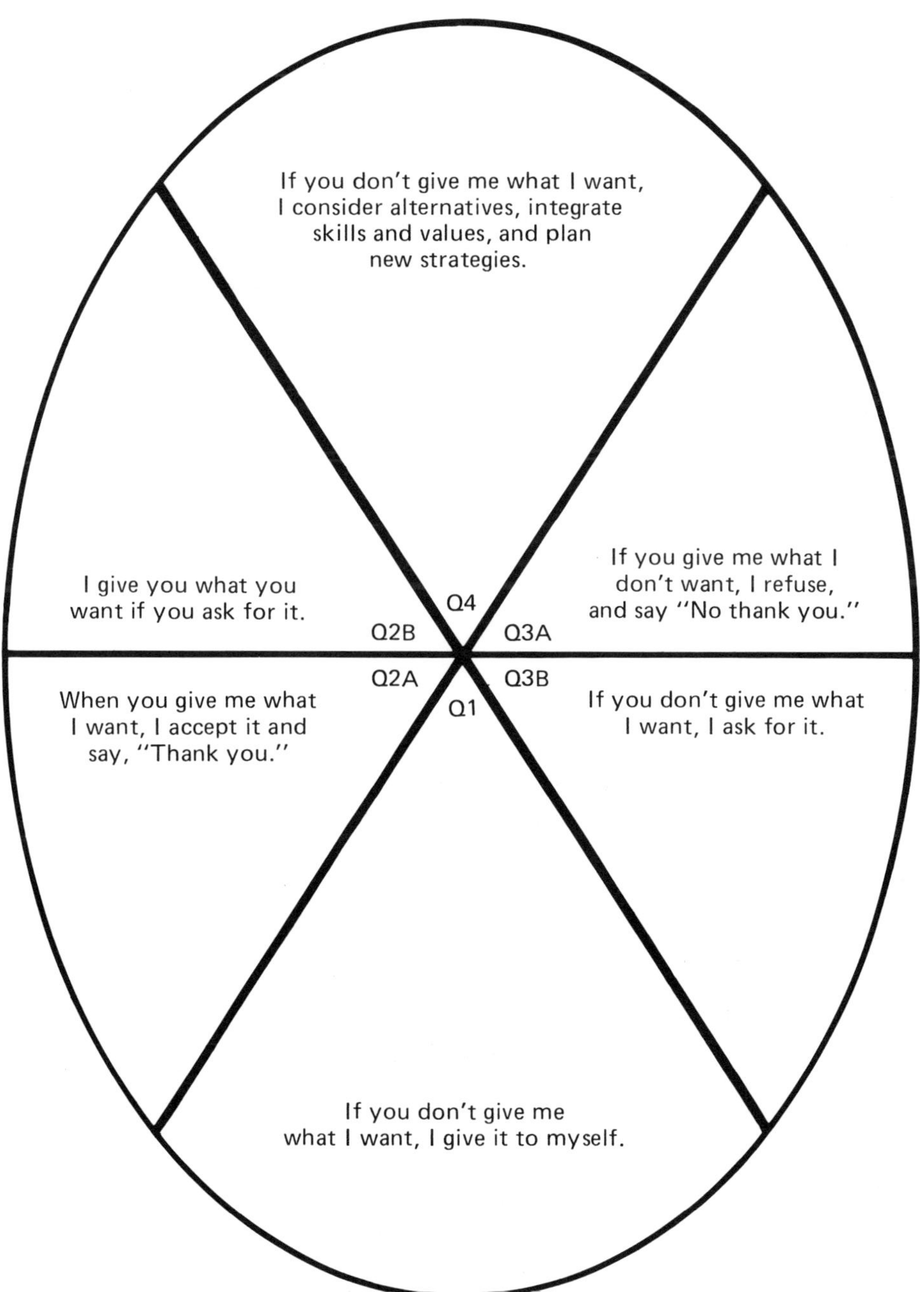

situation. Distress means that you put on a mask to hide the real you. Distress means that you feel substitute and not authentic feelings. When you distress yourself, you do not feel genuine pleasure, only glee, a perverse kind of joy that you derive from feeling uncomfortable and painful feelings. You derive glee or pseudo-pleasure from feeling sad, frustrated, resentful, angry, worried or guilty.

Distress means that you contaminate your thoughts. When you distress yourself, you believe that there is only one answer to a question, whatever the question may be, and you lock yourself into a system of logic that seeks only to justify and defend your answer.

Distress means that you alienate yourself and make your relationships with other people adversarial and, therefore, difficult if not impossible. You act so that either you win and the other person loses or the other person wins and you lose. You are willing to concede one other possibility: both of you must lose.

Distress means that your life attitude is inappropriate to the here and now. While you live in the present, you continue to be controlled by the Decision-responses that you made in the past and that you insist must shape your future. You say to yourself *I must* rather than *I want.* You deny yourself the Permission to be yourself. You live by the Prescriptions of your parents. You avoid giving yourself the Protection you want and need. You comfort yourself with the Prohibitions of your parents. You emasculate your Power.

The feelings, thoughts and behaviors characteristic of Distress (either-or) are illustrated in Diagram 4.8.

Eustress

Eustress is the constructive use of your life energies. Eustress invites a process which elicits a *both/and* mentality. You participate in Chicken *and/or* Egg situations. Eustress means that you shed all masks and become the real you.

Table 4.1
REVIEW

DISTRESS		EUSTRESS
	ATTITUDE	
Inappropriate to the here and now		Appropriate to the here and now
	FEELINGS	
Substitute		Authentic
	THOUGHTS	
Contaminated		Uncontaminated
	BEHAVIORS	
Alienation		Relationship-building
	PERSONALITY TYPES	
Either-or		Both/And

Diagram 4.8
DISTRESS ELLIPSE (EITHER-OR)
Feelings, Thoughts and Behaviors

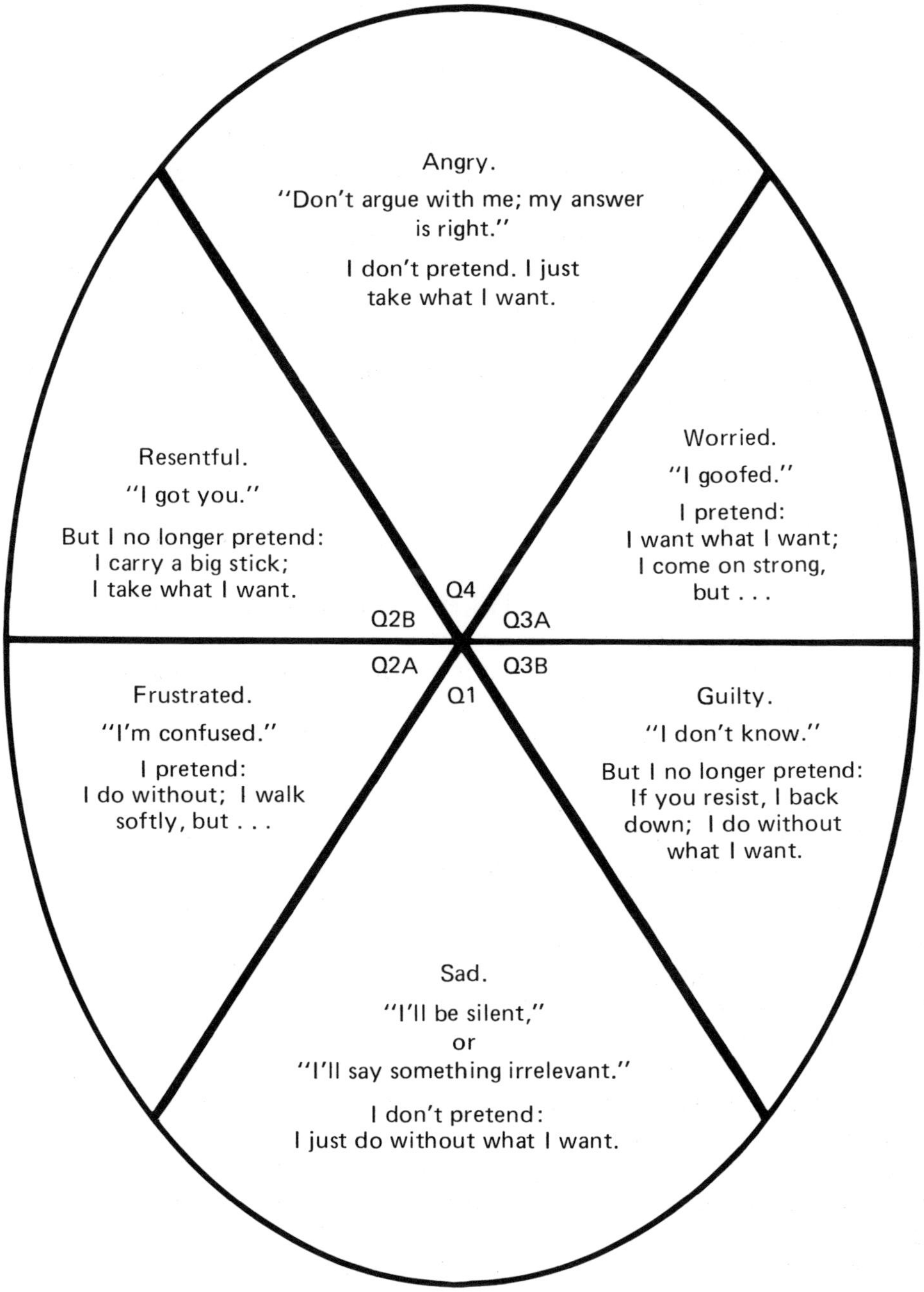

Eustress means that you feel authentic feelings. When you Eustress yourself, you experience genuine pleasure and genuine pain. Eustress feelings usually come in pairs; you are able to feel combinations of comfortable and uncomfortable feelings as well as multiple feelings of comfort and multiple feelings of discomfort.

Eustress means that your thoughts are uncontaminated. When you Eustress yourself you hold your thoughts tentatively, check them out regularly as you test their usefulness, and, when appropriate, you doubt, question and admit mistakes.

Eustress means that your behaviors are relation-building behaviors. When you Eustress yourself, you are Assertive. You enhance your personal self-esteem as well as the other person's.

Eustress means that your life attitude is appropriate to the here and now. You live in the present, and your Decision-responses are of the present, too. You say I *want*. . . , rather than I *must*. . . . You learn from the past, and you design your future. You give yourself Permission, Protection and Power.

The feelings, thoughts and behaviors characteristic of Eustress (both/and) are illustrated in Diagram 4.9.

DISTRESS LIMITATIONS AND EUSTRESS OPPORTUNITIES

When you lock yourself into an *either-or* mentality, you both Distress yourself and limit your life-energy potential to cope with personal and relationship problems. It is as though you put yourself behind psychological prison bars. Either you conform or you defy; you give yourself no other alternative. The either-or mentality is an attack-and-defend mentality. You must choose the Chicken *or* the Egg.

When you choose a *both/and* mentality, you both Eustress yourself and maximize your life-energy potential to cope with personal and relationship problems. It's as though you emancipate yourself and throw off the shackles of psychological imprisonment. Instead of restraining your opportunities, you liberate them. Instead of limiting yourself to attack and defend, you now invest your primary life energies in problem-solving and restrict the strategies of defense and attack to appropriate times and places. You may choose the Chicken *and* the Egg.

A winner is a person who, if one solution does not work, has a second—and even a third and fourth—alternative available. A loser knows but one way and follows blindly in that way.

Both the either-or and the both/and mentalities are incorporated into the Quadrants. The either-or mentality with its limitations on coping capacities is included in the Distress Ellipse (see Diagram 4.10). The both/and mentality with its maximization of coping opportunities is included in the Eustress Ellipse (see Diagram 4.11).

Distress Limitations emphasize Q1 Negative Distortions; Q2 Unfulfilled Expectations: Q4 Positive Distortions; and Q3 Violations of Personal Values. Eu-

Diagram 4.9
EUSTRESS ELLIPSE (BOTH/AND)
Feelings, Thoughts and Behaviors

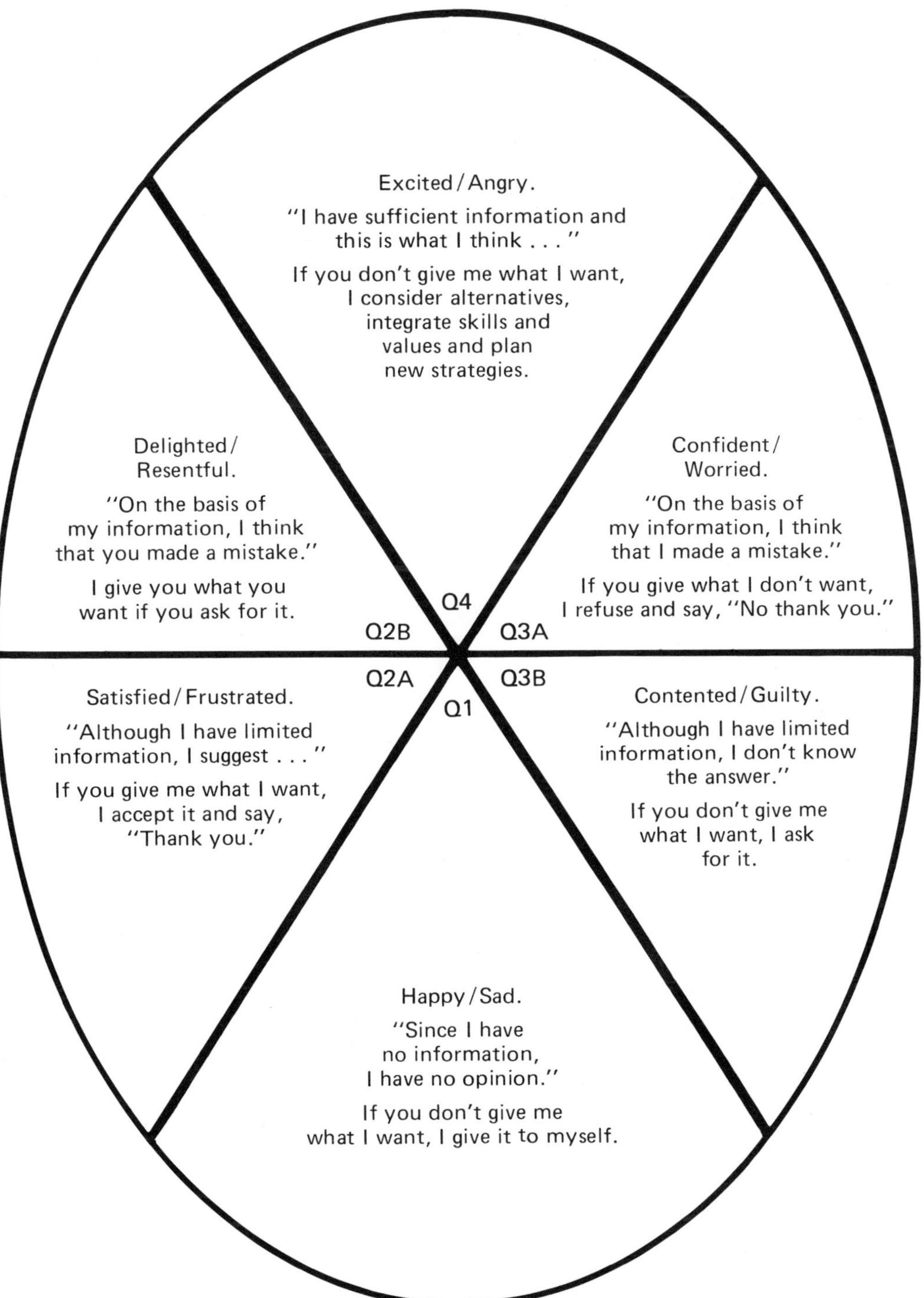

Diagram 4.10
DISTRESS ELLIPSE (EITHER-OR)
Limitations of Coping Capacities

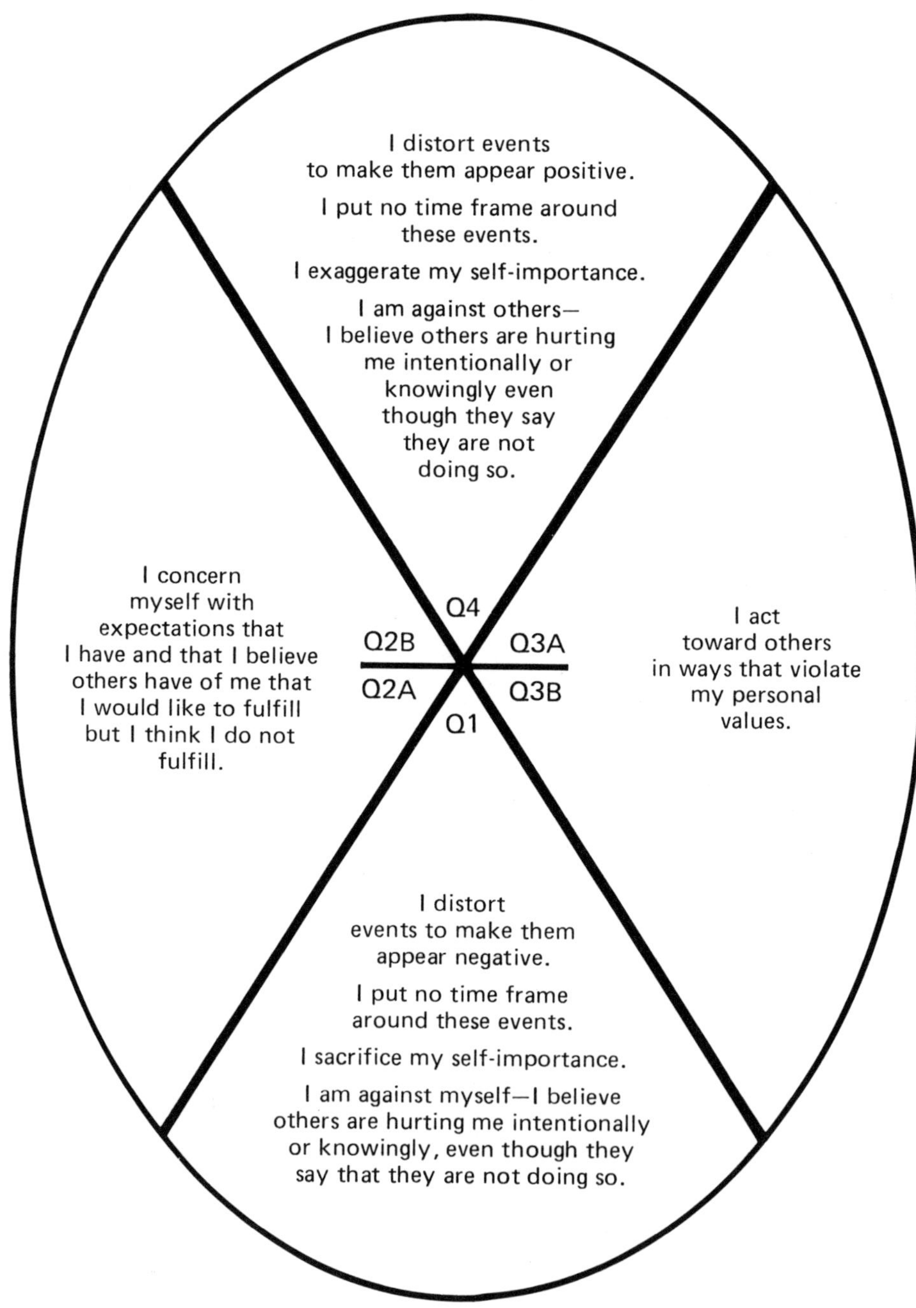

Diagram 4.11
EUSTRESS ELLIPSE (BOTH/AND)
Maximization of Coping Opportunities

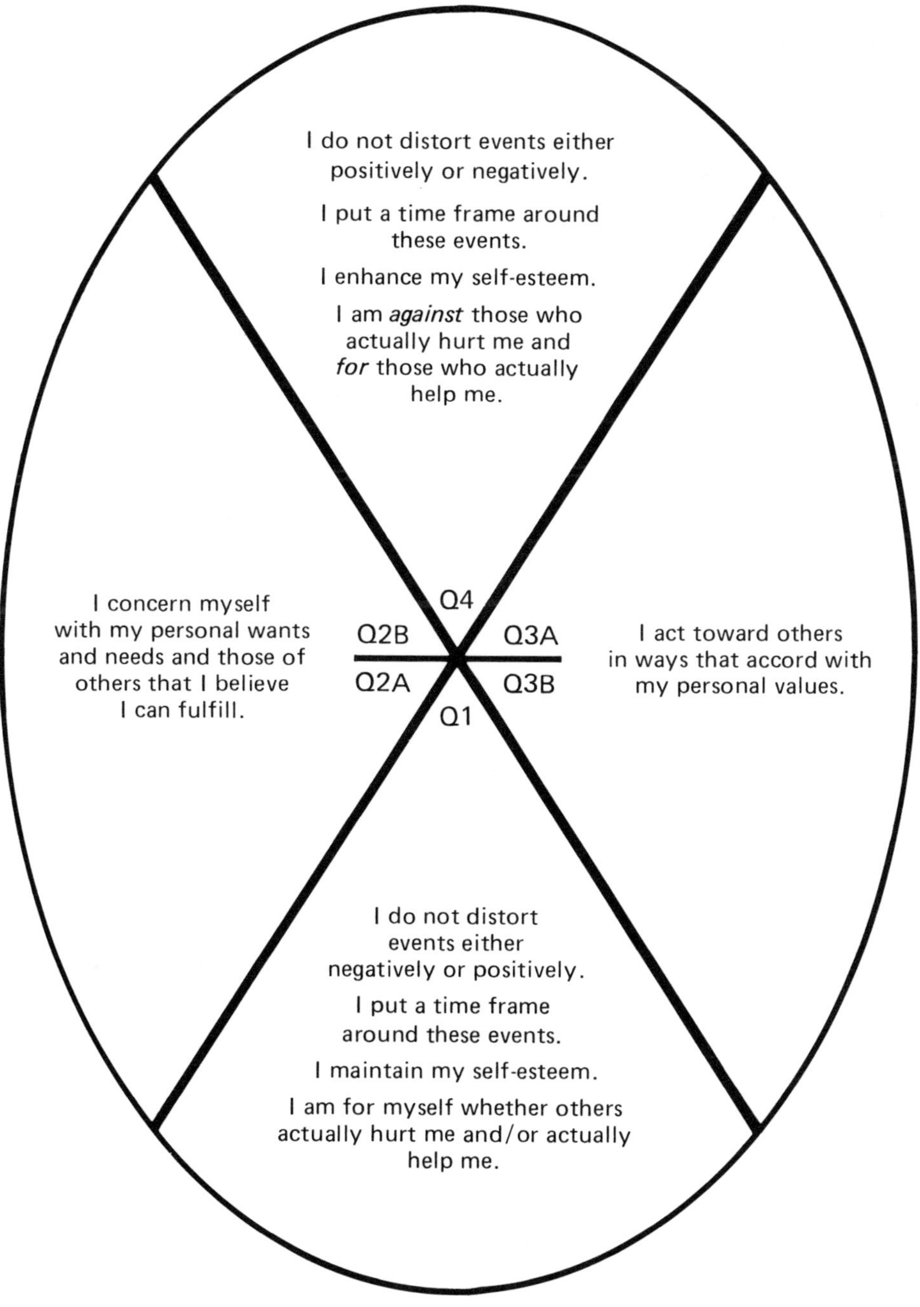

stress Options deal with Q1 Realities; Q2 Wants and Needs; Q4 Realities; and Q3 Integrity of Personal Values.

PUTTING IT ALL TOGETHER AGAIN

The time has come to look once again at the two ellipses and see how they work together. You will recall that when you look inward from the Distress Ellipse to the Eustress Ellipse, you find, in each Eustress Quadrant, ways to use your life energies more constructively and to manage your Stress more effectively. The Eustress Quadrants are the well-being Quadrants and offer you ways to enrich yourself and to grow with others.

This time, review the inappropriate feelings, thoughts and behaviors in the outer Distress Ellipse. Then move into the Eustress Ellipse, following each Quadrant, and find the appropriate feelings, thoughts and behaviors that make for well-being and the management of Stress. Also review, in the same way, the inappropriate Distress Limitations and then look inward to the Eustress Opportunities.

V:

WHO PUSHES YOUR STRESS BUTTONS?

 SIX DISTRESS PERSONALITY TYPES THAT PUSH YOUR STRESS BUTTONS

Six Distress Personality Types are described in this chapter. Each Personality Type is assigned to a Quadrant. Each Quadrant represents a locked-in pattern, which includes a Decision-response, a Feeling, a Thought, a Behavior, a Life Attitude and Limitations.

The Decision-responses are either Compliant or Defiant.

The Feelings are substitute feelings.

The Thoughts are contaminated thoughts.

The Behaviors are Alienation behaviors.

The Life Attitudes are inappropriate to the here and now.

Each of the Personality Types is an Either-or type seeking Guarantees.

The six Distress Personality Types are labeled (see Table 5.1) and illustrated (see Diagram 5.1) below.

Table 5.1
SIX DISTRESS PERSONALITY TYPES

QUADRANT		LABEL
Q1	Personality Type	Rejected
Q2A	Personality Type	Inadequate
Q2B	Personality Type	Vengeful
Q4	Personality Type	Hostile
Q3A	Personality Type	Fearful
Q3B	Personality Type	Insecure

The following diagrams (5.2 through 5.5) summarize the characteristics and behaviors of the Distress Personality Types.

Diagram 5.1
SIX DISTRESS PERSONALITY TYPES

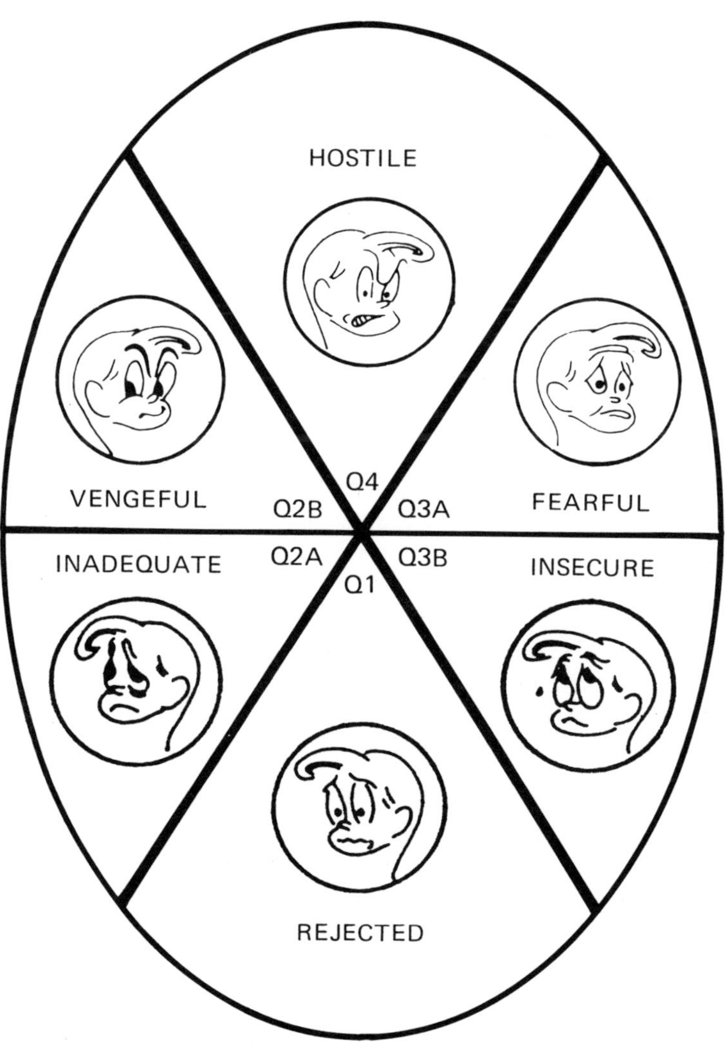

Diagram 5.2
DISTRESS PERSONALITY TYPE: Q1

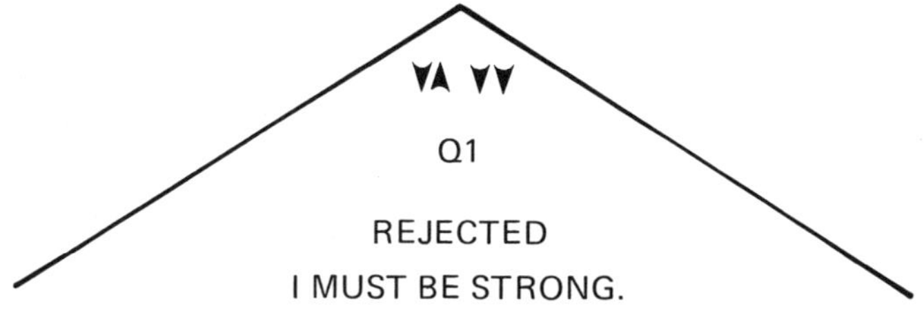

I must not be.
I must not feel.
I must not be me.
I must not belong.
I must not be close.
I must not want.

I FEEL SAD.

"I'll be silent," or "I'll say something irrelevant."
I do without what I want.
I am timid. I am passive. I am compliant.

I distort events to make them appear negative.

I put no time frame around these events.

I sacrifice my self-importance—I believe others are
hurting me, even though they say that they are not
doing so.

Diagram 5.3
DISTRESS PERSONALITY TYPES: Q2B AND Q2A

I MUST HURRY UP (IMPULSIVE).
I must not succeed.
I must not be a child (I must do chores and postpone fun.

BUT . . .

I FEEL RESENTFUL.

"I will get you."
I take what I want.
I am sly. I am aggressive. I am defiant.
I direct my life energies to expectations coming from others
that I believe I cannot fulfill.

VENGEFUL Q2B

INADEQUATE Q2A

I MUST TRY HARD.
I must not succeed.
I must not be sick (insane).
I must go away to succeed.

I FEEL FRUSTRATED.

"I am confused."
I do without what I want.
I am sneaky. I am passive. I am compliant. BUT . . .
I direct my life energies to expectations coming from
within me that I believe I cannot fulfill.

Diagram 5.4
DISTRESS PERSONALITY TYPE: Q4

I distort events to make them appear positive.
I put no time frame around these events.
I exaggerate my self-importance—I believe that others
   are hurting me intentionally or knowingly even
   though they say they are not doing so.
     I am pushy. I am aggressive. I am defiant.
     I take what I want.
     "My answer is right. Don't argue with me."

I FEEL ANGRY.

I must not think.
I must not . . .

I MUST BE PERFECT.

HOSTILE

Q4

▲▼

Diagram 5.5
DISTRESS PERSONALITY TYPES: Q3A AND Q3B

I MUST HURRY UP (COMPULSIVE).
I must not be important.
I must not grow up.
   I FEEL WORRIED.
   "I goofed."
   I take what I want.
   I am sneaky. I am aggressive. I am defiant. BUT . . .
      I direct my life energies against others by acting
      against them in a way that violates my personal
      standards.

FEARFUL Q3A

INSECURE Q3B

I MUST PLEASE OTHERS.
I must not be important.
I must not be well.
I must not be sane.
   BUT . . .
      I FEEL GUILTY.
      "I don't know."
      I do without what I want.
      I am sorry. I am passive. I am compliant.
         I direct my life energies against myself for acting
         against others in a way that violates my personal
         standards.

 # 6 ONE EUSTRESS PERSONALITY WITH SIX OPTIONS

The Eustress Personality cannot be given only one label because it is one personality with many options, or variations. Six options characteristic of the Eustress Personality are described in Table 6.1. Each is assigned to a Quadrant (see Diagram 6.1) and contains a Decision-response, a Feeling, a Thought, a Behavior, a Life Attitude and Options. These are elaborated on in diagrams 6.2–6.5.

The Decision-responses are both Active and Passive responses.

The Feelings are authentic feelings.

The Thoughts are uncontaminated thoughts.

The Behaviors are relation-building behaviors.

The Life Attitude is appropriate to the here and now.

The Eustress Personality is a *Both/And* personality and is invested in options.

While the Eustress Personality itself is not to be labeled, the patterns in each of the six Eustress Quadrants represent Options rather than locked-in Guarantees and are characterized by identifiable qualities.

Table 6.1
ONE EUSTRESS PERSONALITY

QUADRANT		LABEL
Q1	Eustress Option	Self-Accepting
Q2A	Eustress Option	Self-Reliant
Q2B	Eustress Option	Self-Competent
Q4	Eustress Option	Self-Approving
Q3A	Eustress Option	Self-Confident
Q3B	Eustress Option	Self-Responsible

PUTTING IT ALL TOGETHER AGAIN

It is appropriate once again to look at the Eustress Ellipse within the Distress Ellipse (see Diagram 6.6). By looking inward you discover ways to turn the Distress misuse of your Life Energies into the Eustress constructive use of your Life Energies. You also learn how to maximize your personality potential. You become a *both/and* Personality type instead of an *either-or* Personality Type.

Diagram 6.1
ONE EUSTRESS PERSONALITY

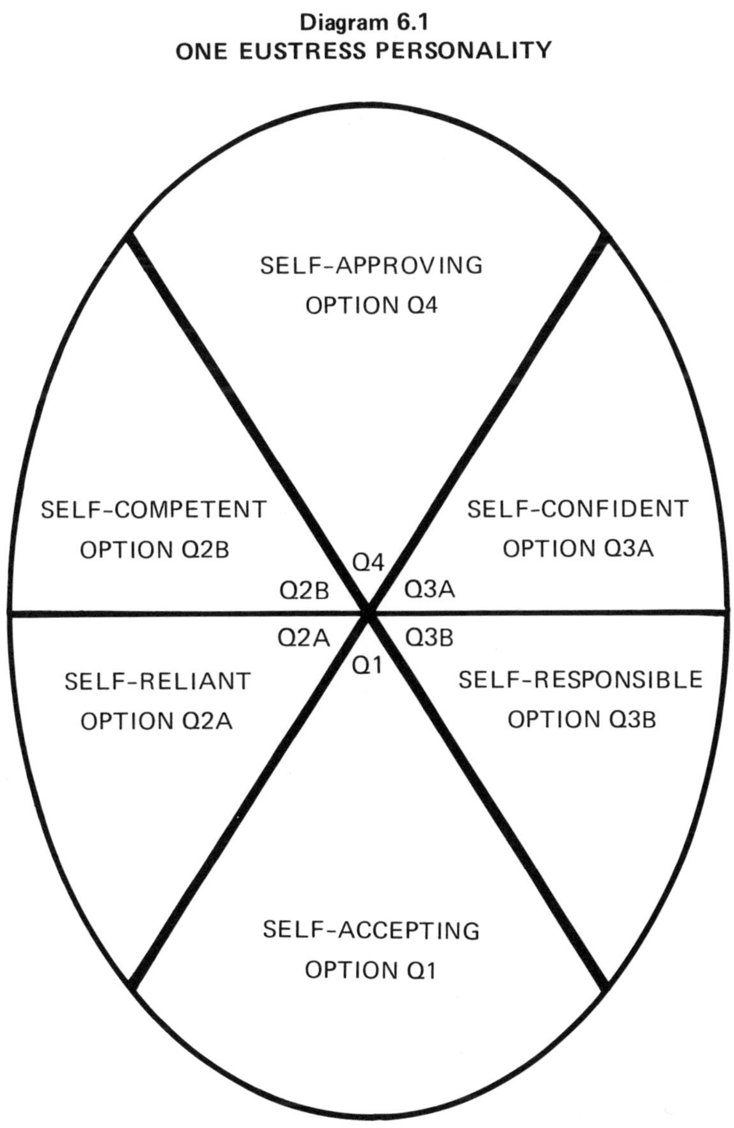

Diagram 6.2
EUSTRESS PERSONALITY OPTIONS: Q1

Q1
SELF-ACCEPTING

I AM HUMAN—I share my feelings *and* I keep my feelings to myself.

I won't be *and* I will be.
I won't feel *and* I will feel.
I won't be me *and* I will be me.
I won't belong *and* I will belong.
I won't want *and* I will want.

I feel happy *and* I feel sad.
"Since I have no information, I have no opinion."

If you don't give me what I want, I give myself what I want.

I AM ASSERTIVE.

I direct my life energies to positive and negative events which I do not distort.

I put a time frame around the events.

I maintain my self-esteem whether others actually hurt me and/or help me.

Diagram 6.3
EUSTRESS PERSONALITY OPTIONS: Q2A AND Q2B

I AM FLEXIBLE.

I won't succeed *and* I will succeed.
I won't be a child (I will do my chores) *and* I will
be a child (I will have fun).

I feel delighted *and* I feel resentful.
"On the basis of my information, I think that you
made a mistake."
I give you what you want if you ask for it.

I AM ASSERTIVE.

I direct my life energies to wants that come from
others which can be fulfilled.

SELF-COMPETENT Q2B   ▲▲

SELF-RELIANT Q2A   ▲▲

I AM SUCCESSFUL.

I won't succeed *and* I will succeed.
I will stay at home and succeed *and* I will go away
and succeed.

I won't be sick and succeed *and* I will succeed
even though I may be sick.

I feel satisfied *and* I feel frustrated.
"Although I have limited information, I suggest."
When you give me what I want, I accept and I say
"thank you."

I AM ASSERTIVE.

I direct my life energies to wants that come from
within me that can be fulfilled.

Diagram 6.4
EUSTRESS PERSONALITY OPTIONS: Q4

I direct my life energies for and against
others depending on whether they actually
help and/or hurt me.

I AM ASSERTIVE.

If you don't give me what I want, I consider
alternatives, integrate skills and values and
plan new strategies.

"I have sufficient information and this is
what I think."

I feel excited *and* I feel angry.

I won't do *and* I will do.
I won't think *and* I will think.

I AM HUMBLE.

SELF-APPROVING

Q4

Diagram 6.5
EUSTRESS PERSONALITY OPTIONS: Q3A AND Q3B

I AM CARING.

I won't be important *and* I will be important.
I won't grow up (I will take care of others) *and*
I will grow up (I will take care of myself).

I feel confident *and* I feel worried.
"On the basis of my information, I think that
I made a mistake."
If you give me what I don't want, I refuse and
say, "No, thank you."

I AM ASSERTIVE.

I direct my life energies to others by acting
toward them in ways that accord with my
personal standards.

▲▲ SELF–CONFIDENT Q3A

▲▲ SELF–RESPONSIBLE Q3B

I AM IMPORTANT.

I won't be important *and* I will be important.
I won't be sane and be important *and* I will be
sane and be important.
I will be important even though I am not well
and I will be well and be important.

I feel contented and I feel guilty.

"Although I have limited information, I don't
know the answer."

If you don't give me what I want, I ask for it.

I AM ASSERTIVE.

I direct my life energies to myself by acting
toward others in ways that accord with my
personal standards.

Diagram 6.6

DISTRESS ELLIPSE
Six Distress Personality Types
With Six Distress Guarantees
HOSTILE
GUARANTEE
VENGEFUL
GUARANTEE
FEARFUL
GUARANTEE
Self-Approving
Option
Self-Competent
Option
Q4
Self-Confident
Option
Q2B
Q3A
Q2A
Q3B
Self-Reliant
Option
Q1
Self-Responsible
Option
INADEQUATE
GUARANTEE
INSECURE
GUARANTEE
Self-Accepting
Option
REJECTED
GUARANTEE
EUSTRESS ELLIPSE
One Eustress Personality with Six Options

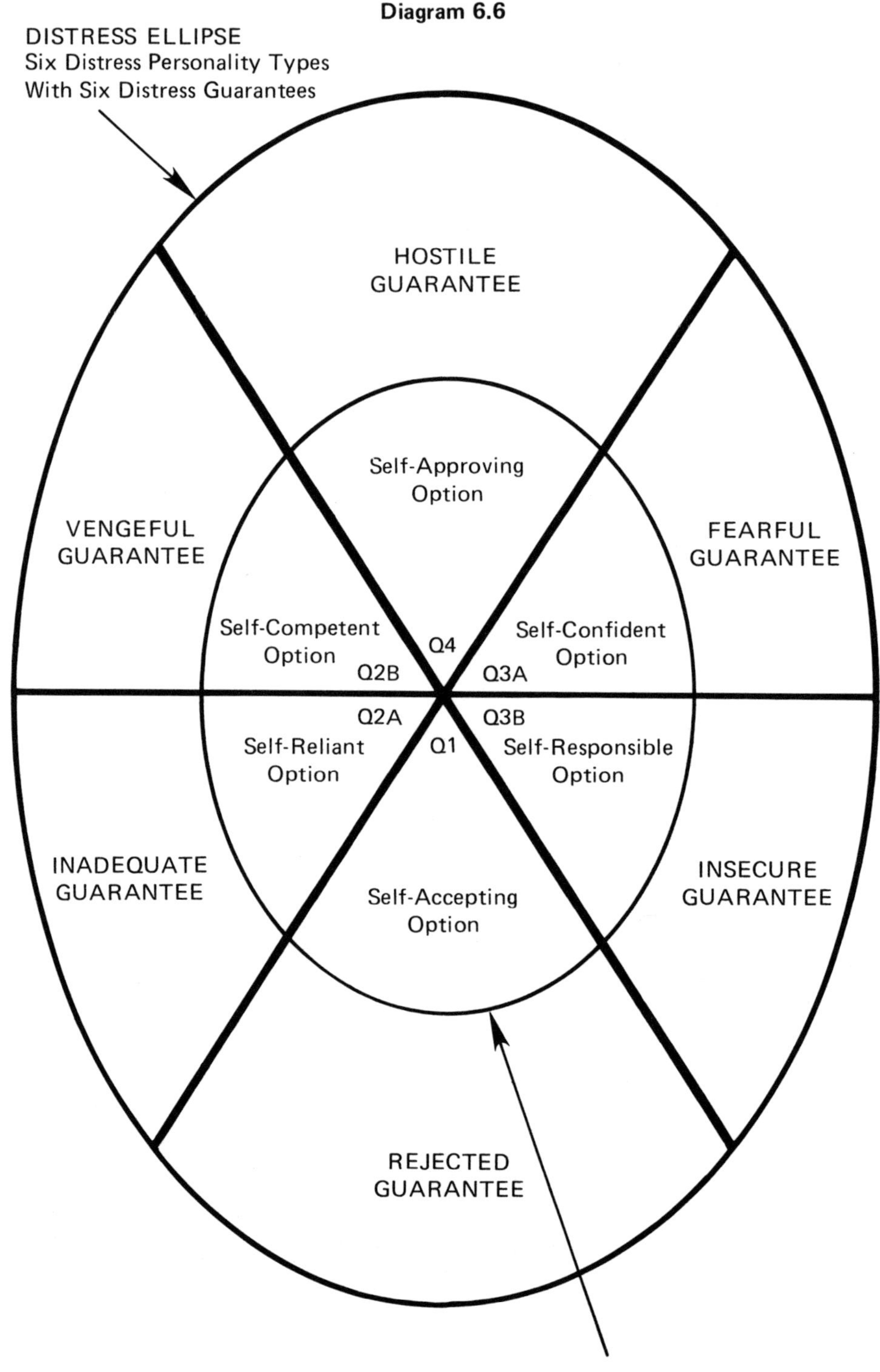

CHAPTER 7

COPING WITH DISTRESS

AFFECTION AND APPRECIATION

Distress reflects psychological hungers, which sap your essential life energies: 1) to trust and be trustworthy, 2) to exercise hope, 3) to exercise drive, 4) to be autonomous, 5) to exercise willpower and 6) to exercise self-control. These six life capacities emerge within the first three years of infancy, and they set the tone for your childhood, adolescent and adult patterning. The degree to which they emerge depends initially upon the psychological nourishment that you receive from others. In the beginning, these nourishments are prescribed by your parents in the form of Positive and Negative Conditional Messages. Your Decision-responses to these psychological nourishments reflect your ability to cope with Distress. Later as your neural connections mature and as you develop skills and grow in experience, you increasingly become the source of your own Positive and Negative Messages, and your Decision-responses demonstrate your ability to cope with Distress.

There are two essential psychological hungers: 1) the Hunger for Affection and 2) the Hunger for Appreciation. The Hunger for Affection is the more primary of the two hungers and the foundation upon which all Appreciation hungers are based.

The Hunger for Affection is a twofold hunger: 1) to be trusted and be trustworthy and 2) to be autonomous. It is the hunger to be accepted as one is—that your parents and the significant others in your life will be consistent and continuous in their support of you as you cope with the internal and external pressures in your life. Without such nourishment, you lock yourself into either the Rejected or the Hostile Personality Type. Your feelings lose their authenticity. You contaminate your thoughts. You alienate yourself from yourself and from others. No matter how distressful your feelings, thoughts and behaviors are, you hold onto them because you must have guarantees to sustain you. You begin to mistrust yourself and others, and you sacrifice your autonomy to choose, as you surrender your responsibility to integrate your skills and values into meaningful strategies.

With psychological nourishment, you take on the Self-Accepting and the Self-Approving opportunities of the Eustress Personality. Your feelings are authentic. Your thoughts are uncontaminated. Your behaviors strengthen your network of interdependent relationships. You are aware of your life energies, and you integrate your skills and values into meaningful strategies.

The Hunger for Appreciation is also a twofold hunger: 1) the Hunger to Succeed and 2) the Hunger to be Important.

The Hunger to Succeed precedes the Hunger for Importance. It is satisfied best in an atmosphere of trust where the life energy capacities for hope and drive are fostered. Hope is the expression of your self-reliant desire to succeed.

Drive is your fulfillment of that hope, an expression of your self-competent performance.

The Hunger for Importance is nurtured in an atmosphere of autonomy where the life energy capacities for will power and self-control are nourished. Will power is the behavioral expression of your self-confidence—that you are important and that you commit your feelings, thoughts, and behaviors to relationships. Self-control is the exercise of your self-responsibility—that you are important and will monitor the use of your will-power.

If the Hunger to Succeed is not satisfied, you lock yourself into the Inadequate and Vengeful Personality Types. You become disillusioned and lose your incentive, or you divert your life energies into getting even and being spiteful. You cease to be self-reliant and self-competent.

When the Hunger for Importance remains unfulfilled, you lock yourself into the Fearful and Insecure Personality Types. Shamed by the thought that you might tip your hand prematurely, you emasculate your will-power and become manipulative, or you begin to doubt your own importance, give up your capacity for self-control and surrender the exercise of your will power to others.

If you cannot satisfy your Hungers for Affection and Appreciation, you will seek Attention. You will not allow yourself to be ignored, no matter what the cost, even if your Attention-seeking proves to be counterproductive. The more severe your deprivation, the more extreme your Hunger for Attention becomes, and the more serious becomes the nature of your Distress.

The Hungers for Affection and Appreciation are diagrammed in the Distress Ellipse (see Diagram 7.1), and the nourishments of Affection and Appreciation are recorded in the Eustress Ellipse (see Diagram 7.2). Affection is placed in Q1 and Q4, with Q1 indicating the concern with Trust and Q4 the concern with Autonomy. Appreciation is noted in Q2 and Q3, with Q2 signifying Success Issues and Q3 problems of Being Important.

PERMISSIONS AND PROTECTIONS

When you cope with Distress, it is important to keep the Hungers for Affection and Appreciation in mind. Most people are unable to satisfy their Hungers for Affection and Appreciation. First, they require Permission and Protection. They need Permission, or authority, to nourish themselves, to provide the psychological food which they are lacking. They also need Protection, or reassurance, against their internal and external pressures while they satisfy their hungers. So often, the capacity to cope with Distress is in direct proportion to the quantity and the quality of Permissions and Protections which people possess.

At the outset, most parents seek to satisfy the Hungers for Affection and Appreciation by providing their children with Permissions and Protections through Conditional Positive and Negative Messages. Later, as the parents make the transition from Conditional to Unconditional Messages, they encourage their family members to give themselves the necessary Permissions and Pro-

Diagram 7.1
AFFECTION AND APPRECIATION
Distress Ellipse

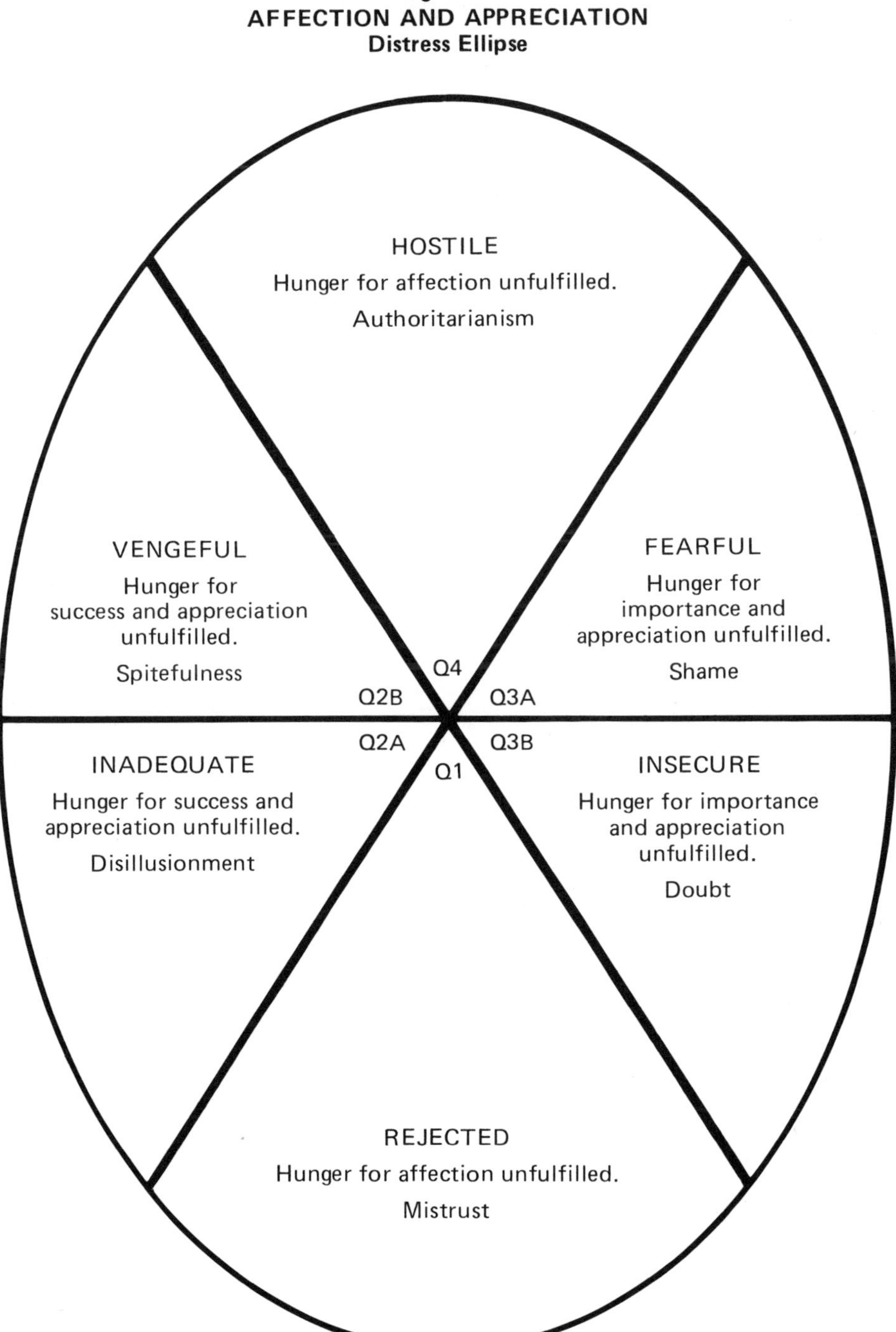

Diagram 7.2
AFFECTION AND APPRECIATION
Eustress Ellipse

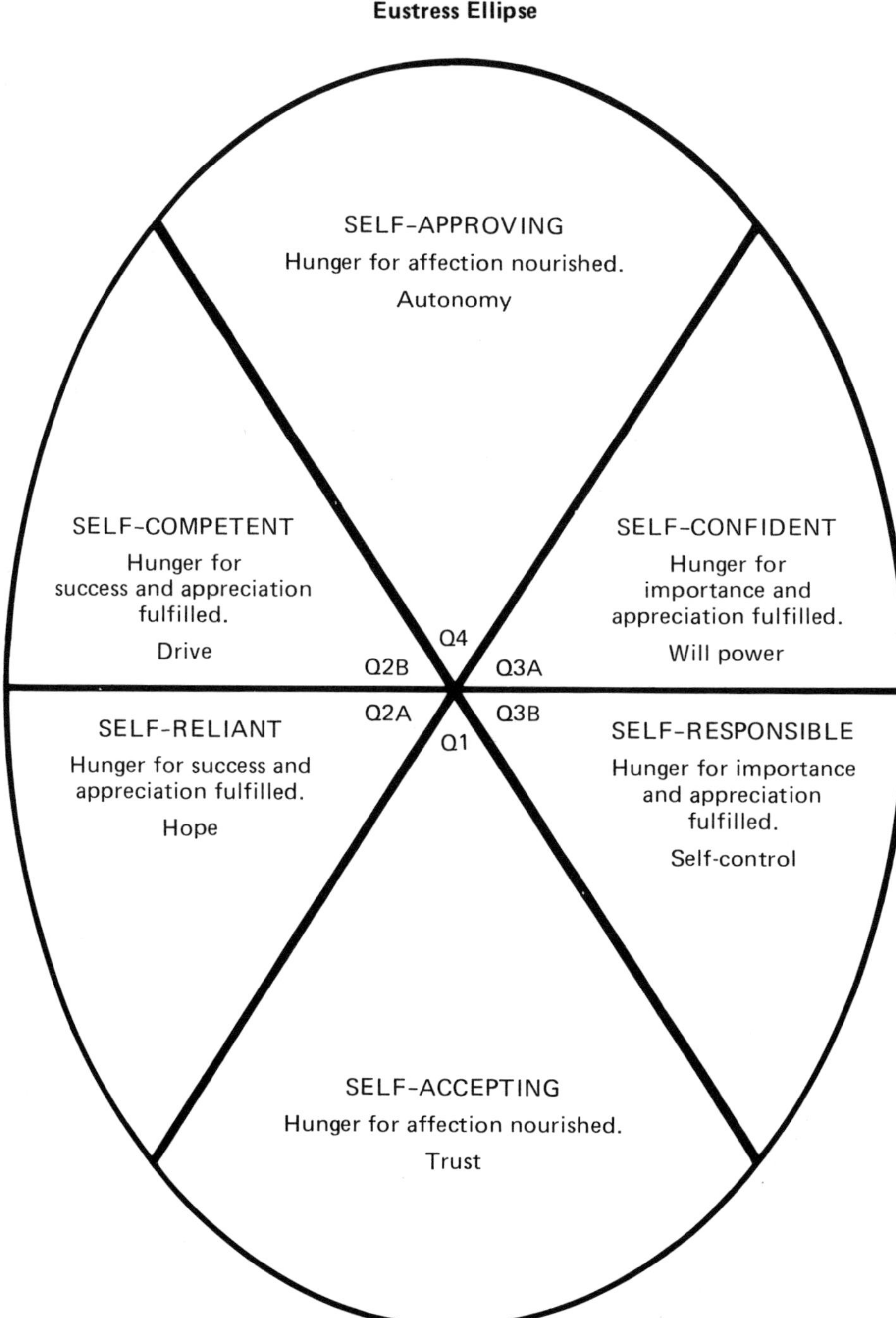

tections to satisfy their hungers. Some parents, however, never make the transition, and many do so only with great difficulty. As a result, many people have limited capabilities to give themselves the necessary authority and basic safety to cope with their Distress. These limitations are expressed either through the compliance with which they cling to their parental Conditional Prescriptions and Prohibitions or through the defiance with which they reject their parental Conditional authority and support. Whether they comply or defy, the psychological result is the same: they distress themselves.

When you cope with your personal Distress, you give yourself Permission and Protection to satisfy your Hunger for Affection—to trust, to be trusted and to be autonomous—and your Hunger for Appreciation—to succeed and to be important. When you cope with the Distress of other people, you offer them Permission and Protection so that they, too, can satisfy their Hunger for Affection—to trust, to be trusted and to be autonomous—and their Hunger for Appreciation—to succeed and to be important.

Sometimes it is necessary to help people relive their early childhood experiences before they can cope with their Hungers for Affection and Appreciation. Chronologically they may be adult; however, psychologically they still live with their memories of an emotionally impoverished childhood with which they continue to distress themselves. This reliving process frequently requires professional guidance. More often, however, your awareness of the hungers within you and within others and the supplying of limited Permission and Protection may suffice to transform a Distress situation into a Eustress experience.

Each Distress Personality Type calls for specific Permissions and specific Protections, because each Personality Type received different Conditional Positive and Negative Messages when young, and, as a result, made different Decision-responses.

The Permission messages or options are divided into four groups, based upon the developmental stage in which hunger may have occurred. The four stages and their corresponding age ranges are: 1) Infancy (0–36 months); 2) Early Childhood (3–6 years); 3) Late Childhood (6–12 years); and Adolescence (12–18 years).

The Infancy Stage, moreover, is sub-divided into four sub-periods, corresponding to the Four Quadrants: Q1: 0–6 months (see Diagram 7.3); Q2: 6–18 months (see Diagram 7.4); Q4: 18–24 months (see Diagram 7.5); and Q3: 24–36 months (see Diagram 7.6). Q1 and Q2 correlate with what has been called the Oral Stage of Development, and Q4 and Q3 correlate with what has been called the Anal Stage of Development.

POWER

There are three Distress *P*'s which go together: Prescriptions, Prohibitions and Powerlessness (see Diagram 7.7).

Distress Prescriptions and Distress Prohibitions produce Distress Powerlessness. Distress Powerlessness is life energy which is used inappropriately in the here and now. Distress Powerlessness is the life energy which the RE-JECTED, INADEQUATE, VENGEFUL, HOSTILE, FEARFUL and INSECURE Personality Types exercise in order to be either Compliant or Defiant.

Distress Powerlessness is characterized by substitute feelings, contaminated thoughts and alienation behaviors. It is painful and uncomfortable. At best it elicits only glee. It exploits a Life Attitude that either you must be one-up and I must be one-down, or I must be one-up and you must be one-down, or both of us must be down.

Distress Powerlessness intensifies the Hungers for Affection and Appreciation. It does not assert awareness of the life energies. It does not explore values and develop skills. It does not integrate optional values and skills into a meaningful plan.

Distress Powerlessness does not commit integrated values and skills to an interdependent network of human relationships.

There are three Eustress *P*'s which go together: Permissions, Protections and Power (see Diagram 7.8).

Diagram 7.3
EUSTRESS COPING WITH Q1 DISTRESS PERSONALITY TYPE

ENCOURAGE *REJECTED* TO BUILD SELF-ESTEEM AND BECOME *SELF-ACCEPTING.*

PERMISSIONS

Recognize the existence of *REJECTED.*

(0–6 mos.)	You have a right to be here. Your needs are okay with me. I'm glad you're you (Boy/Girl). I like to be near you/hold you. You can want.
(3–6 yrs.)	It's important for you to find out what you are about as a boy/girl.
(6–12 yrs.)	It's okay to do things your own way, to have your own morals and methods. It's okay to trust your own feelings to guide you.
(12–18 yrs.)	You can be a sexual being and still have needs.

PROTECTIONS (for all ages):

BUILD *BASIC TRUST.*

Be available;
be non-judgmental;
be accepting;
listen.

Eustress Permissions and Eustress Protections produce Eustress Power.

Eustress Power is life energy which is used appropriately in the here and now. It consists of the life energy Options that the Eustress Personality utilizes in order to be both Active and Passive.

Eustress Power is characterized by authentic feelings, uncontaminated thoughts and relation-building behaviors. It is both painful and pleasurable, uncomfortable and comfortable; it can elicit joy. It builds upon a Life Attitude in which all persons are up. It nourishes the Hungers for Affection and Appreciation.

Eustress Power asserts personal awareness of one's life energies. It explores personal values and develops personal skills. It integrates optional values and skills into a meaningful personal plan.

Eustress Power commits and negotiates integrated personal values and skills in an interdependent network of human relationships.

Diagram 7.4
EUSTRESS COPING WITH Q2A AND Q2B DISTRESS PERSONALITY TYPES

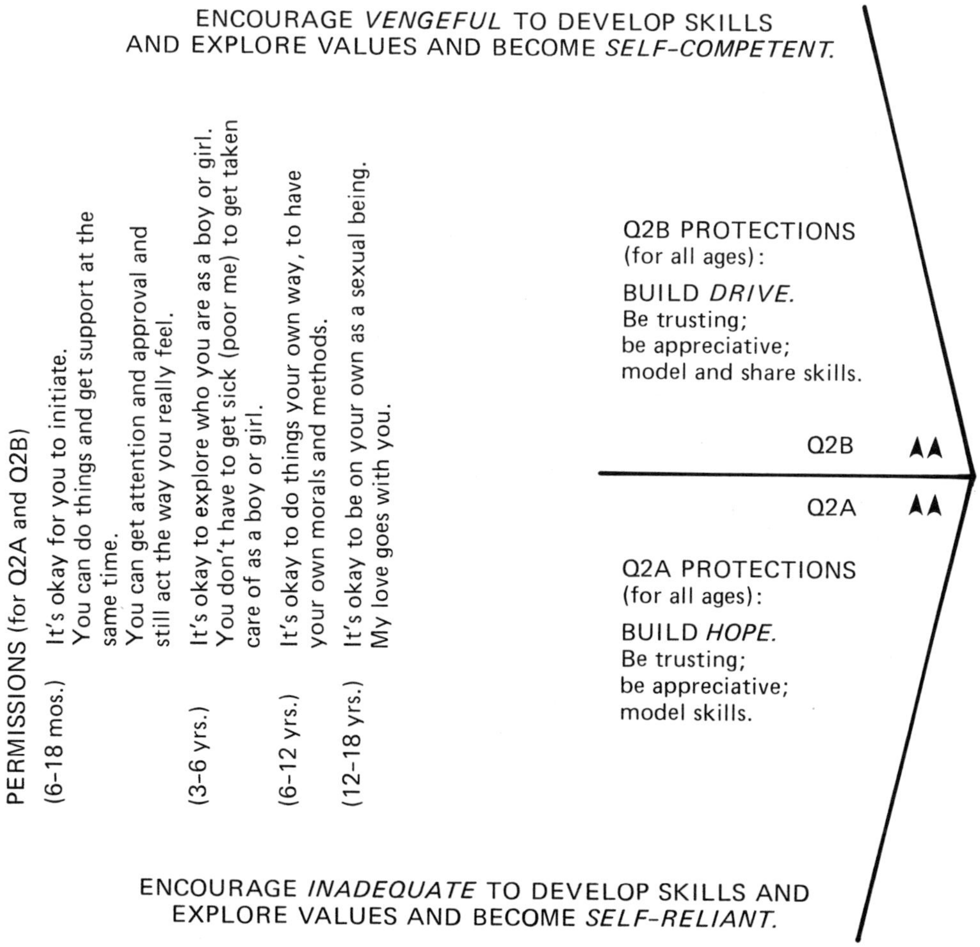

PUTTING IT ALL TOGETHER AGAIN

It is time to look inward again. However, this time you will examine the Hungers for Affection and Appreciation as well as the three *P's* of Distress: Prescriptions, Prohibitions and Powerlessness. As you go toward the source of your life energies, you will discover innumerable options to live creatively. Instead of being locked-in with no exit, you will find innumerable passages to new adventures and excitement. By turning inward, you have an opportunity to nourish your Hungers for Affection and Appreciation and to turn your Prescriptions into Permissions, your Prohibitions into Protections and your Powerlessness into Power.

Diagram 7.5
EUSTRESS COPING WITH Q4 DISTRESS PERSONALITY TYPE

ENCOURAGE *HOSTILE* TO EVALUATE REASONS FOR ANGER, TO THINK OF ALTERNATIVE SOLUTIONS AND TO BECOME *SELF–APPROVING.*

Q4 PERMISSIONS

(12–18 yrs.)	It's okay to be responsible for your own thoughts, feelings, behaviors and needs as a sexual being.
(6–12 yrs.)	You can think before you make that your own way.
(3–6 yrs.)	It's okay to imagine things about your being a boy or girl without being afraid that you will make them come true.
(18–24 mos.)	You can be sure about what you need. You can feel about your thinking and think about your feelings. You can think for yourself. You can let people know you're angry. I'm glad you're growing up.

Q4 PROTECTIONS

BUILD *AUTONOMY.*

Confront and challenge;
be consistent;
be direct.

SELF–APPROVING

Diagram 7.6
EUSTRESS COPING WITH Q3A AND Q3B DISTRESS PERSONALITY TYPES

ENCOURAGE *FEARFUL* TO CHECK OUT CONSEQUENCES
AND BECOME *SELF-CONFIDENT.*

Q3A PROTECTION
(for all ages):

BUILD *WILL POWER.*

Be caring;
be important;
stay in the here and now.

▲▲ Q3A

▲▲ Q3B

Q3B PROTECTION
(for all ages):

BUILD *SELF-CONTROL.*

Be important;
be caring;
stay in the here and now.

PERMISSIONS (for Q3A and Q3B)

(24-36 mos.) You don't have to act scary, sick, sad, or mad
to get taken care of.
You can be powerful and still have needs.
It's okay to find out what you are about.
It's okay to imagine things without being afraid that
you will make them come true.
It's okay to find out the consequences of your
behavior.

(3-6 yrs.) You can be powerful and still have needs as a boy
or girl.
You don't have to act scary to be taken care of as
a boy or girl.

(6-12 yrs.) You don't have to suffer to get what you want.

(12-18 yrs.) You are welcome to come home again.

ENCOURAGE INSECURE TO TAKE *RISKS*
AND BECOME *SELF-RESPONSIBLE.*

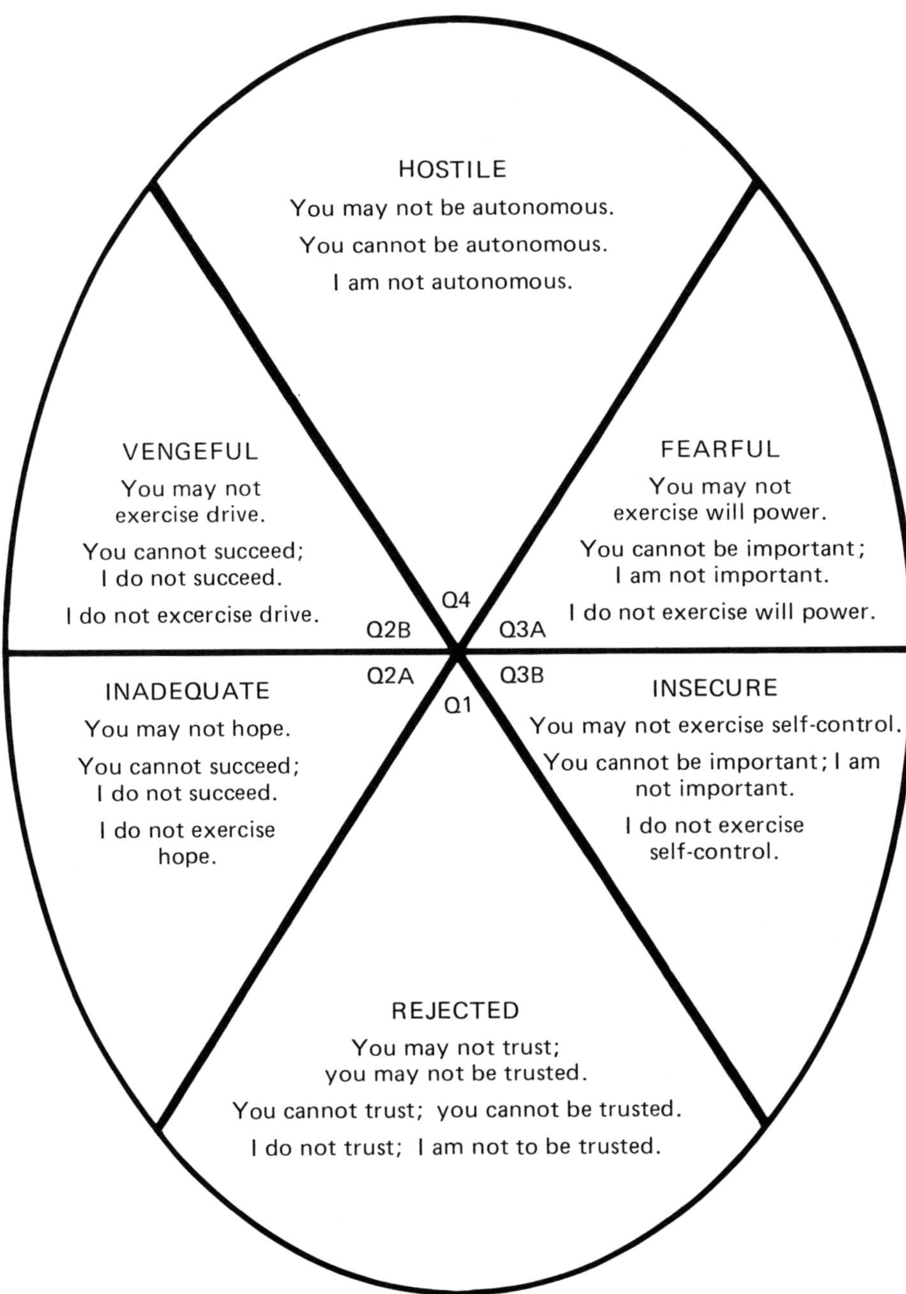

Diagram 7.7
DISTRESS ELLIPSE
Prescriptions, Prohibitions, Powerlessness
HOSTILE
You may not be autonomous.
You cannot be autonomous.
I am not autonomous.
VENGEFUL
You may not exercise drive.
You cannot succeed; I do not succeed.
I do not excercise drive.
FEARFUL
You may not exercise will power.
You cannot be important; I am not important.
I do not exercise will power.
Q4
Q2B
Q3A
Q2A
Q3B
Q1
INADEQUATE
You may not hope.
You cannot succeed; I do not succeed.
I do not exercise hope.
INSECURE
You may not exercise self-control.
You cannot be important; I am not important.
I do not exercise self-control.
REJECTED
You may not trust; you may not be trusted.
You cannot trust; you cannot be trusted.
I do not trust; I am not to be trusted.

Diagram 7.8
EUSTRESS ELLIPSE
Permissions, Protections, Power

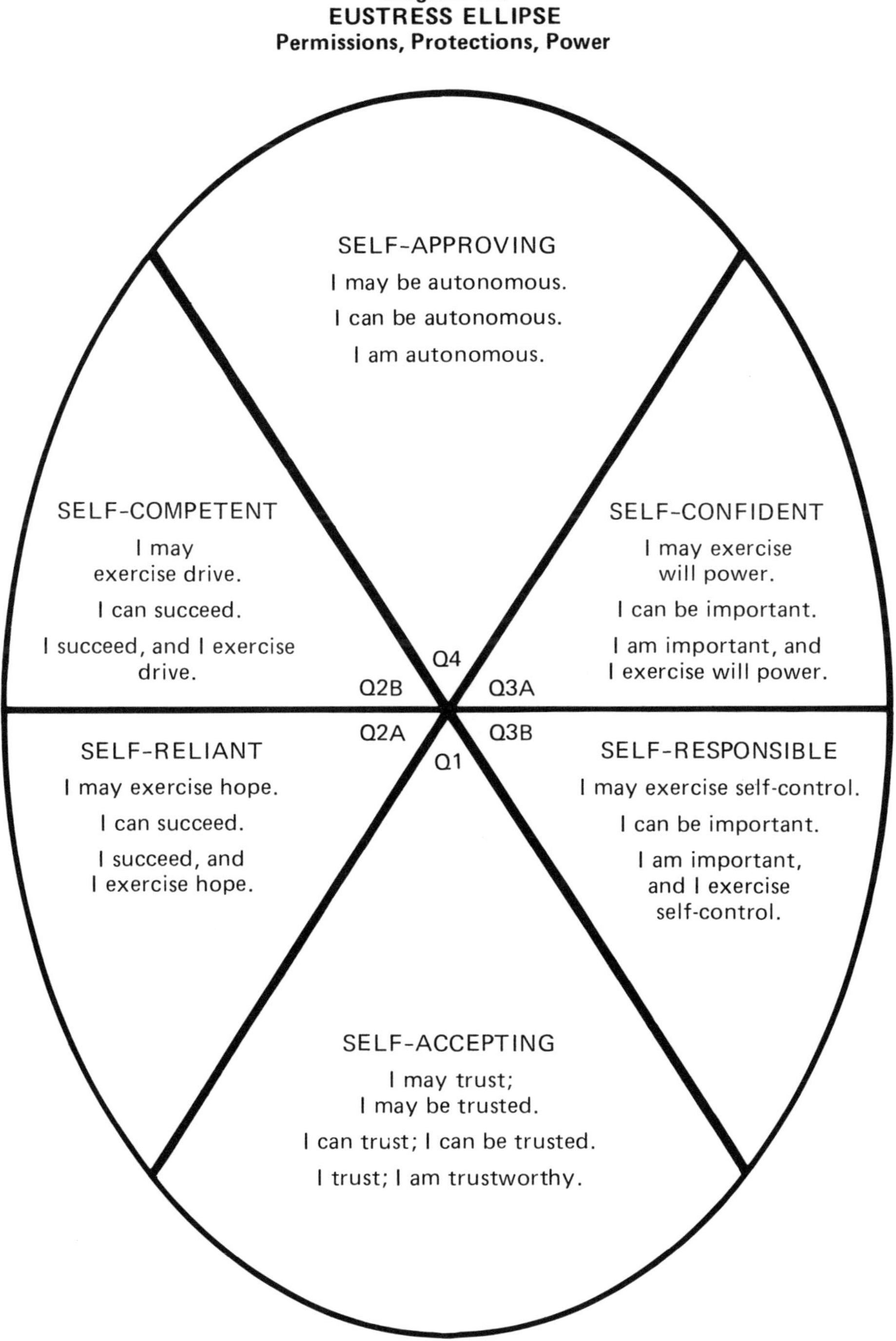

VI:
THE EFFECTIVE MANAGEMENT OF STRESS

 8 **YOU BECOME A PLAYWRIGHT**

FOUR DISTRESS DRAMAS

Once you lock yourself into your Distress Life-Attitude and your Distress Decision-responses with their Distress feelings, thoughts and behaviors, you begin to make your decisions come true, like a self-fulfilling prophecy. You now seek to prove that the Chicken or the Egg came first.

In fact, you become a playwright, and you write the drama of your life. You pick a theme to heighten the drama. You select the players who will be your actors and attribute to them their mannerisms, including such things as their tone of voice, their facial expressions, their postures and their gestures. You determine the time sequence as well as the scenarios for each act. You predict the games and the make-believe in which the players will involve themselves. Finally, you write the denouement, the payoff, the self-fulfilling prophecy—which you create. Your life is ended. The play is over.

All of the themes you choose, however, will be inappropriate, and the roles that you and the other characters play will also be inappropriate. You may believe that what you are doing is appropriate and that you may be deriving genuine joy; however, once you lock yourself into a Life Attitude in which someone must be one-down, you begin to prove that the Chicken or the Egg came first and you condemn yourself to play-act a life of Distress.

Just as there are characteristic Personality Types for each of the Distress Quadrants, so there are characteristic life dramas for each of the Distress Quadrants. There are four Distress dramas, each with its own perspective: A Q1 Distress life drama is a Monologue or a Fairy Tale without a happy ending. "Woe is me, for I am undone. Hear me out, and let me tell you my tale, for without a hearing I cannot live. Once upon a time . . ." A Q2 Distress life drama is an Adventure Story without success. "There is a pot of gold at the end of every rainbow. You will love me when I return." A Q4 Distress life drama is a Melodrama without laughter. "The forces of good are in constant struggle with the forces of evil. I have no choice. I will be evil. I will be good. I dare you to stop me." A Q3 Distress life drama is a Psychological Case Study without resolution. "You and I are drifting apart. We are strangers to each other. If only I understood, I could love you and you could love me. So, tell me why."

Each of the six Distress Personality Types is locked into one of the four Distress life dramas (see Diagram 8.1): Q1 REJECTED is locked into a Monologue or Fairy Tale without a happy ending. Q2A INADEQUATE and Q2B VENGEFUL are locked into an Adventure Story without success. Q4 HOSTILE is locked into a Melodrama without laughter. Q3A FEARFUL and Q3B INSECURE are locked into a Psychological Case Study without resolution.

Diagram 8.1
FOUR DISTRESS DRAMAS
Each With One Perspective

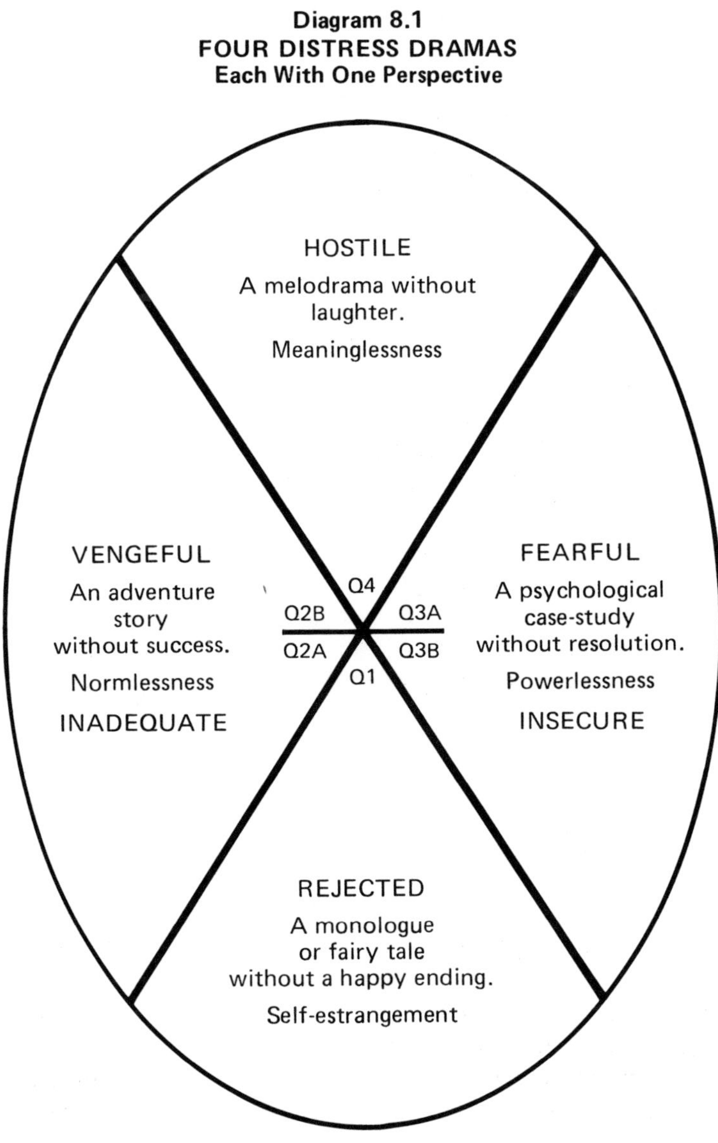

ONE EUSTRESS DRAMA

A Eustress life drama is one drama with four perspectives. A Eustress life drama is not a locked-in drama (see Diagram 8.2). Unlike Distress life dramas, a Eustress life drama involves one Eustress personality that "chooses" appropriately from among multiple patterns. These patterns are selected from whichever Eustress Quadrant is appropriate in the immediate context.

There are no guarantees in a Eustress life drama except the guarantee of the constructive use of your life energies. Whether your feelings are painful or pleasurable, they are authentic. Your life energies are expressing themselves appropriately. You are Eustressing yourself. A Eustress life drama reflects Q1 self-awareness. It is your Personal Story and relates THAT YOU ARE. You are *Self-Accepting*. A Eustress life drama illustrates Q2 exploration and the development of values and skills for success. It is your Adventure Story and relates HOW YOU ARE. You are *Self-Reliant* and *Self-Competent*. A Eustress life drama exemplifies Q4 consideration of alternatives and the integration of values and skills. It is your Identity Story and relates WHO YOU ARE. You are *Self-Approving*. A Eustress life drama demonstrates Q3 commitment of your integrated values and skills to relationships. It is your History Story and relates WHAT YOU ARE. You are *Self-Confident* and *Self-Responsible*.

PUTTING IT ALL TOGETHER AGAIN

As you become a Playwright, it is important that you keep in mind the differences between the Four Distress Dramas, each with a locked-in perspective and the One Eustress Drama with four optional perspectives (see Diagram 8.3).

It is even more important for you to turn inward from the Distress Ellipse to the Eustress Ellipse and invest your life energies for the rewriting of your Life Drama. The power to transform your life is available to you, because when you give yourself Permission, when you exercise Protection, and when you give yourself Power, you are using your Life Energies constructively. You are Eustressing yourself.

DISTRESS THEMES

The drama unfolds.

Just as a play has a script that tells what will happen throughout the play, so every life drama has a theme. Life dramas may have a Distress Theme or a Eustress Theme. Distress Themes are locked-in themes with locked-in Distress feelings, thoughts and behaviors. Distress Themes, therefore, have a predictable monotony to them. They repeat themselves again and again. The Games, the Make-Believe, the Signals, the Escapes and the Outcomes, all remain the same.

Diagram 8.2
ONE EUSTRESS DRAMA
With Four Perspectives

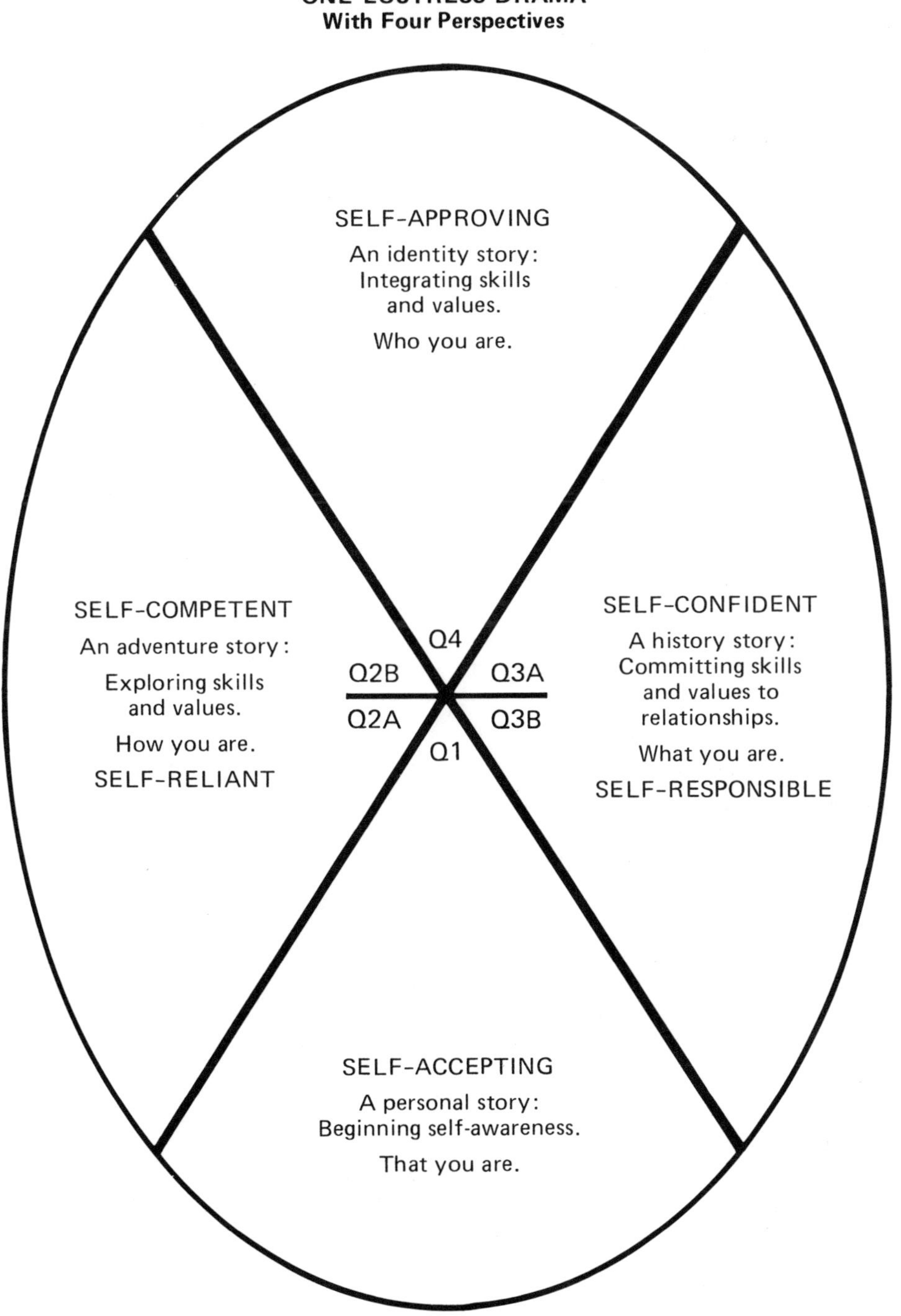

Diagram 8.3

FOUR DISTRESS DRAMAS
Each With One Perspective

HOSTILE
A melodrama without laughter.
Meaninglessness

SELF-APPROVING
An identity story:
Integrating skills
and values.
Who you are.

SELF-
COMPETENT
An
adventure
story:
Exploring
skills and
values.
How you
are.
SELF-
RELIANT

SELF-
CONFIDENT
A history
story:
Committing
skills and
values.
What you
are.
SELF-
RESPON-
SIBLE

VENGEFUL
An
adventure
story
without
success.
Normlessness
INADEQUATE

FEARFUL
A psycho-
logical
case-study
without
resolution.
Powerlessness
INSECURE

Q4
Q2B
Q2A
Q3A
Q3B
Q1

A
personal
story:
Beginning
self-awareness.
That you are.
SELF-ACCEPTING

A monologue or fairy tale without
a happy ending.
Self-estrangement
REJECTED

ONE EUSTRESS DRAMA
With Four Perspectives

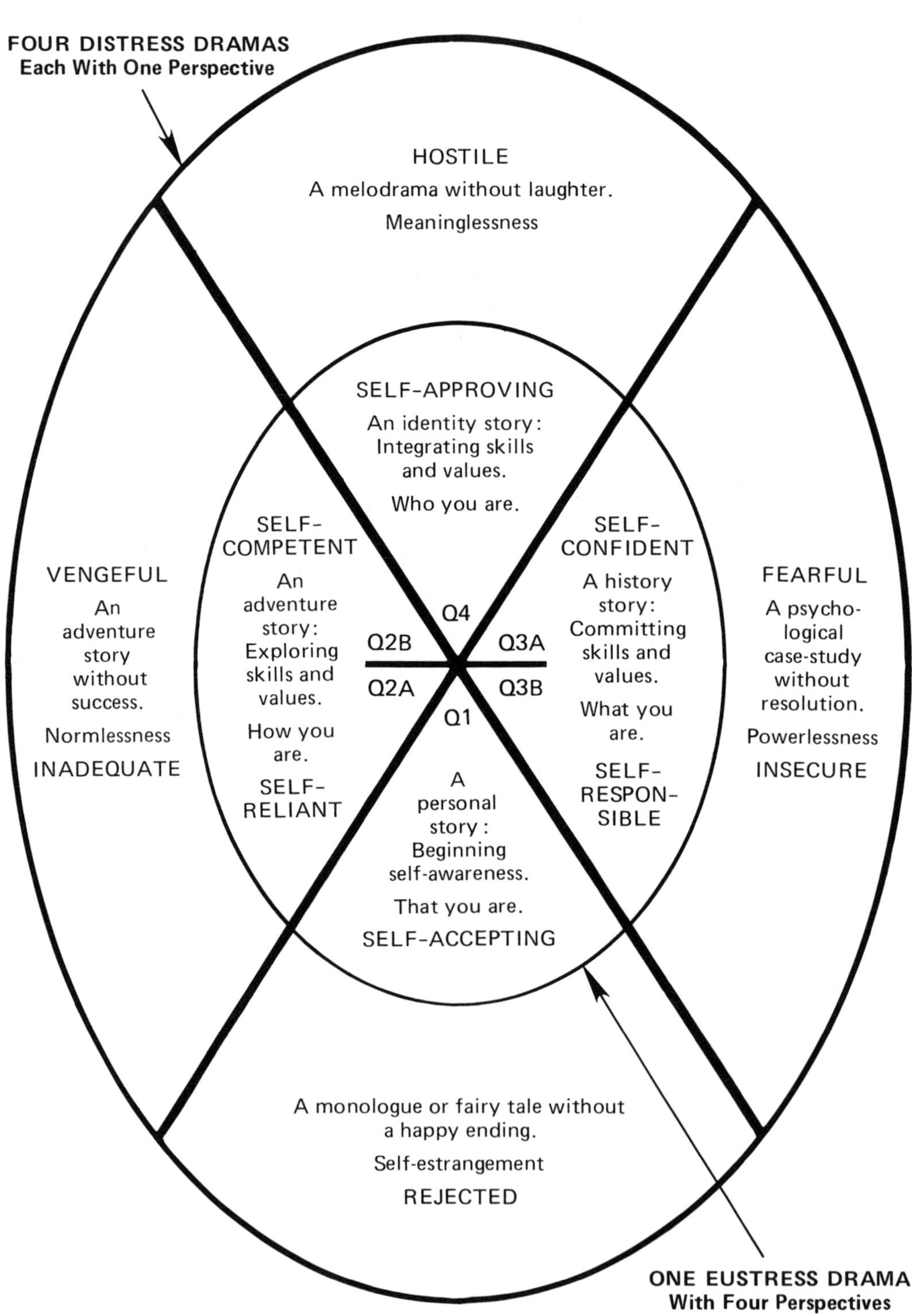

Even the players, though they bear different names, are the same because they play the same roles. The times and places may vary, yet they are the same because the theme remains the same. Distress Themes are self-fulfilling prophecies, and each Distress Personality Type selects his/her favorite Distress prophecy to fulfill.

There are six Distress Themes into which you can lock yourself. Which one you follow will depend upon the Distress Personality Type into which you locked yourself when you made your Distress Decision-responses to your parental Messages. Like the six Distress Personality Types, each of the six Distress Themes is diagrammed according to the Quadrants of the Distress Ellipse (see Diagram 8.4). Each of the Distress Themes also has a parallel in Greek Mythology. The Q1 theme is: You can *never* have what you want. You are like

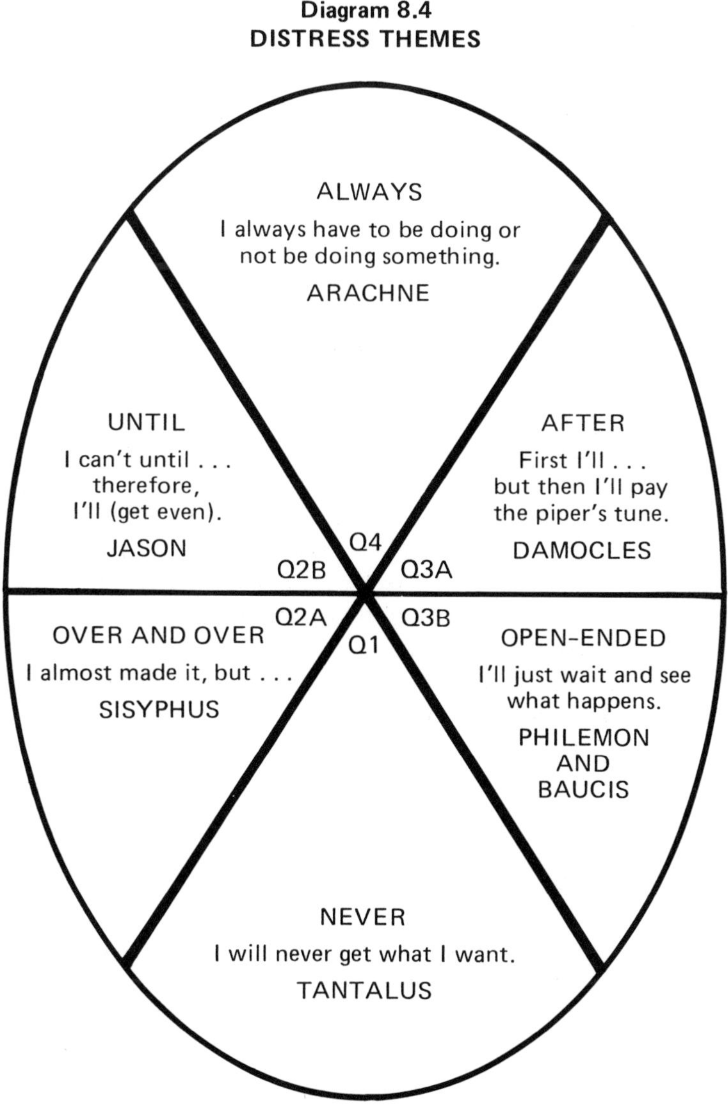

Tantalus who saw an abundance of food spread out before him but had to suffer from hunger because he was forbidden to eat. The Q2A theme is: You *almost* make it but not quite. You will keep doing it *over and over.* You are like Sisyphus who was condemned to roll a heavy stone up a hill; just as he was about to reach the top, the stone rolled back, and he had to start over again. The Q2B theme is: You can't have what you want *until* . . . You are like Jason who could not be king until he had performed certain tasks. The Q4 theme is: You do what you do because that is what you have been told to do and have *always* done. You are like Arachne who was turned into a spider and condemned to spend all her time spinning webs because she had challenged a goddess. The Q3A theme is: *After* you have done what you want, you will have to pay for it. You are like Damocles who enjoyed himself but lived with a sense of impending doom, because while he sat on the throne a sword, dangling by a thread, was hanging over his head. The Q3B theme is: Even though it's not fair, it's best to leave this *open-ended* and not make a disturbance. You are like Philemon and Baucis who were turned into laurel trees as a reward for their good deeds and condemned to spend the rest of their lives rustling in the wind waiting to see if they would ever be appropriately rewarded.

EUSTRESS THEMES

Eustress Themes are not locked-in themes. Unlike Distress Themes, they reflect both the possibilities (implying opportunities) and the probabilities (implying limitations) inherent in the use of the life energies. Eustress Themes are rich with multiple possibilities and probabilities. Each Eustress Theme, however, provides a direction encouraging the individual to pattern the details of his/her own life (see Diagram 8.5). In Q1 you deal with the Theme of *Possibilities.* You are aware of what is possible. In Q2A you deal with an *Exploratory* Theme. You explore what is possible. In Q2B you deal with a *Beforehand* Theme. You test the possible against the probable. In Q4 you deal with the Theme of *Probabilities.* You choose between what is and is not probable. In Q3A you deal with an *Afterward* Theme. You check-out the probable against the possible and the probable. In Q3B you deal with a *Tentative* Theme. You commit yourself to the checked-out probable.

DISTRESS PLAYERS

Not only do you pick the theme of your life drama; you also select the players who are to be the actors in your life drama. More important, you give them specific roles which you expect them to play with you. You also assign a role to yourself. You and all the other players may switch from one role to another; however each of you will be locked into a primary role.

You are either a Victim, a Persecutor or a Rescuer. *Victims* are persons who maintain a *one-down* position by inviting others to become Rescuers and to do for them what they can do for themselves or inviting others to become Persecutors and to control or punish them. *Persecutors* are persons who maintain a *one-up* position by controlling or putting others down. Persecutors look for Victims to blame. *Rescuers* are persons who maintain a *one-up* position by doing for others what the others can do for themselves. Rescuers find some way of being helpful to others, even without being asked, so that the others become or remain the Victims.

An interesting way to discover what your favorite role may be is to look at your favorite fairy tale. If you are not into fairy tales, then you can examine your favorite TV program or movie, or, if you prefer, your favorite book. Ask

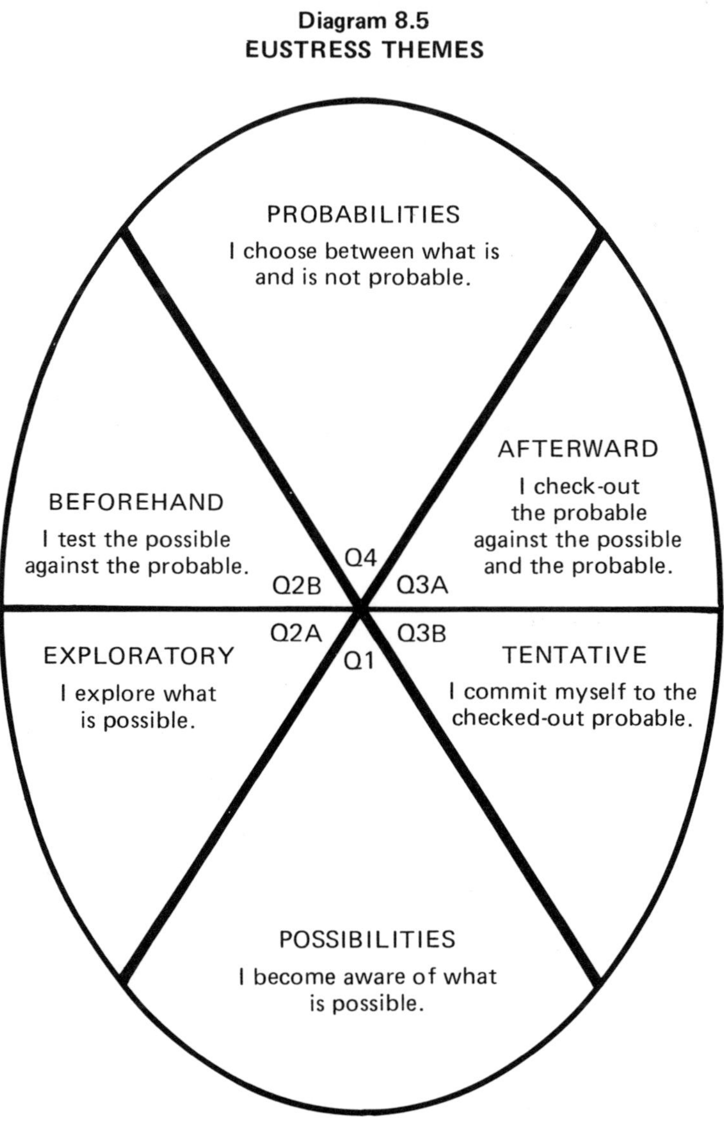

yourself: "Who is my favorite character?" Or ask yourself: "With whom do I identify most?" Then ask: "What role does this character play in the story?" By asking these questions you also can discover what roles you have assigned to the other people in your life.

One of the most popular fairy tales which people use to explore the roles which they and the other people in their lives play is Little Red Riding Hood. The wolf, of course, is a Persecutor; the Grandmother, a Victim; and the Hunter, a Rescuer. Little Red Riding Hood's mother frequently is seen in two roles: She is regarded by some as Rescuer who sends her daughter on a mission of mercy; or by others as a Persecutor who sends her little daughter out on a dangerous journey aware that there may be a wolf lurking in the forest. Little Red Riding Hood is regarded by most people as a Rescuer; however, some see her only as an innocent little girl who is victimized by a big bad wolf.

Another favorite fairy tale is Cinderella. Here the roles generally are more precise. Cinderella is a Victim; the prince and the fairy godmother, the Rescuers; and the stepmother and the sisters, the Persecutors.

Your favorite fairy tale or TV characters are, of course, only symbols. They really are projected images of you and the people in your life. In your fantasies you are freer to see yourself as you think you are and as you expect others to be.

The three roles are points on a triangle (see Diagram 8.6). At the bottom is the Victim; at the top are the Persecutor and the Rescuer.

Not all Victims, Persecutors and Rescuers operate from the same motivation. There are three Victim roles, two Persecutor and two Rescuer roles diagrammed in the Distress Ellipse (see Diagram 8.7).

All the Victim roles are below the center line. The Persecutor and Rescuer roles are above the center line. The Persecutor roles, however, are on your

Diagram 8.6
DISTRESS ROLES

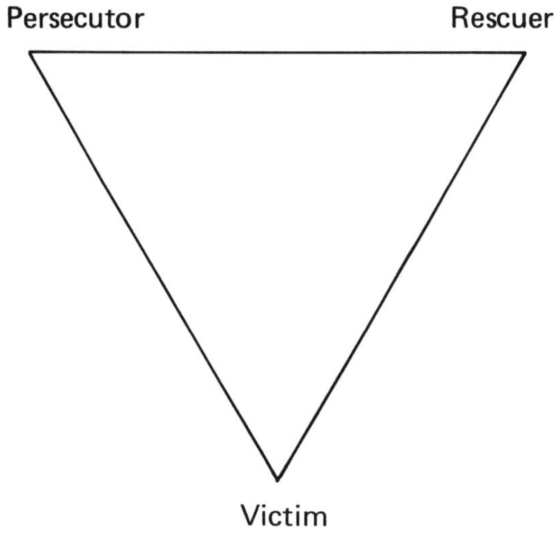

Diagram 8.7
DISTRESS PLAYERS

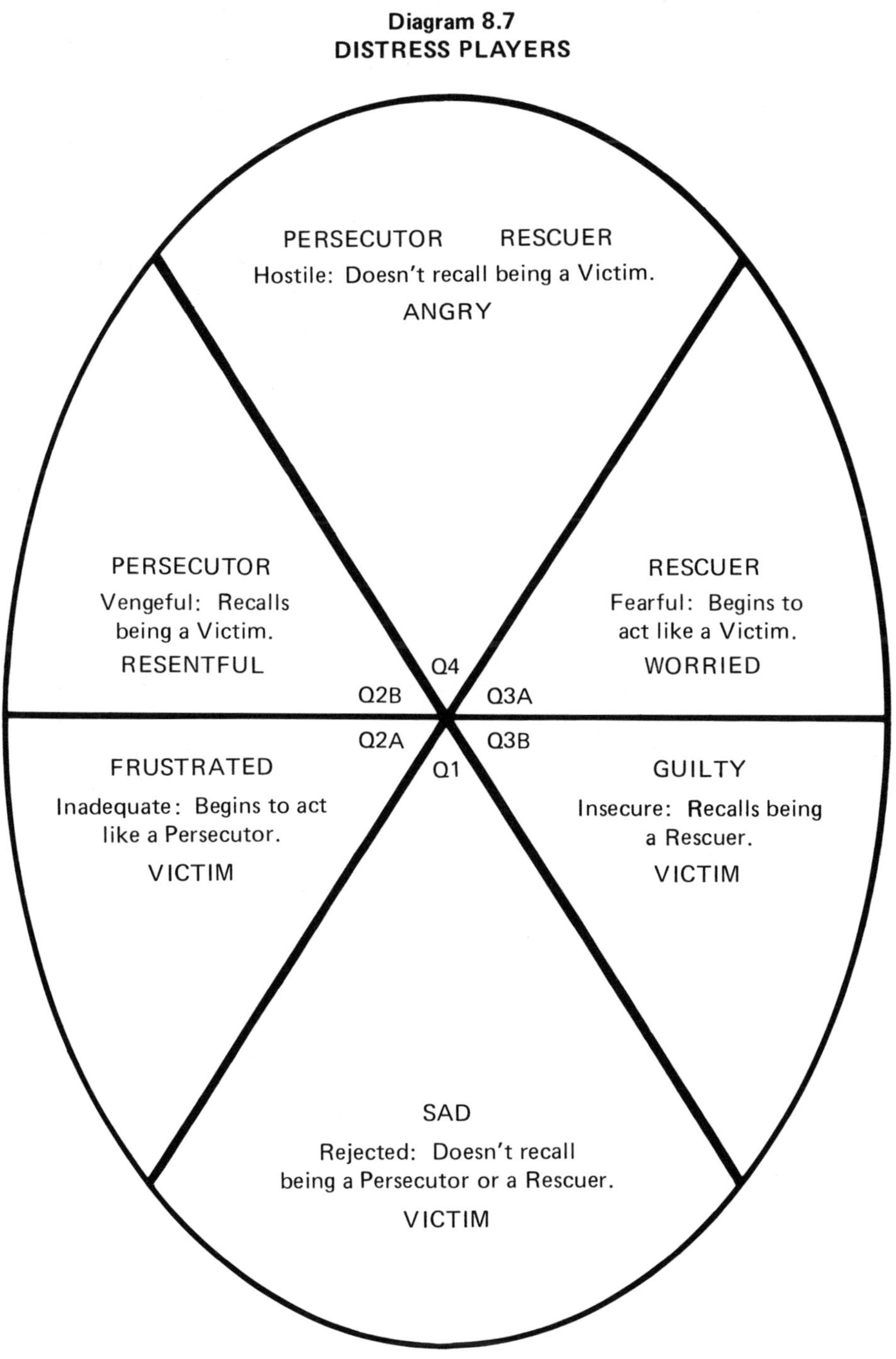

left as you face the ellipse. The Rescuer roles are on your right as you face the ellipse. Each role correlates with a particular Quadrant and is characterized by a specific feeling, thought, behavior pattern and Life Attitude.

There are three basic Distress Victim roles: Q1: When you are a Victim in Q1 you lock yourself into the REJECTED Personality Type without thinking of yourself either as a Persecutor or as a Rescuer. You feel Sad, and your Life Attitude is either ↓↑ or ↓↓. You do nothing to resolve your problems, or, if you do, it is only to put yourself down. Q2A: When you are a Victim in Q2A you lock yourself into the INADEQUATE Personality Type, but you begin to think of yourself as a Persecutor. You feel frustrated, and your Life Attitude is ↓↑. You begin to agitate and keep your motor running. Q3B: When you are a Victim in Q3B you lock yourself into the INSECURE Personality Type, but you recall the time when you were a Rescuer. You feel Guilty, and your Life Attitude is ↓↑. You give in and adapt your ways to other people.

There are two basic Distress Persecutor roles: Q2B: When you are a Persecutor in Q2B you lock yourself into the VENGEFUL Personality Type, but you still recall the time when you were a Victim. You feel Resentful, and your Life Attitude is ↑↓. Your motor really is revved up, and you are into all kinds of agitated activities. Q4A: When you are a Persecutor in Q4A you lock yourself into the HOSTILE Personality Type, without thinking of yourself as a Victim. You feel Angry, and your Life Attitude is ↑↓. You throw a temper tantrum, put your fist through the wall or even become dangerous to others or to yourself.

There are two basic Distress Rescuer roles: Q4B: When you are a Rescuer in Q4B you lock yourself into the HOSTILE Personality Type, without thinking of yourself as Victim. You feel Angry, and your Life Attitude is ↑↓. You get involved in causes, and you test all kinds of waters, presumably to help others but primarily to save yourself, even if it means to incapacitate yourself. Q3A: When you are a Rescuer in Q3A you lock yourself into the FEARFUL Personality Type, but you begin to think of yourself as a Victim. You feel Worried, and your Life Attitude is ↑↓. You continue to test the waters, but you also look back over your shoulder telling those whom you Rescue that it is for their own good. You are ready to give in if the pressure is too much.

SWITCHING DISTRESS ROLES

If you are like most people, sooner or later you will look for ways to become comfortable and to get out of being bottom dog. One way that you can escape is to shift from one role to another. Instead of being a Victim, you become a Persecutor or a Rescuer. Or, if you are a Persecutor, you become a Rescuer or a Victim, or, if you are a Rescuer, you become a Persecutor or a Victim. However, no matter to what role you move, you still distress yourself because someone remains a bottom dog.

Once you begin to switch, sometimes you will play two roles. The odds are, however, that you will play all three roles. You may even play a second Victim, Persecutor or Rescuer role before you return to the favorite role with which you began. Altogether there are twelve main switches, which are illustrated in Diagram 8.8. Each Victim has four switches in combination with one Persecutor and one Rescuer role.

If, for example, your favorite Distress role is to be a Q1 REJECTED Victim, you probably will lock yourself into one of the following patterns:

1) Q1   REJECTED Victim → to Q2B   VENGEFUL Persecutor → to Q3A FEARFUL Rescuer → to Q1   REJECTED Victim.

2) Q1   REJECTED Victim → to Q2B   VENGEFUL Persecutor → to Q4B HOSTILE Rescuer   → to Q1   REJECTED Victim.

3) Q1   REJECTED Victim → to Q4A   HOSTILE Persecutor → to Q4B HOSTILE Rescuer   → to Q1   REJECTED Victim.

4) Q1   REJECTED Victim → to Q4A   HOSTILE Persecutor → to Q3A FEARFUL Rescuer → to Q1   REJECTED Victim.

In Part IV of this book you learned that each Personality Type is locked into a substitute uncomfortable (painful) feeling and into a Distress Life Attitude. Switching from one role to another, however, will not make your life less painful nor will it help you escape from your Distress Life Attitude. Getting rid of an old role with its uncomfortable feeling may feel comfortable to you for a moment or two, but before long you will discover that the discomfort associated with your new role will have caught up with you. Moreover, you will be switching from one Distress Life Attitude to another where either you or the other person will be *one-down.* You are switching from one locked-in Personality Type to another locked-in Personality Type.

Not only will you switch from one role to another, you also will select other actors who will play roles complementary to your role and who will switch roles whenever you switch your role. For example, if you are a Victim who is expecting someone to help you (i.e., to do for you what you can do for yourself), you will lock yourself into a Distress behavior pattern with a Rescuer who seemingly will be grateful for the opportunity to assist you. Or, if you are expecting someone to criticize, you will lock yourself into a Distress behavior pattern with a Persecutor who is ever-ready to criticize you for whatever you do or don't do. If, on the other hand, you switch to the role of Persecutor or Rescuer, in both instances you will expect the other person to be a Victim with whom you can lock into a Distress behavior pattern.

Once you lock yourself into one of the three Distress roles, you also switch your expectations of other people. For example, if you are a Victim and expect the other person to be your Rescuer and the individual refuses to play that role, you now will regard that other person as a Persecutor. Alternatively, you yourself will become a Persecutor and expect that other person to be a Victim. On the other hand, if you are Victim and expect the other person to be your Persecutor, you will switch your own role to that of a Rescuer in the hope that by Rescuing that other person s/he also will switch roles and likewise become your Rescuer instead of your Persecutor. Whenever you switch roles as a Victim, Persecutor or Rescuer, you distress yourself.

Diagram 8.8
SWITCHING DISTRESS ROLES

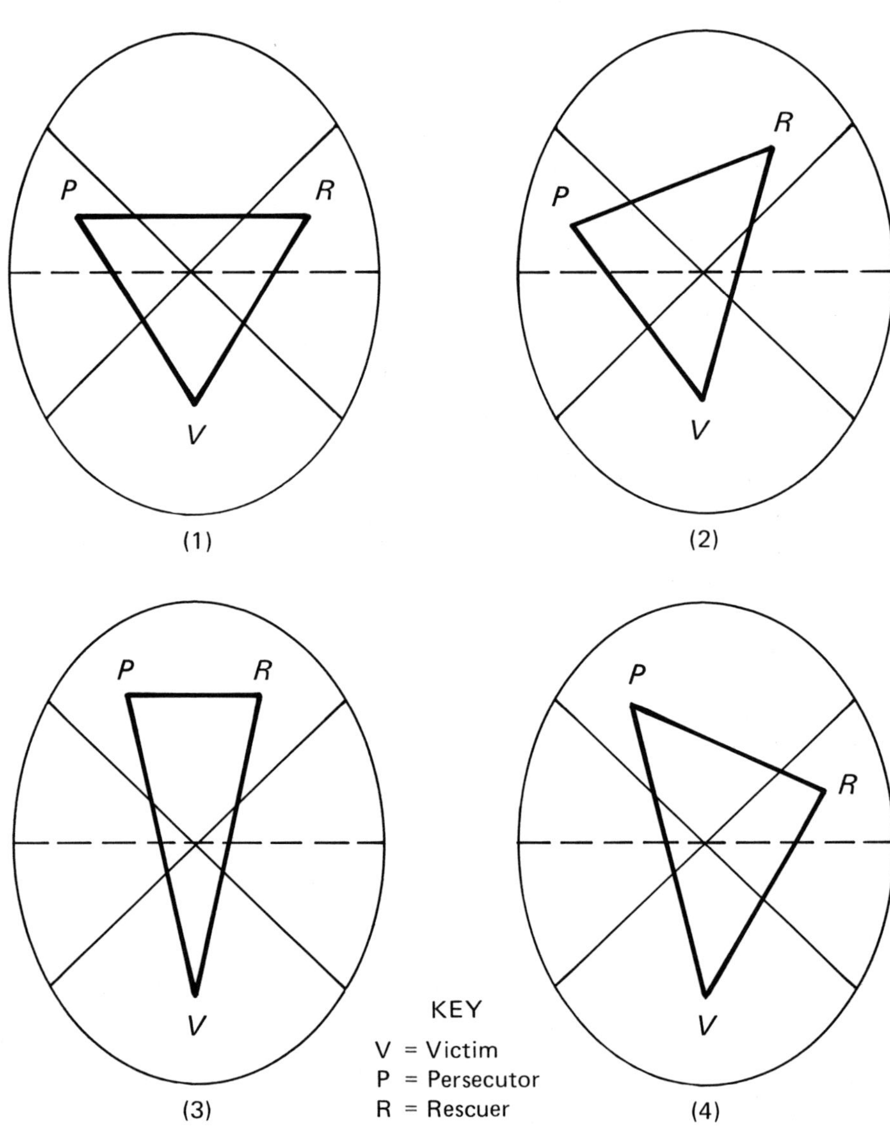

FINISHING UNFINISHED BUSINESS

The Distress role into which you lock yourself probably was established a long time ago when you were very young. In section three of this book you learned about the Conditional Positive and the Conditional Negative Messages which you received from your parents. You also learned about the Decision-response which you made in reply to your parents.

When you made a Decision-response to a parental message you also locked yourself into your Distress role. You decided at that time what you could expect of your parents and what the best way was to deal with them. You chose either to be a Victim, a Persecutor or a Rescuer. Sometimes you decided to switch to different roles for different situations; however, no matter what the circumstance, your new role was a locked-in role with fixed feelings, thoughts and behaviors.

What at first seemed to be freedom for you as a child became your prison as you grew older. What once had worked with your parents no longer seemed to work either with them or with others, especially your peers. Success, if it came at all, was achieved outside your family and then only when you learned to switch your Decision-responses. If you were a Victim in your family, you learned how to become a Persecutor or Rescuer outside your family. If you were a Persecutor in your family, you learned how to become a Rescuer or a Victim outside your family. If you were a Rescuer inside your family you became a Persecutor or a Victim outside your family. You learned to handle your external situation just as you had handled your original family situation, only this time you reversed your role. You switched your family role to a new role—although it was still a Distress role—which enabled you to survive.

Then you married and you expected that this time you would succeed inside your family life. You were in love, and your spouse was expected to fulfill all the unfinished business you had with your parents. Everything that you ever wanted to feel, think and do now would be possible.

If you were a man who had difficulty with your father and turned to your mother for help, you now expected your wife to be your Rescuer whenever you were in trouble. If she did not Rescue you, you saw her as your Persecutor or you switched and became her Persecutor.

If you were a man who had difficulty with his mother, now you expected your wife to be everything your mother was not. If she did not measure up to your expectation, either you remained a Victim and saw her as your Persecutor, just as you saw your mother as your Persecutor, or you switched and became her Persecutor and made her into your Victim.

If you were a woman who had difficulty with your mother and turned to your father for help, now you expected your husband to be your Rescuer whenever you were in trouble. If he did not Rescue you, you saw him as your Persecutor or you switched and became his Persecutor.

If you were a woman who had difficulty with your father, now you expected your husband to be everything that your father was not. If he did not measure up to your expectation, either you remained a Victim and saw him as your

Persecutor, just as you had thought that your father was your Persecutor, or you switched and became his Persecutor and made him into a Victim.

Finishing, with your spouse and especially with your children, the unfinished business of your family of origin is reliving locked-in Distress roles. In the process you may be creating a self-fulfilling prophecy. By concentrating on what you expect rather than on what you want, you may wind up with a dreaded rather than a desired outcome.

EUSTRESS CONTRACTS

There are no locked-in Eustress roles. Instead, you have many options as a Eustress Personality. You may choose to be a small "*v*" victim, or a small, "*p*" persecutor or a small "*r*" rescuer. The difference between the small-letter and the big-letter roles is that the big-letter roles are the inappropriate Distress roles into which you lock yourself in an immediate context. The small letter roles are the appropriate roles for specific occasions, and you give them up as soon as they have served your purpose.

Small "v" victims recognize that they are in uncomfortable situations. Instead of expecting someone to punish them or to help them, however, they make a contract to get what they want. They do not lock themselves in a Q1 REJECTED, Q2A INADEQUATE or Q3B INSECURE Distress Personality Type and lament "how terrible," "poor me," or "help me." They contract with small "p" persecutors to evaluate them and their situation and with small "r" rescuers to assist them. They do not live with the expectation that it is wrong to have limitations or that it is incumbent upon others to take care of them. On the contrary, they arrange openly to take care of their wants. They make agreements with themselves to give themselves what they want, especially if they don't get what they want from others. Small "v" victims are neither hopeless, nor helpless nor harmless.

Eustress contracts, explained below, are illustrated in Diagram 8.9. Q1 small "*v*" victims exercise the SELF-ACCEPTING option: whenever they contract with others for whatever purpose, they maintain their self-esteem. Q2A small "*v*" victims exercise the SELF-RELIANT option: whenever they contract to learn skills and explore values, they learn on their own and from others. Q3B small "*v*" victims exercise the SELF-RESPONSIBLE option: whenever they negotiate contracts they take responsibility for their 50 percent and hold the other contractors responsible for the remaining 50 percent. Q2B small "*p*" persecutors exercise the SELF-COMPETENT option: whenever they contract to give evaluations or to pass judgment on others, they continue to respect the others whether they agree or disagree with them. Q4 small "*p*" persecutors exercise the SELF-APPROVING option: whenever they contract to teach others what not to do, they do not put the others down; instead, they offer enlightened friendship and encourage the others to come up with alternatives to solve their own problems. Q4 small "*r*" rescuers exercise the SELF-APPROVING option: whenever they contract to teach others what to do, they do not put the others down; instead, they offer enlightened friendship and encourage the

Diagram 8.9
EUSTRESS CONTRACTS

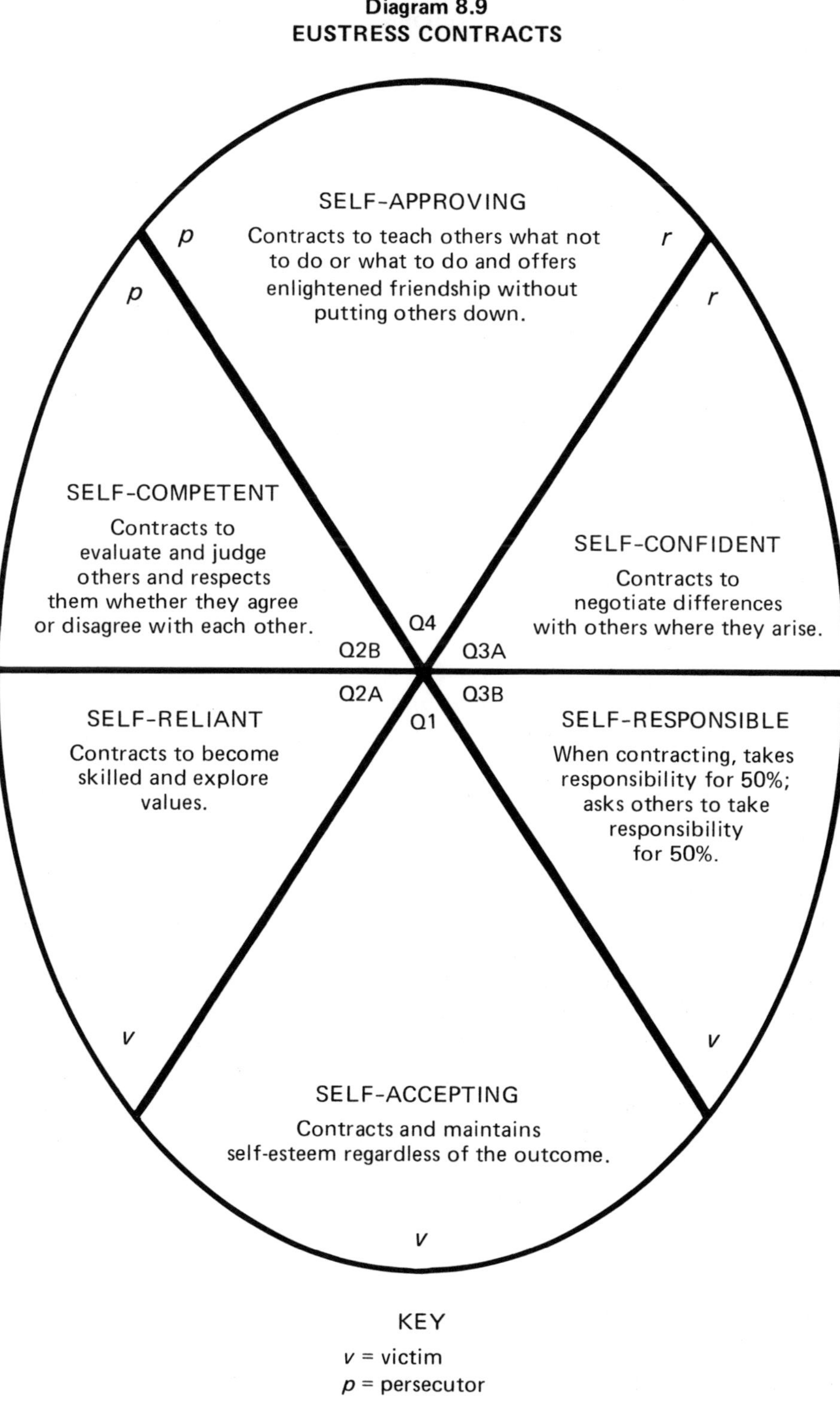

KEY
v = victim
p = persecutor
r = rescuer

others to come up with alternatives to solve their own problems. Q3A small "*r*" rescuers exercise the SELF-CONFIDENT option: whenever they contract with others, they press their own issues to a conclusion, and they negotiate differences which may arise.

DISTRESS SIGNALS

You and the Players in your life drama are identified not only by the roles that you and the others play but also by the non-verbal signals that your bodies send out. You communicate with *gestures, postures, facial expressions* and *tones of voice* as well as with *words*. Your body language reveals as much about what you think and feel as your verbally expressed thoughts and feelings. Of course, no one knows for sure what your signals are communicating; however, your body is betraying powerful hints about your Personality Type, whether you are locked into one of the Six Distress Personality Types or you are a Eustress Personality with six options.

Whenever you distress yourself, you lock in your non-verbal gestures, postures, facial expressions and tone of voice. The other players do the same whenever they distress themselves.

Non-verbal Distress behaviors are suits of armor that your body, like the knight of old, wears to defend and assert itself. Armor is helpful, often necessary; however, it also can be a hindrance and a self-defeating encumbrance. For example, when the medieval knight and his adversary, each with a lance poised for the thrust, bore down upon each other, their protective armor was essential because it provided them with security. When one of the knights was thrown from his horse, however, he was often imprisoned in his armor and lay helpless upon the ground. He was weighted down and burdened by his armor's inflexibility and became subject to the mercy of his opponent. Even when helped to his feet by his supporters, he remained at a disadvantage, fighting unmounted with a mounted foe.

Distress signals are expressions of Defiance or Compliance. They reflect Prescriptions, Prohibitions and Powerlessness. Distress Signals are listed in the Distress Quadrants (see Diagram 8.10; read in conjunction with Diagram 8.6: Distress Players) in the order of (1) gestures, (2) postures, (3) facial expressions and (4) tones of voice, and each is marked by a dash (—). Sometimes the Signals are externally influenced, growing out of Messages which say "You Must...". Other times the Signals are internally influenced, growing out of Decision-responses which say "I Must...".

EUSTRESS SIGNALS

Eustress gestures, postures, facial expressions and tones of voice, while they may resemble characteristic Distress signals, are neither Defiant nor Compliant. They are Active signals, and they are Passive signals; however, above all they

Diagram 8.10
DISTRESS SIGNALS

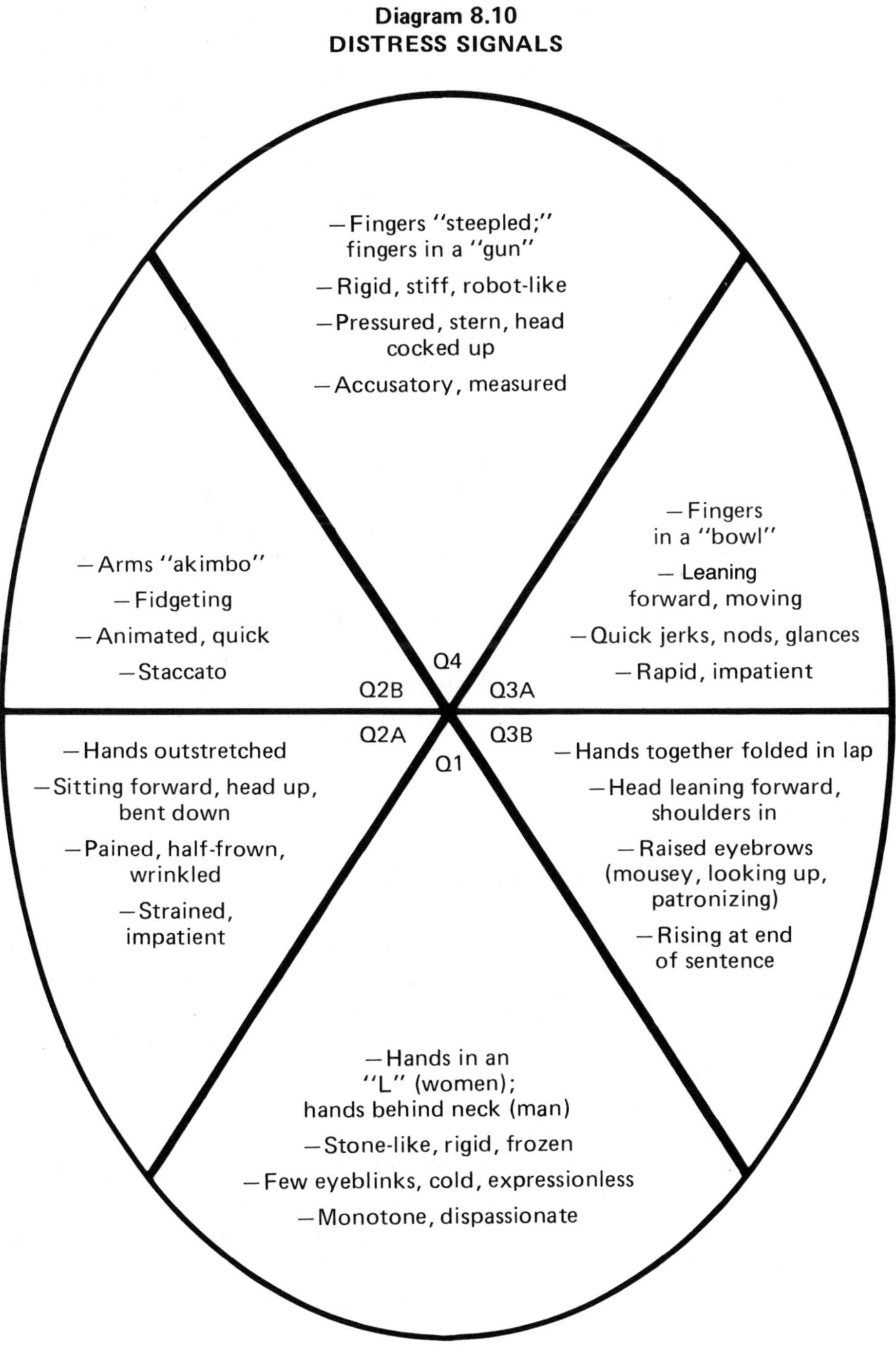

are signals that are expressed selectively, so that they are both appropriate to a specific occasion and compatible with the accompanying spoken words.

Unlike the Distress signals, which are locked-in and, therefore, limited in scope, the Eustress signals are as limitless as the individual's ability to show imagination and capacity to be aware of his/her thoughts, feelings and behaviors. Eustress signals provide Permission and Protection on the deeper psychological level for the Permissions and Protections expressed verbally on the social level. When the psychological level signals and the social level verbalizations are congruent with each other, the individual is able to create a powerful Eustress life drama. Eustress signals express Permission, Protection and Power.

When you send out Eustress signals your entire being is proclaiming that you are SELF-ACCEPTING, SELF-RELIANT, SELF-COMPETENT, SELF-APPROV-ING, SELF-CONFIDENT and SELF-RESPONSIBLE. Most important, you are making your life an unfolding Personal Story *That You Are*, an Adventure Story *How You Are*, an Identity Story *Who You Are* and a History Story *What You Are*.

Sometimes non-verbal signals are externally influenced. Distress signals grow out of Distress Conditional Messages, both Positive and Negative, which say *You must* or *You must not*. Eustress signals develop from Eustress Unconditional Messages both Positive and Negative, which say *You may* and *you may not*.

Other times non-verbal messages are internally influenced. Distress signals grow out of Distress Conditional Distress-responses, both Positive and Negative, which say *I must* or *I must not*. Eustress Unconditional Distress-responses develop from Eustress Decision-responses, both Positive and Negative, which say *I want* and *I don't want*.

A WORD ABOUT THE NERVOUS SYSTEM

Your body acts as an integrated whole, and, under ordinary circumstances, the brain oversees everything that goes on in your body. Every thought, every feeling and every behavior, whether with your awareness or without, begins with an electrochemical event in the brain. In a very real sense, all of psychology is the study of the brain processes.

To simplify the complex, the nervous system in your body can be divided into a Central Nervous System—consisting of the brain, the brain stem and the spinal cord—and the Peripheral Nervous System, which includes all the nerve fibers to and from the rest of the body. The Central Nervous System always acts on the world via the Peripheral Nervous System. A brain without a mouth cannot talk. Similarly, the Central Nervous System learns about the world through the Peripheral Nervous System. Again, a brain without eyes can see nothing.

The Peripheral Nervous System is broken down further into two systems: 1) a Somatic Nervous System, which consists of the nerves going to and from the sensory (taste, touch, smell, sight and hearing) and motor (hands and feet) organs, and activates the voluntary muscles. The Somatic Nervous System requires the direct involvement of the person for its operation. 2) an Autonomic Nervous System, which controls the internal organs of the body and innervates the involuntary smooth muscles without a person's awareness or active involvement. The heart and the glands are examples of organs controlled by the Autonomic Nervous System. While recent experiments in biofeedback and the studies of Eastern mystics suggest that under special conditions the so-called involuntary muscles can become voluntary, the fact still remains that you do not ordinarily exert conscious control over the internal organs. Nature has so provided that it is not necessary for you to tell your heart to beat so many times per minute for the rest of your life. Imagine what it would be like if you had to keep your internal systems under everyday control. You would be so busy with the complicated business of keeping yourself alive that you would have little, if any, time left to do anything else.

The Autonomic Nervous System again is divided into two systems: 1) the Sympathetic Nervous System and 2) the Parasympathetic Nervous System. These two systems are antagonistic to each other; yet they work together to maintain stable conditions within the body in the face of an ever-changing world.

The function of the Sympathetic Nervous System is to mobilize the body for action to meet an emergency by making the energy stores of the body available. The person is essentially in a producing posture. There is a flow of adrenalin and noradrenalin into the bloodstream, and the system is called the Adrenergic system. These chemicals are not quickly destroyed once they have performed their functions of setting the electrical mechanisms into operation. This complex body pattern, called the "fight or flight reaction," involves the entire body and acts quickly, is all of a piece and is maintained for a relatively long period of time. The adrenergic response is probably a holdover from primitive times when people lived at the mercy of the elements and hostile forces.

The Parasympathetic Nervous System, on the other hand, functions to conserve and maintain bodily resources. The person is essentially in a receiving posture. This time the chemical, acetylcholine, is discharged into the bloodstream and deactivated quickly once its role in the electrical system is carried out. The actions, therefore, are localized and of short duration. This system is also called the Cholinergic system.

There also is a structural difference between the Adrenergic (Sympathetic) and the Cholinergic (Parasympathetic) systems. The nerve fibers of the Adrenergic system that deliver the electrochemical impulses emerge from the middle regions of the spinal column and pass through a chain of closely connected ganglia or nerve centers before they reach the target organ. In the ganglia much "cross-talk" takes place between the nerve fibers so that all the organs of the Sympathetic System become activated. Thus, there ensues the "fight or flight" of the entire body.

The nerve fibers of the Parasympathetic System, however, have only one linkage, which goes from the brain, brain stem or spinal cord directly to the target area. The ganglia are far from each other, and there is very little "cross-talk" so that the action is more specific and limited to a single organ.

Despite the differences in function and structure, the Sympathetic and Parasympathetic Nervous Systems are designed to maintain an exquisite balance between the adrenergic and the cholinergic responses, and, when not interfered with, this balancing process contributes to the longevity and health of all body systems. Because of external environmental demands in our contemporary society, however, many individuals interfere with this delicate balance by maintaining themselves either in self-defeating adrenergic "fight or flight" gestures, postures, facial expressions and tones of voice or in self-defeating vegetative cholinergic gestures, postures, facial expressions and tones of voice. Both, however, are inappropriate and represent locked-in responses.

When your non-verbal behaviors are congruent with your verbal expressions, both send the same message. When your balance is disrupted, however—when you maintain either an inappropriate adrenergic or an inappropriate cholinergic response—your non-verbal is incongruent and sends a message which is different from your verbal message. Since your response is involuntary, your non-verbal reveals what you think, feel and do even more than your verbal message, which you speak with control. Your verbal messages usually tell what you would like to be or would like to happen. They are your beliefs, your explanations, your defenses. They are the social messages designed for the other person to hear and accept. Your non-verbal messages, however, tell what is happening in the inner you. They are the psychological messages designed to express what deep down you hear and accept and want for yourself.

TWO SPECIAL WORDS: *YES* AND *NO*

There are two special words which reveal whether you and the players in your life drama are Distress players or Eustress players. These two words are *yes* and *no*. They are powerful words. Though made up of only two and three letters, both words signal your ability and that of your life drama players to carry out three very important functions on the social level of your life:

1) the ability to give yourself Permission.
2) the ability to give yourself Protection.
3) the ability to give yourself Power.

"*Yes*" is both a Prescription and a Permission word. "*No*" is both a Prohibition and a Protection word. "Yes" and "no," when used together, are both Powerless and Power words.

In part III of this book, you will recall, there was a discussion about Positive and Negative Conditional and Unconditional Messages from parents and the Decision-responses which you as a child made to these messages. The Positive and Negative Conditional Messages are the *either-or* Distress messages. Either you are compliant and accept your parents' Permission and thus receive their so-called Protection, or you are Defiant and reject their Permission and as a consequence you believe that you are deprived of their Protection. In both instances you place the Power to exercise your life energies to think, feel and behave under their and not your jurisdiction.

The Positive and Negative Unconditional Messages are the *both/and* Eustress messages. You are able both to accept and to reject their Permission by choosing what is appropriate Permission for you and, at the same time, give yourself genuine Protection. Both you and your parents share Power. They have the Power to provide you with guidelines, and you have the Power to choose. As you grow older, the Power to choose increasingly shifts to you as you become more and more responsible for your Permissions and Protections. Simultaneously your parents' Power to guide decreases, as they, too, shift from providing guidelines to offering suggestions and advice when requested.

These childhood messages and decisions most often were translated into the two words *yes* and *no*, and they are repeated as *yes* and *no*, in your life drama to this day. Learning to say *Yes* and *No*, therefore, is very important. You and the players in your life drama say *yes* and *no* to each other. Whether your *yes* and your *no* is a Distress or a Eustress *yes* and *no* depends, however, upon whether you and your players still have unfinished business from your childhood that you act out in the life drama.

The words *yes* and *no* determine the Prescriptions, Prohibitions and the Powerlessness that you and the other players assign to yourself and to each other. They also determine your capacity to give to yourselves and to receive from others Permission, Protection and Power.

A WORD ABOUT HUMAN DEVELOPMENT

Before a person can exercise Permission, Protection and Power, s/he must receive Permission from parents to learn each of these three functions. Altogether there are six necessary Permissions: 1) to say *yes*, 2) to say *yes* to yourself, 3) to say *yes* to another person, 4) to say *no*, 5) to say *no* to yourself and 6) to say *no* to another person.

When a child is given Permission and enabled to experience each of these Permissions, psychologically s/he learns to Eustress him/herself. If, however, the child is deprived of these Permissions or receives this information as Prescriptions, then an important link is missing in that child's life chain, and that child grows chronologically but not psychologically and distresses him/herself as a consequence.

Each of these six Permissions is a developmental task to be completed before the next task is undertaken. Whenever a task is not completed satisfactorily, the individual continues to hold onto the last successfully completed developmental task and becomes fixated, using the last successfully completed task again and again whether appropriate or not to the succeeding developmental situations.

The six developmental tasks do not emerge all at once. Learning how to say *yes* comes before learning how to say *no*, and learning how to say *no* precedes learning how to say *yes and no* in combination.

The tasks of saying *yes* and *no* develop during the first three years of life while the child is growing through two developmental phases, which Freud called the Oral Stage and the Anal Stage. The tasks of saying *yes* and *no* in combination emerge in the third-fourth year with the onset of what Freud called the Oedipal Stage. The Oral Stage is also called the Stage of Early Infancy; the Anal Stage, Late Infancy; and the Oedipal Stage, Early Childhood.

Learning how to say *yes* begins with the very first moment of life and belongs to the Early Infancy Stage from the time of birth until approximately the second year in the child's life. The first *yes* Permission is given with the mother's milk and her nurturing warmth and care. This is the time when trust is established. This is followed by the infant's first *yes* Permission to explore and learn as the infant begins to sit up, then to stand, and finally to walk in order to examine the world around him/her. Initially, the infant practices Permission to say *yes* to him/herself and later experiments with Permission to say *yes* to the other person. What appears to be, during this period, a *no* is not so much a *no* as it is a desire to learn how to say *yes* to oneself and to others. If these opportunities to say *yes* are denied to the infant by the parent, when the time to learn how to say *no* does arrive, the child will enter the *no* stage with a deficient capacity to say *yes*.

Learning how to say *no* is a function of the Late Infancy Stage, the time of the *terrible two's. Yes* provides Permission. *No* provides Protection. *No* sets the boundaries. *No* establishes the *don't's* just as *yes* offers the *do's*. Before the child can lay the groundwork for giving him/herself Protection, however, s/he must receive Permission from the parents that it is appropriate to set boundaries and to live with *don't's* and to give oneself Protection.

In the Late Infancy Stage the parents give the child Permission to say *no*. When the child does say *no*, there is no judgment intended by the child at this point. Learning how to say *no* is a necessary psychological developmental task just as walking is a necessary motor developmental task. Once the parents give the child Permission to practice saying *no*, the next parental Permission is to enable the child to say *no* to one's self and then to say *no* to others. As the child learns and exercises these Permissions, s/he is able to enter the world of relationships with increasing Power. Exercising the Power to say *no*, just as exercising the Power to say *yes*, is essential to establishing intimacy with another person.

In the Early and Late Infancy Stages *yes* and *no* are established in one-to-one relationships between the child and a parent. While there may be more than two people present, the relationships are *dyadic*, involving, from the child's point of view, only one other person, whether a father, a mother, a sibling, a relative or a friend.

By the time the child approaches age three, however, the relationships become *triadic*. The child has entered the Early Childhood Stage, dealing simultaneously with the mother and the father, with both a parent and a sibling, with two friends and so on. Instead of being a time for building independent and simple one-to-one relationship skills, the third developmental period is devoted to developing multiple-relationship tools.

The child no longer tests his/her individual *yes* against another's individual *no*. The child now tests *yes* and *no* against the collective *yes* and *no* of a group. The child learns, moreover, that not everyone says *yes* and that not everyone says *no* at the same time. Choices now become necessary and strategies increasingly essential. In this new world of multiple-relationships the child needs parental Permission to recycle and reexperience, in the new context, the Permissions received in the earlier two stages. The granting of these Permissions and the fulfillment by the child of these Permissions determine the Permission, Protection and Power the child takes with him/her into the multiple-relationships of puberty, adolescence and adulthood.

DISTRESS AND EUSTRESS *YES* AND *NO*

The Three developmental stages in the life of a child before the age of six are diagrammed in the Quadrants of both the Distress and Eustress Ellipses (Diagrams 8.10–8.13). *Stage 1* (Early Infancy) is represented by Q1, Q2A and Q2B, where the emphasis is on learning to say *yes*, to saying *yes* to oneself and to others in one-to-one situations. *Stage 2* (Late Infancy) is represented by Q4, where the emphasis is on learning how to say *no* and in Q3A and Q3B on experiencing saying *no* to oneself and to another person in one-to-one situations. Both of these stages are placed on one ellipse. There is one Distress Ellipse (see Diagram 8.11) which combines both the Early and Late Infancy Stages and shows six Distress locked-in ways of saying *yes* or *no*. There is one Eustress Ellipse (see Diagram 8.12) which combines both the Early and Late Infancy Stages and shows six Eustress options for saying *yes* and *no*. *Stage 3* (Early Childhood) is diagrammed on two separate ellipses, one to indicate the Distress locked-in ways of saying *yes* or *no* in multiple-relationship situations (see Diagram 8.13) and one to indicate the Eustress options for saying *yes* and *no* in multiple-relationship situations (see Diagram 8.14).

DISTRESS SCENARIOS

Not only do you pick the players in your life drama, you also determine how you will spend your time acting out your life drama theme. Time is the tabula rasa or slate on which you record the scenarios of your life—the record of how you use and misuse your life energies. When you lock yourself into feelings, thoughts and behaviors and into a life attitude, you also lock in your misuse of time. Your time is Distress Time.

Distress Time

Distress Time is expressed in one of six different ways. Each is an effort to secure psychological intimacy; however, the intimacy that you seek is illusive.

Diagram 8.11
DISTRESS: YES OR NO
Early / Late Infancy

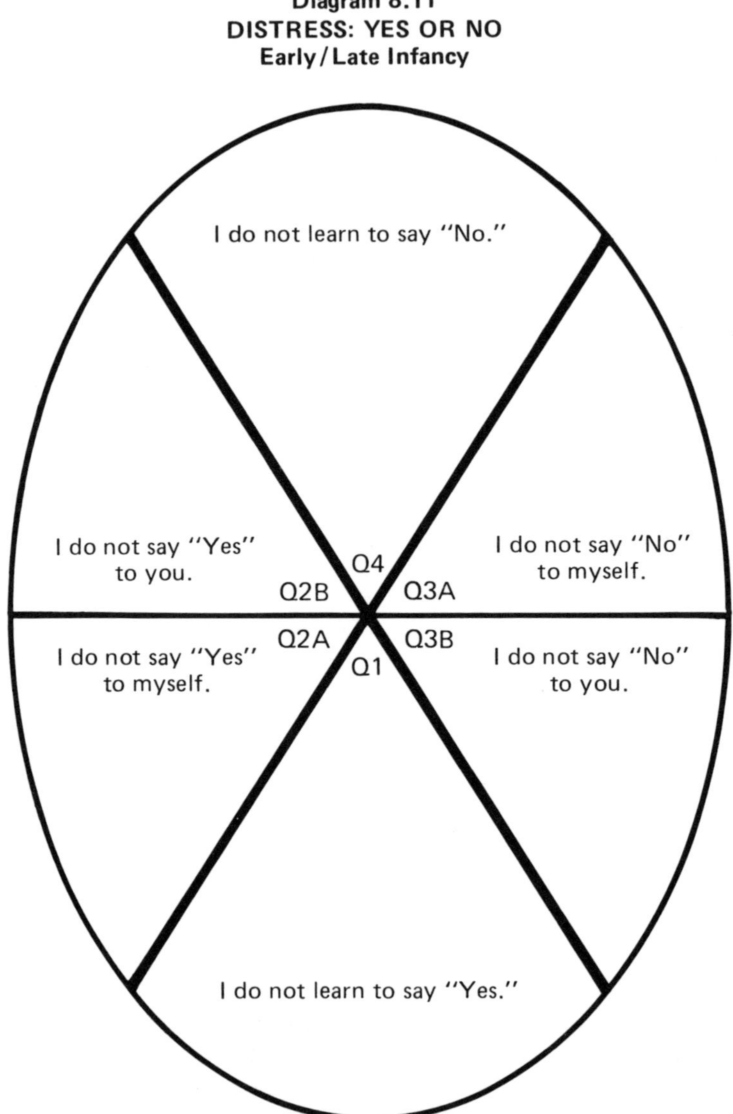

Diagram 8.12
EUSTRESS: YES AND NO
Early / Late Infancy

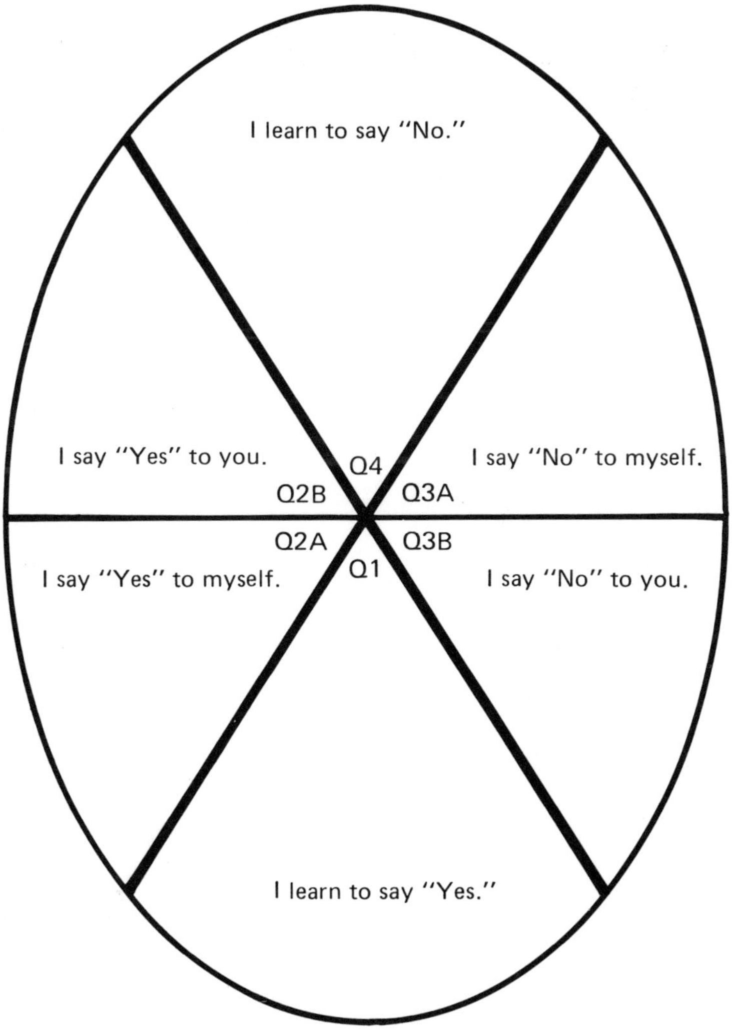

Diagram 8.13
DISTRESS: YES OR NO
Early Childhood

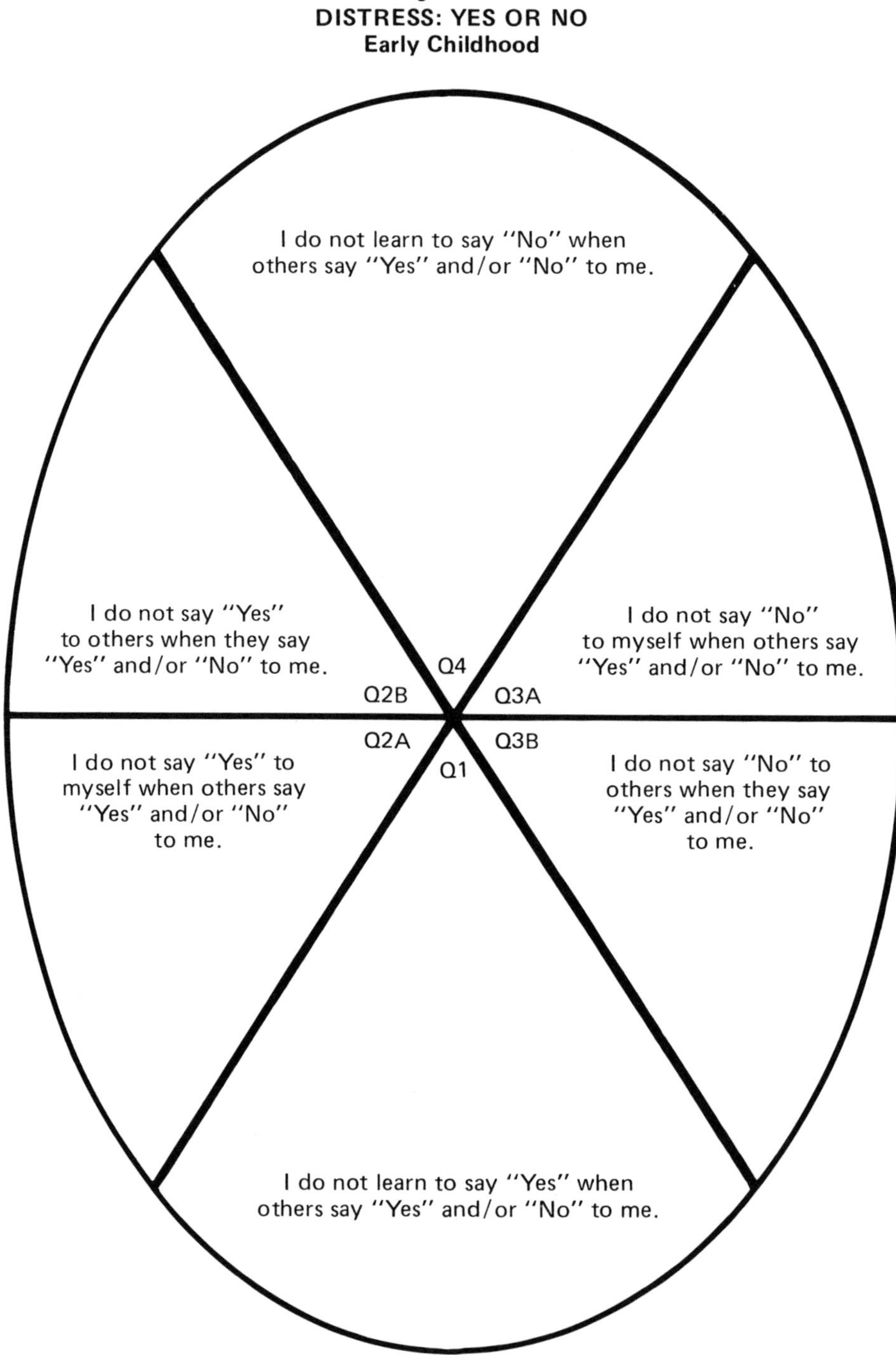

Diagram 8.14
EUSTRESS: YES AND NO
Early Childhood

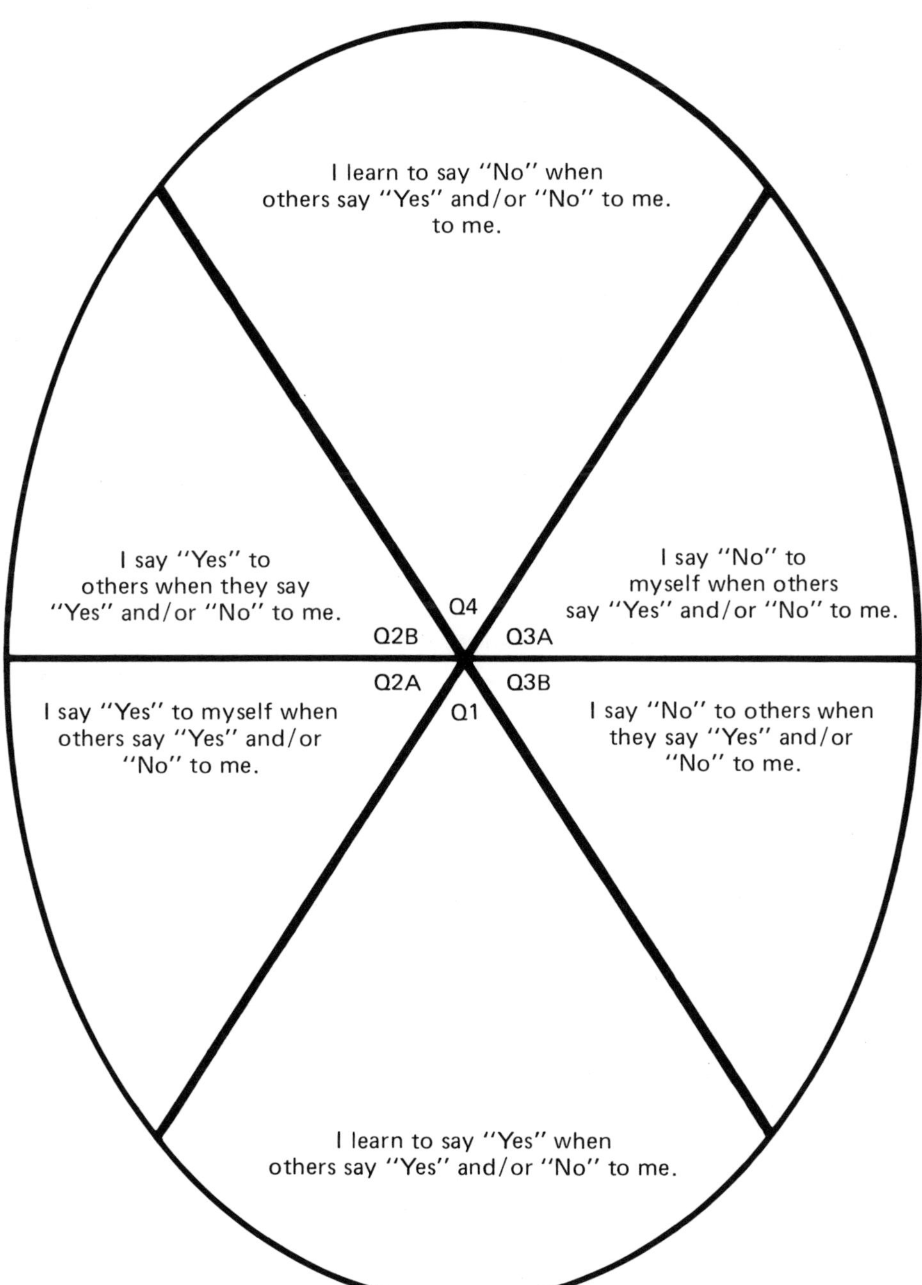

Psychological intimacy deals more with the fulfillment of the Hungers for Affection and Appreciation than it does with physical closeness. You can be physically close to another person, yet removed psychologically. On the other hand, you can be psychologically intimate, yet physically removed.

A case in point is the frequently heard complaint of a wife that her husband does not listen. They see each other every morning and every night before and after he returns from work, and their sex relationships are frequent and satisfying. Yet, she remains unfulfilled. In her opinion, he primarily feeds her Hunger for Appreciation, making ever more demands on her time and praising her only when she has accomplished the tasks he considers important. He leaves her Hunger for Affection unfulfilled, however, because he neither shares his feelings with her nor acknowledges her feelings. Her time with him is Distress Time.

Six Distress Scenarios are incorporated into the Distress Ellipse (see Diagram 8.15). Each is a bid for psychological intimacy; yet when locked-in, each becomes counterproductive and constitutes Distress Time.

Q1. *Withdrawal*: The REJECTED Personality Type withdraws into him/herself and is physically away from the other players. The hideaway may be far away in a distant Shangri-la or as close as a darkened room before a TV screen. REJECTED makes no effort to become aware of his/her life energies, nor is there a bid whatsoever for psychological intimacy with others.

Q2A. *Pastime*: The INADEQUATE Personality Type goes from one player to another, chit-chatting with each along the way. The physical connection is greater than in Withdrawal, but INADEQUATE's intention is to be only passingly sociable and no more. S/he does not seek to spend time exploring values and developing skills.

Q2B. *Activity*: The VENGEFUL Personality Type spends time with the other players only when work or a program arises suddenly, so that the goal of the undertaking and not the relationship governs the management of time. There is no pre-planning, and the action is impulsive.

Q4. *Activity*: The HOSTILE Personality Type also spends time with others in activity; however, HOSTILE's activities are competitive. There generally is considerable physical contact with other people, but HOSTILE's intention is not to be close but to get excitement at the other person's expense. S/he does not spend time planning meaningful activities so that both can get excitement from the activity.

Q3A. *Activity*: The FEARFUL Personality Type spends time with the other players when the work of the program is obligatory. As in the Activity of the Vengeful Personality Type in Q2B, the goal of the Q3A obligation outweighs the relationships involved and governs the management of time. While there is no pre-planning, the action is compulsive.

Q3B. *Ritual*: The INSECURE Personality Type spends time with the other players by participating in ceremonial behavior prescribed by tradition, etiquette or authority. INSECURE may participate side-by-side with the other player, but enters only into a parallel relationship with them.

Diagram 8.15
DISTRESS SCENARIOS

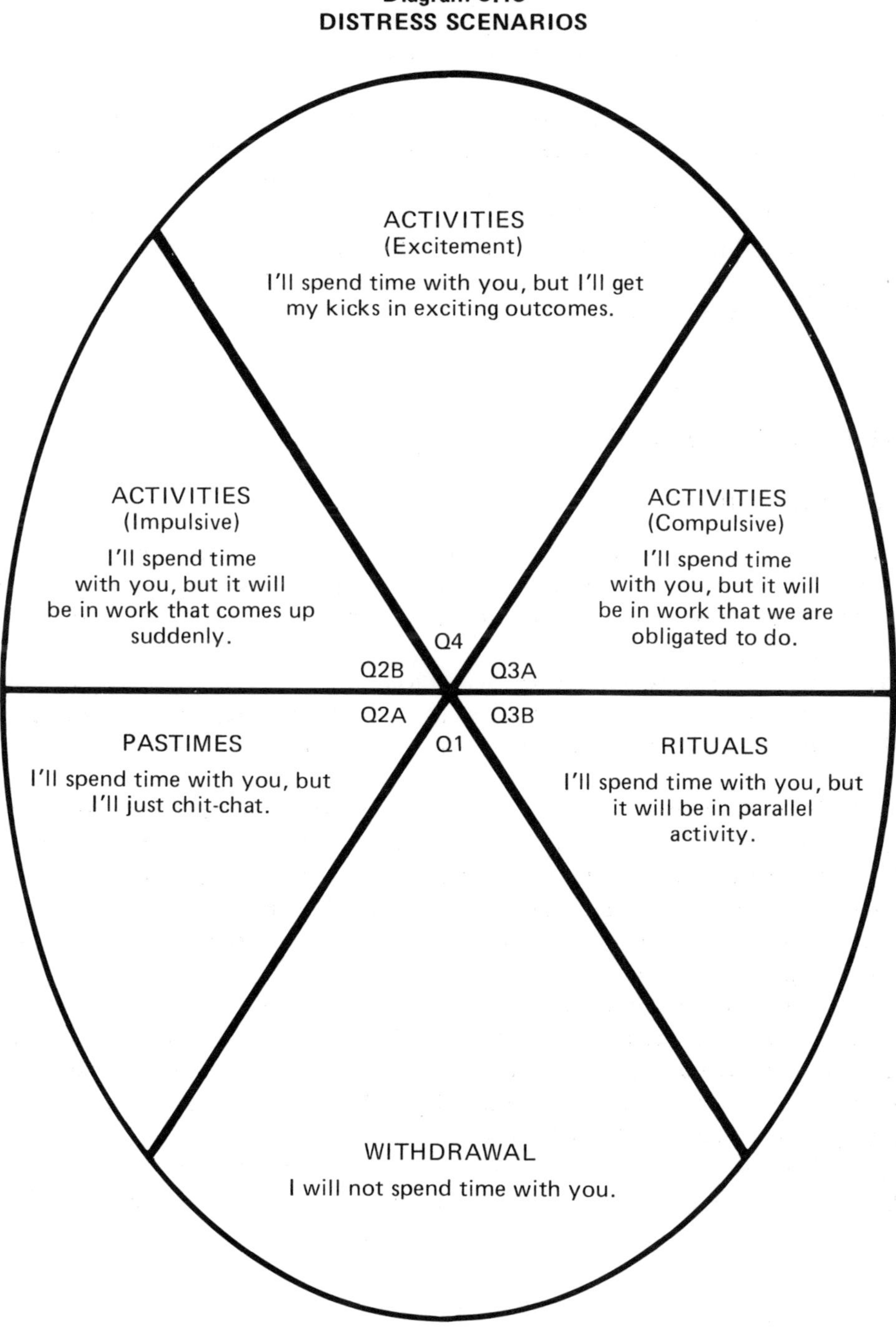

The six Distress misuses of time can be graphed on a continuum (see Table 8.1) from the least intimacy-producing time to the most intimacy-producing time. When you misuse your time, you set the pattern for each scene in your life, and the scene repeats itself in every act. You lock in your time, and you lock in your life energies. You Distress yourself, and your time becomes Distress Time.

These six Distress misuses of time are not to be confused with Game-Playing, about which you will learn in the next part of the book. Game Playing is an even more intense (and fruitless) bid for psychological intimacy and is diagrammed by the switches that you and the players in your life drama make from one locked-in Personality Type to another locked-in Personality Type. The six Distress misuses of time described above do not involve switches. Each Personality Type is locked into his/her Distress scenario.

EUSTRESS SCENARIOS

Eustress Time

The alternative to Distress Time, however, is not the disregard of time. It is Eustress Time, the constructive use of your time that brings a special kind of intimacy born out of the feeding and the nurturing care of the Hungers for Affection and Appreciation.

Six Eustress options for the constructive use of time, in contrast to the Distress scenarios, are available to you and to the players in your life drama (see Diagram 8.16). To be constructive is to be creative.

Q1. The Self-Accepting use of time is the creative use of *Aloneness.* Being alone is not the same as being lonely. Aloneness is the Eustress Time for meditation, for making that inward exploration of the human pulling and tugging between the good and the good, between the bad and the bad and between the good and the bad that goes on in every player. Aloneness is an opportunity for becoming aware of the Self *That You Are.*

Q2A. The Self-Reliant use of time is the creative use of *Informality.* Being informal is not the same as being casual. Informality permits relaxed involvement, allowing you to make an outward exploration and discovery of what you consider to be essential for success. Informality affords the opportunity for exploring and developing *How You Are.*

Q2B. The Self-Competent use of time is the creative use of *Spontaneity.* Being spontaneous is not the same as being impulsive. Spontaneity facilitates

Table 8.1
DISTRESS TIME

Q1	Q3B	Q2A	Q2B	Q3A	Q4
Withdrawal	Ritual	Pastime	Activity (Impulsive)	Activity (Compulsive)	Activity (Excitement)

Diagram 8.16
EUSTRESS SCENARIOS

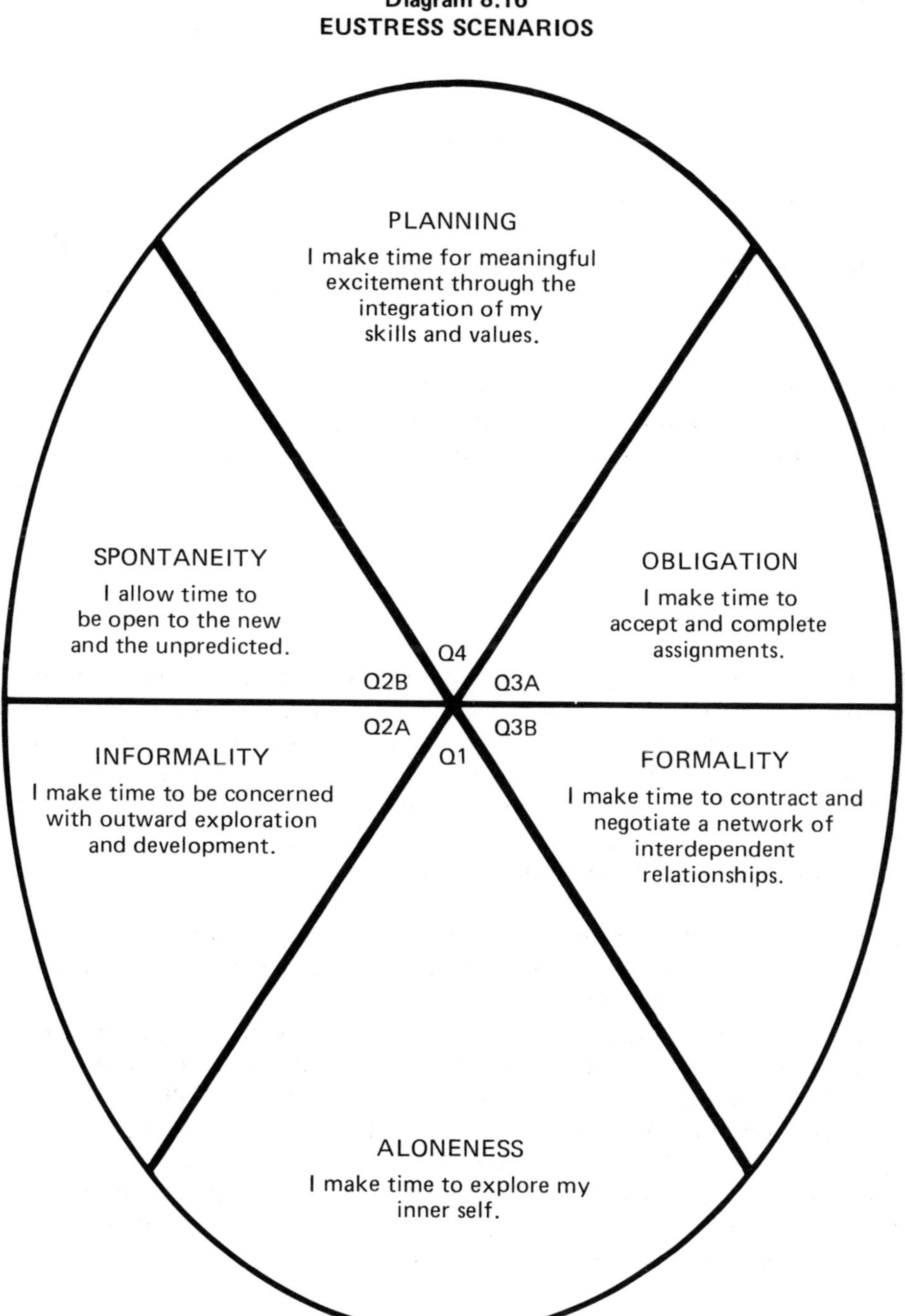

the unpremeditated and the unplanned, allowing the new and the unpredicted to become viable alternatives for your success. Spontaneity affords the opportunity for learning and developing *How You Are.*

Q4. The Self-Approving use of time is the creative use of *Planning.* Planning is not the same as rigidity and authoritarian control. Planning refers to the putting together of viable alternatives into meaningful purposes so that the intimacy that is born out of the experience is exciting for all parties. Planning your time affords the opportunity for expressing *Who You Are.*

Q3A. The Self-Confident use of time is the creative use of *Obligation.* Being obligated is not the same as being compulsive. Obligation allows for the taking on of duties and assignments with the assurance that one has the ability to complete them. Fulfilling your obligations affords the opportunity for expressing *What You Are.*

Q3B. The Self-Responsible use of time is the creative use of *Formality.* Formality is not the same as convention and custom. Formality facilitates the entering into contractual arrangements and negotiating when necessary in order to establish interdependent networks of relationships. Formality affords the opportunity for expressing *What You Are.*

DISTRESS GAMES

Psychologically speaking, there are two kinds of games: Distress Games and the Eustress game. The two are not the same. Distress Games are goal-oriented games that are adversarial in character. They are played, however, without awareness, and they lead to unpleasant pay-offs. The Eustress game, on the other hand, emphasizes goals to be achieved through cooperative human relationships and involves an awareness of psychological insight.

There are three aspects to a Distress Game:

1. You are an *either-or* player. You play for all or nothing. Either you win and the other person loses, or you lose and other person wins. You are not willing to negotiate your differences with others.

2. You use a psychological *con* or come-on (though without awareness) to "psych out" the other person's *gimmick* or weak spot. You look for their Achilles Heel and go for the kill. You are like a horse with blinders, focusing only upon the goal and the anticipated *glee* that it will bring to you.

3. You make a sudden *switch.* You begin with a below-the-center-line "If it weren't for me" Distress Scenario and end up playing an above-the-center-line "If it weren't for you" Distress Scenario. Sometimes, the switch is in reverse. The switch crosses the center line in both scenarios.

Unless there is a *switch* there is no Distress Game, even though your feelings, thoughts and behaviors seem to resemble the opening moves in a Game. An invitation to structure your time through Withdrawal, Pastime, Activity and Ritual is not the same as a "con" to structure your time through a Distress

Game. In the former case, your invitation remains only an invitation, and there is no switch across the center line. Your invitation does not "hook" someone else's "gimmick." In the latter instance, your "con" does hook someone else's "gimmick," and then you switch across the center line.

There are many kinds of "cons" that you can offer to start a Distress Game (see Diagram 8.17):

Q1. There is the *Ain't-it-awful lament*: "I have to do it your way," or "you're doing it for my good."

Q2A. There is the *Wooden Leg excuse*: If it weren't for my wooden leg, I could have . . ."

Q2B. There is the *NIGYSOB gloat*: "Now I've Got You, [You're getting what you deserve, you] Son of a Bitch."

Q4. There is the *See-What-You-Made-Me-Do decree* or *pronouncement*: "You do it my way or else," or "I'm doing it for my good."

Q3A. There is the *Brinkmanship taunt*: "I'll see what I can get away with. I'm only doing it for your good."

Q3B. There is the *Stupid complaint*: "It's just not fair after all I've done for you. What a dummy I am."

Not all Distress Games are of the same severity. Your game may be a mild one, played out in the open. It may be a more secretive one played behind closed doors away from the public view. Or, it may be a "tissue" game, involving life-and-death outcomes. The severity of your Distress Game, however, will depend upon the Distress Decision-responses you made many years ago to the Conditional Positive and Negative Messages that you believe you received from your parents or authority figures at that time.

THE EUSTRESS GAME

When you and the players in your life drama Eustress yourselves, all of you play The Intimacy game. The Eustress game *is* The Intimacy game (see Diagram 8.18). It is a game with a small "g." When you are a Eustress game player, you have no *cons* with which to hook. You look for no *gimmicks* to be hooked into. Instead, you are an involved player. There are no side-line players in the Eustress game. You start the game and do not wait for the others to begin. You make room for the others to join.

You are creative. You adapt the game to your personal needs and tastes, and, at the same time, you provide a safe and supportive environment for the others to do the same. You are competitive, but only to surpass yourself and to match, but not to overwhelm, the other players. You are a team-player. You include everyone, and you change your role as needed. When appropriate, you are the leader and, when appropriate, you are the follower.

The Eustress Intimacy game is a cooperative game. Flexibility is its benchmark; and high spirit, shared experience and joyous exhaustion are its hall-

Diagram 8.17
DISTRESS GAMES

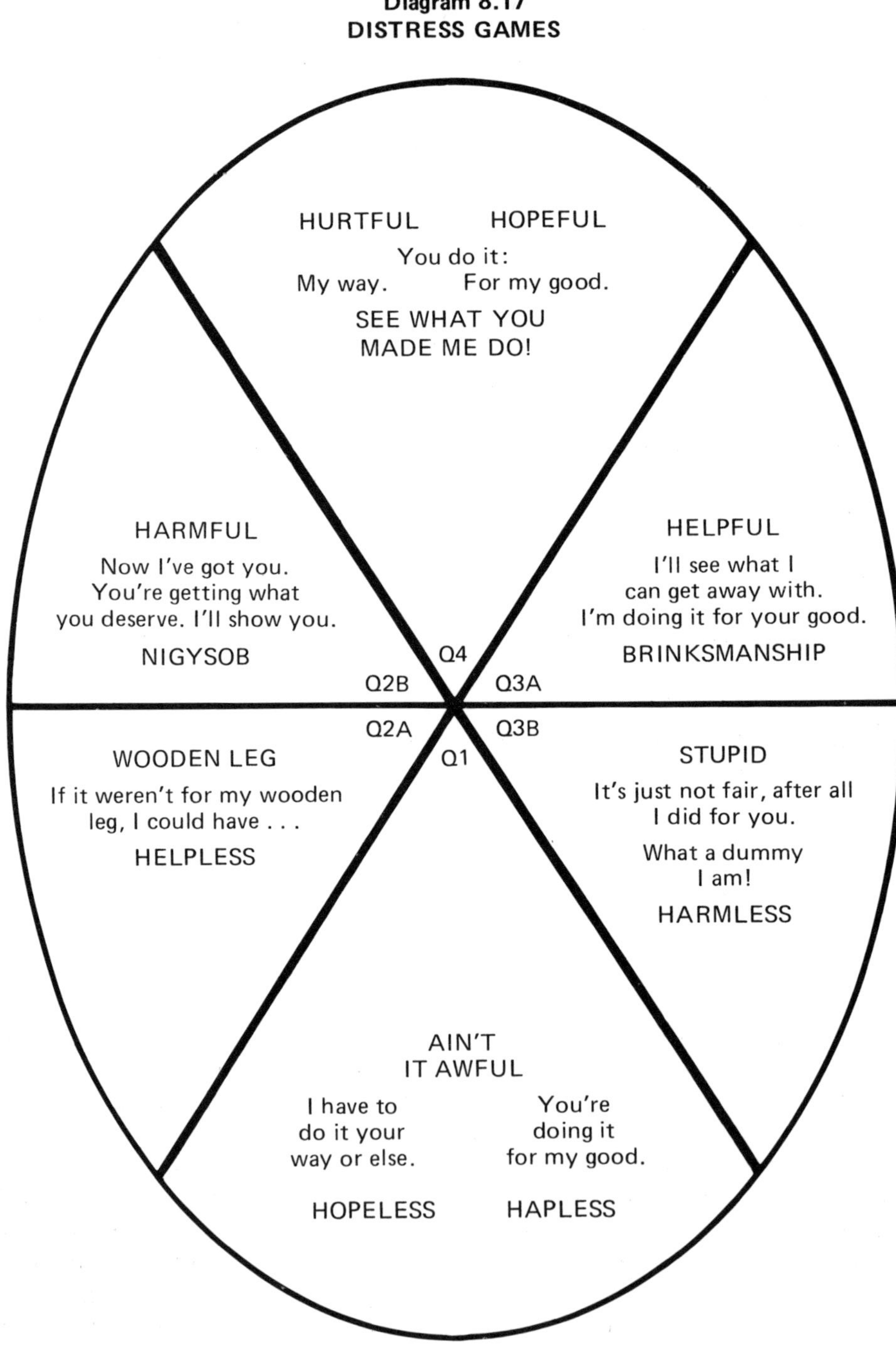

Diagram 8.18
THE EUSTRESS GAME

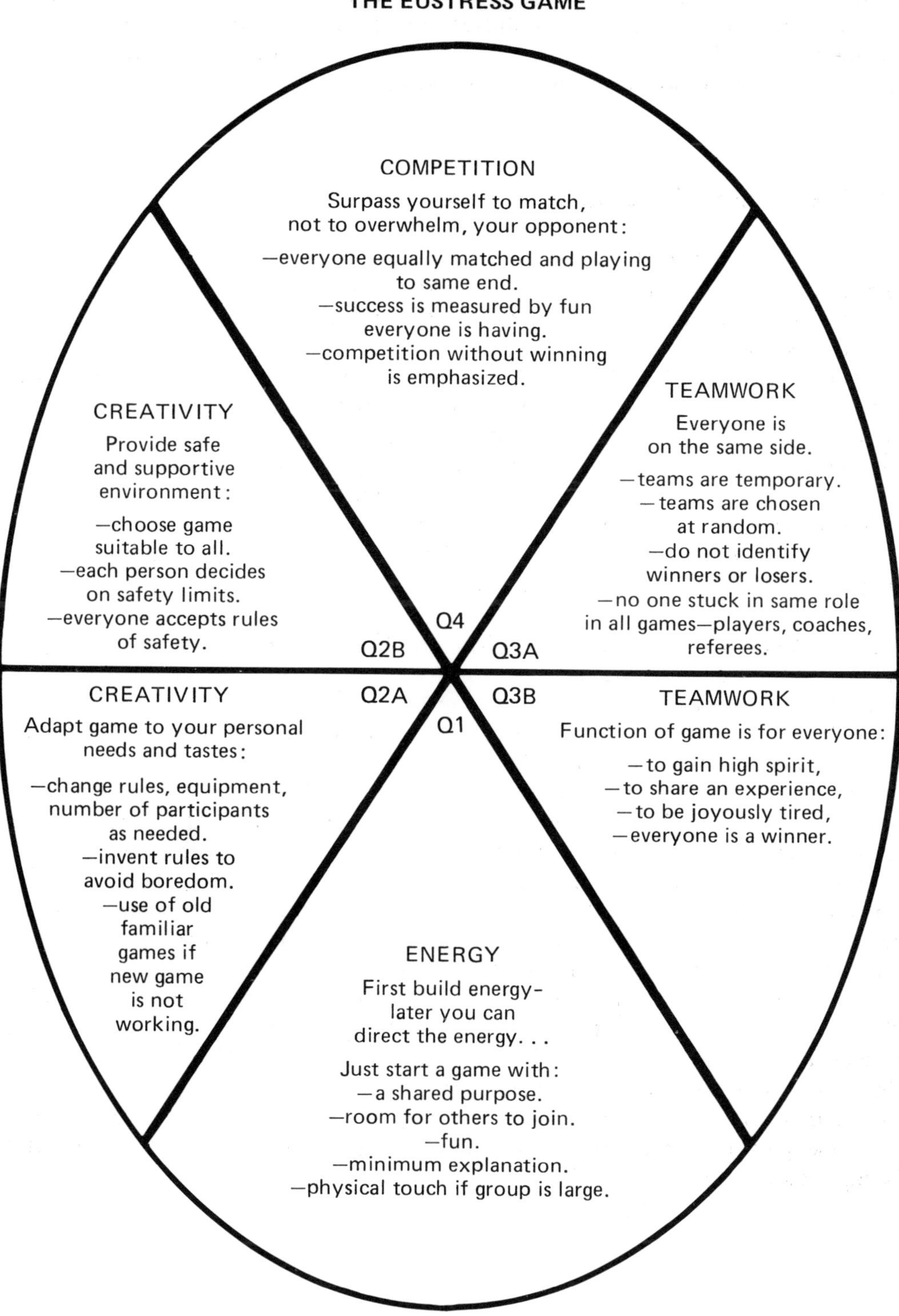

marks. Intimacy is the experience of Affection and Appreciation in an atmosphere of mutual Permission, Protection and Power. Intimacy is living in the here and now with its possibilities and its probabilities. In the Eustress Intimacy game there are no Guarantees. Intimacy is the by-product of what you do with your Opportunities and Limitations.

DISTRESS MAKE-BELIEVE

When you and the players in your life drama distort your internal or external experience, you resort to Make-believe. Make-believe is a powerful tool. It is exciting. It grows stronger and stronger the more that it is used. There is no end to Make-believe.

There are four Make-believe fantasies, however, which are most popular with people who distress themselves: 1) You make believe that what is happening is not happening; 2) If it is happening, you make believe that it is not very important; 3) If it is happening and it is important, you make believe that it is something about which nobody can do anything; and 4) You make believe that it is something about which you, in particular, can do nothing.

To make believe is to lock yourself into one of these four fantasies (see Diagram 8.19) and to live the fantasy as a reality:

Q1. When you lock yourselves into the REJECTED Personality Type, you resort to the first Make-believe. No matter what the issue, it never existed, it doesn't exist now and it never ever will exist.

Q2. When you lock yourself into the INADEQUATE and VENGEFUL Personality Types, you begin your Make-believe by playing down what the other people want. "It is not important," you say to yourself even though it is very important to them. Ignoring what is important to them, you take what you want, because what is of importance is only that which is important to you.

Q4. When you lock yourself into the HOSTILE Personality Type, you are not minded to be mindful. "There is *no* solution," you argue. You abandon all reason and surrender yourself to the only way that you think remains available—force—and you take what is important to you.

Q3. When you lock yourself into the FEARFUL and INSECURE Personality Types, you make believe that you are powerful, but secretly you don't feel powerful at all. Privately, you lack confidence in *your* ability to cope with difficult situations. You play up what supposedly is important to you. When others insist on what is important to them, you surrender yourself to the only way that you think remains open to you—to give in—and you give up what is important to you.

EUSTRESS PROBLEM-SOLVING

Life is full of issues. An issue is something of which you are aware, something which is important to you and something concerning which you make a choice as you relate to the world around you. Stress is the natural expression of your life energies to feel, think and act as you grapple with issues.

Just as Stress can become Distress, so an issue can become a Problem. An issue becomes a problem when you play Make-believe: 1) The issue doesn't exist. 2) The issue exists, but it isn't important. 3) The issue exists and is important, but nobody can do anything about it. And 4) You yourself can't do anything about it.

Just as Stress can become Eustress, so an issue can become a challenge instead of a problem. To avoid turning an issue into a problem, we have found that the words one of us wrote a number of years ago continue to be appropriately useful:

Diagram 8.19
DISTRESS MAKE-BELIEVE

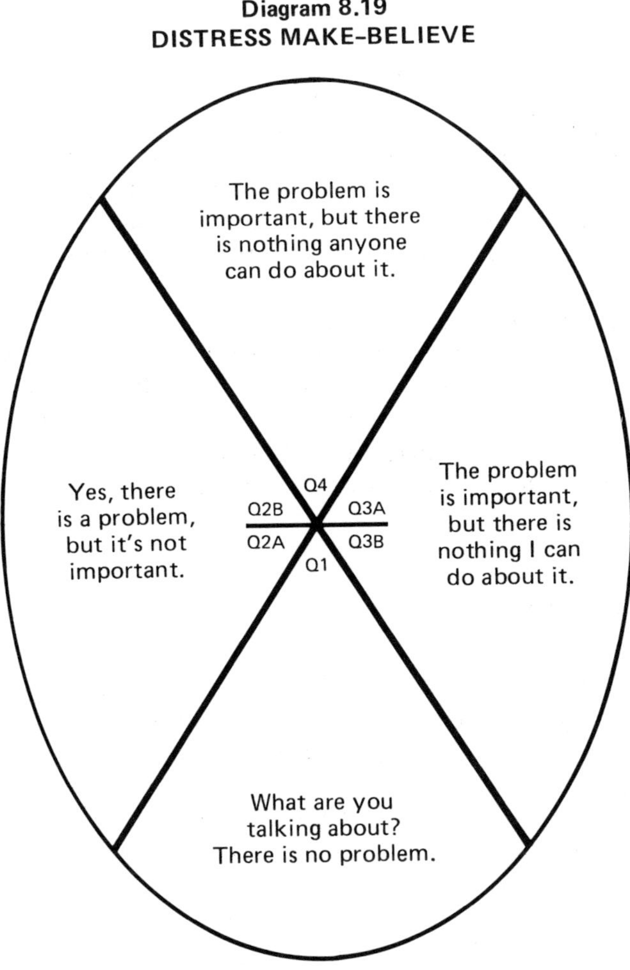

REALITY

Reality
To face—
Not to confront
In anger and arrogance,
Nor to play the meaningless farce
Of distraction and self-deception—

But to face as adventure
The ultimacy of our conscious being.
To transcend
To stand outside ourselves
And consider what we want to be.
And in a world of interdependent beings
Commit what we want to be into being.

Edward Zerin

The attitude expressed in the poem is also expressed in the alternatives illustrated in Diagram 8.20.

In Q1 you face reality and distinguish between problems that exist and those that do not. You acknowledge each of these realities appropriately.

In Q2 you face each reality as an adventure. You develop your skills and explore your values as you differentiate between realities that are important and those that are unimportant.

In Q4 you transcend and you stand outside yourself and consider what meaning there may be to life. As you choose what you want your life to be, you establish your identity and refuse to play your life as a meaningless farce of distraction and self-deception fraught with anger and arrogance.

In Q3 you enter into a world of interdependent beings, committing into being what you have chosen to do about your problems.

DISTRESS ESCAPES

How is your life drama going to end?

When you distress yourself, you guarantee your fate. You lock yourself into your life drama Quadrant (see Diagram 8.21). You must carry out your Theme. You must interact with players who endlessly switch their Roles to complement your own switches from Victim to Persecutor to Rescuer. You must repeat the same Scenarios. You must play the same Games. You must engage in the same Make-believe. Destiny takes over, and you make it happen.

When you distress yourself, few surprises are permitted. Your life is either a Monologue or a Fairy Tale without a happy ending, An Adventure Story

Diagram 8.20
EUSTRESS PROBLEM–SOLVING

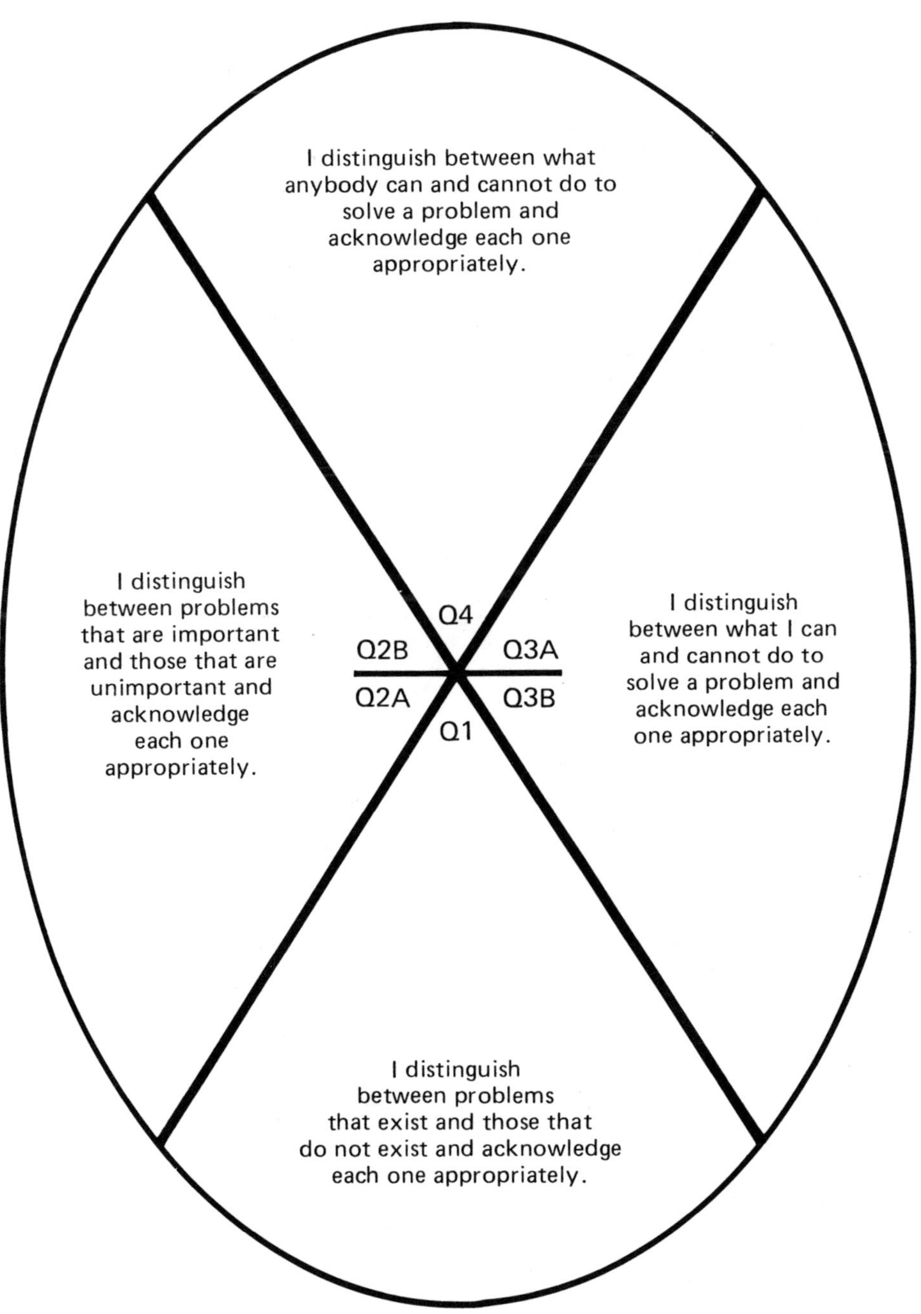

Diagram 8.21
DISTRESS ESCAPES

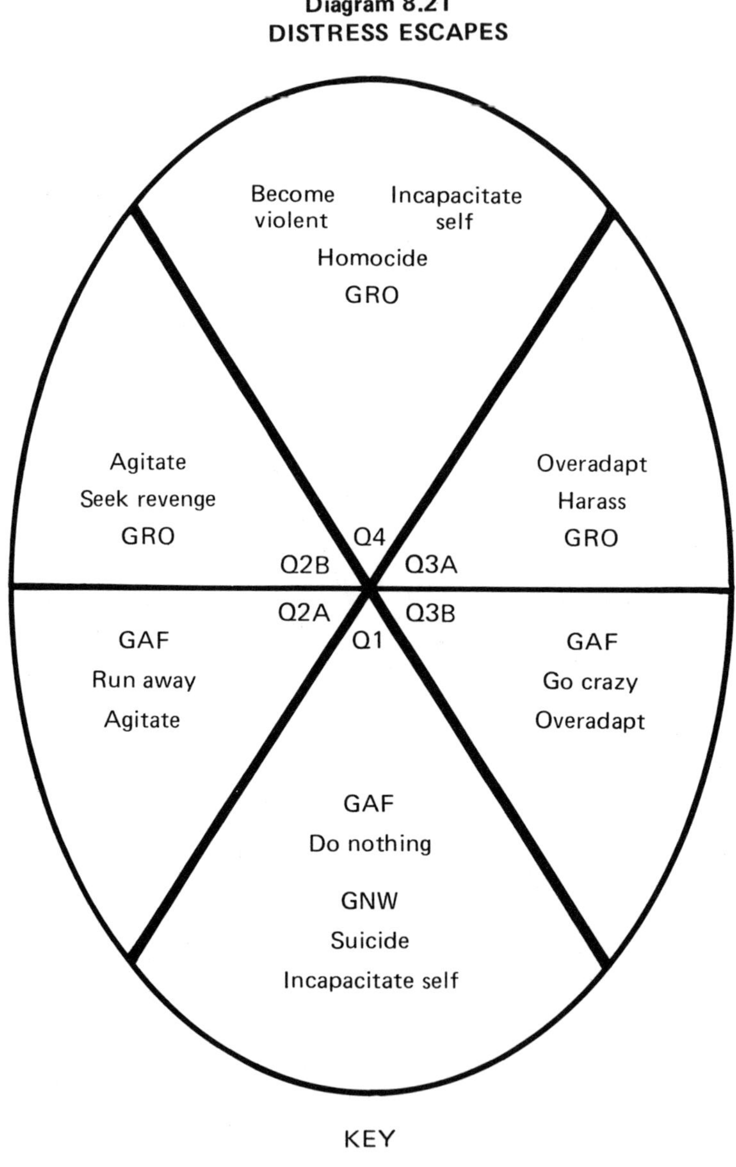

KEY
GAF = Get Away From
GRO = Get Rid Of
GNW = Get Nowhere With

without success, a Melodrama without laughter or a Psychological Case Study without resolution. You enact all the locked-in feeling, thought and behavior patterns of the REJECTED, INADEQUATE, VENGEFUL, HOSTILE, FEARFUL and INSECURE Personality Types.

When destiny takes over, your life will have one of three endings: 1) Your life will be *banal* and just run out with no definable outcome. 2) You will end up as a *non-winner* or 3) You will die a *loser*. A *banal* life is one in which you live without a purpose—your life has no beginning and no end. A *non-winner* life is one in which you have a purpose, but you work hard just to break even. A *loser* life is one in which you do not accomplish your declared purpose. In all three, however, the endings are unrewarding.

A *banal* life is merely dull. A *non-winner* life also is banal, but it has a slight advantage. You can say, "At least I tried." A *loser* life is a tragedy, frequently involving self-destruction or the destruction of another person and calling ultimately for the attention of lawyers, police, health-care personnel and morticians.

When you distress yourself, you convert your life energies into a series of *escape mechanisms* that neither solve your problems nor bring you the joy you desire. Escape mechanisms are techniques you devise in order to avoid dealing with the realities of your situation in the here and now. Escape mechanisms are designed to keep distance between you and the other people in your life.

You distance yourself by "getting away from" (GAF) them or by "getting rid of" (GRO) them so that they "get away from you." When you lock yourself into the REJECTED, INADEQUATE or INSECURE Distress Personality Types you tend to "get away from" others. When you lock yourself into the VENGEFUL, HOSTILE or WORRIED Distress Personality Types, you "get rid of" others. When you are Compliant, you remove yourself. When you are Defiant, you remove others. Sometimes you are able neither to "get away from" nor to "get rid of" the others. You seem to "get nowhere with" (GNW) them. You are stuck. There is no way out. There are no more ways to escape. Whether you "get away from," "get rid of" or "get nowhere with" the others, however, the outcome of your relationship is unpleasant and the payoff for your life drama is unrewarding. The Distress Escapes are illustrated in Diagram 8.21.

If you are a loser, and not just living out a *non-winner* or *banal* life, your outcome is more tragic and your payoff more catastrophic. When you "get away from," either you disappear from the scene (flip out) or you go crazy so that you have to be removed from the scene (hospitalized). When you "get rid of" others, you are capable of the ultimate tragic act of homicide; and when you "get away from" others, you are capable of the equally tragic act of suicide. When you "get nowhere with" others, you immobilize yourself so that you are among the "living dead."

At the same time, escape mechanisms allow you to pretend that you are solving your problems. For example, in Q1 you *do nothing*; however, you cannot do nothing. Paradoxically, to *do nothing* is to "do something," only the something that you do is nothing to solve your problem.

Or, in Q2 you begin to *agitate* and keep your motor running. Your foot begins to move back and forth. You can't seem to sit still, as though you are sitting on pins and needles. You are very active, to say the least, but your activity is repetitious and fruitless. It does have a purpose—to show that you are busy—but not a problem-solving purpose.

Or, you become *violent*. You put your thinking process into deep-freeze. Instead of thinking, you throw a temper tantrum. You hit and hurt people. You break things.

Or, you *overadapt*. While you are in the Defiant stance, you invoke all kinds of subtle maneuvers, including harassing others. When you are in a Compliant stance, you cease and desist, and your defiance dissipates into compliance. You give up your own desires and wants, and you give in to the expectations and demands of others.

Or, you *incapacitate* yourself by turning the anger intended for others against yourself. There are two ways in which you do this. The first way is to make yourself a Victim in Q1 so that you do not have to recall that you are an angry Persecutor or an angry Rescuer. You smoke. You overeat. You undereat. You avoid physical exercise. You abuse alcohol and drugs. The ultimate incapacitation as a Victim, of course, is suicide. The second way is to become a Rescuer in Q4 and sublimate your anger into seemingly socially acceptable endeavors. For example, you become a utopian. You take on an idealized vision of the world, and your vision serves to save the person with whom you are angry. To achieve this utopia, however, you sacrifice and give up much of what you treasure, but you tell yourself that you are happy to do so.

EUSTRESS INVOLVEMENTS

When you Eustress yourself, you are aware that you cannot guarantee your destiny. There is a bit of mystery that veils your life, and each day contains its own wonderment. At the same time, you believe that you are responsible for the outcome of your life. While you do not solicit serendipity and happenstance, when they occur you welcome and make them part of your new awareness as you unravel with each fleeting moment the mystery That You Are, How You Are, Who You Are and What You Are.

By being involved in the fashioning of your destiny, you become a *winner*. A *winner* life has a declared purpose, and when you are a winner you accomplish your purpose. When you miss your mark, you acknowledge your mistakes, and you explore and integrate new strategies. Like the proverbial cat, you land on all fours. The other people with whom you are interacting also land on all fours. All of you are winners.

A *winner* is not an aggressor. An aggressor takes what s/he wants. A *winner* is assertive and recognizes that all participants have their individualized wants. A *winner* negotiates and asks that each party to a contract be responsible for his/her share and be a winner, too. A *winner* exercises the Eustress options of being Self-Accepting, Self-Reliant, Self-Competent, Self-Approving, Self-Confident and Self-Responsible. Eustress Involvements are illustrated in Diagram 8.22.

Diagram 8.22
EUSTRESS INVOLVEMENTS

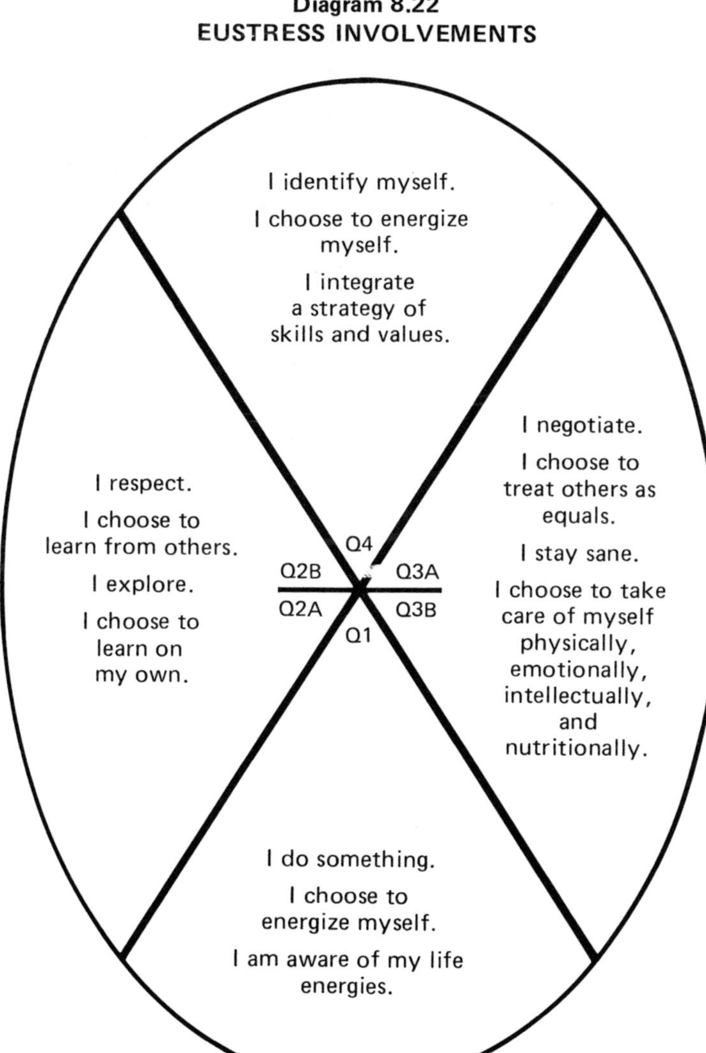

Q1. When you are a *winner*, instead of doing nothing, you do something. You are Self-Accepting and become aware of your life energies.

Q2. When you are a *winner*, instead of agitating, you explore. You are Self-Reliant and develop skills and values on your own. You are Self-Competent and respect others, learning from them as well.

Q4. When you are a *winner*, instead of being violent, you think through your opportunities. You are Self-Approving and choose your identity by integrating your skills and values into meaningful strategies.

Q3. When you are a *winner*, instead of overadapting, you make commitments and, where necessary, negotiate your situations. You are Self-Confident and treat others as equals. You also enjoy your well-being. You are Self-Responsible and take care of yourself physically, emotionally, intellectually and nutritionally even as you become a part of an interdependent network of human relationships.

When you are a *winner*, instead of incapacitating yourself, you energize yourself. You "get on with" (GOW) life and are free to incorporate into your life many dramatic elements. You make it a personal story and an identity story, filled with adventures that satisfy, and highlighted by a history and an outcome of which you are proud.

When you are a *winner*, your life energies are used constructively and appropriately. You manage them effectively. You minimize your Distress. You maximize your Eustress.

CHAPTER 9 PUTTING IT ALL TOGETHER

ONE MORE TIME

This book was not intended to be a big book. However, its contents are big and involve many different ways to enrich yourself personally and to help you grow with others. Once again, it is appropriate to put the two ellipses together so that when you Distress yourself you can look inward toward the source of your life energies and learn how to Eustress yourself and manage your Stress more constructively.

In diagrams 9.1–9.4 are listed the characteristics of each of the four Distress Life-Dramas.

DISTRESS LIFE DRAMAS

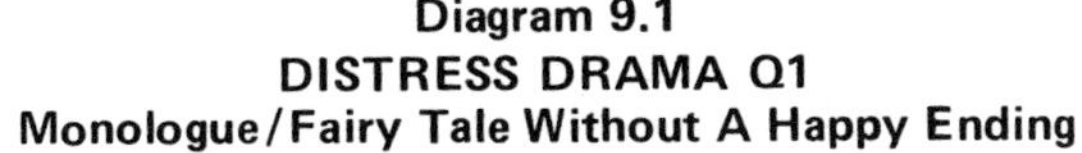

Diagram 9.1
DISTRESS DRAMA Q1
Monologue/Fairy Tale Without A Happy Ending

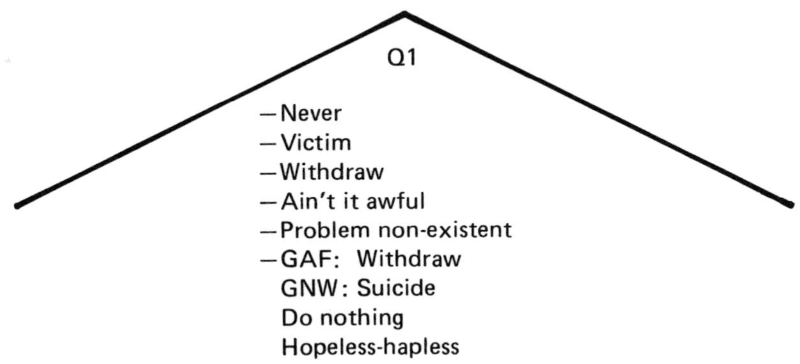

KEY

GAF = Get Away From
GNW = Get Nowhere With

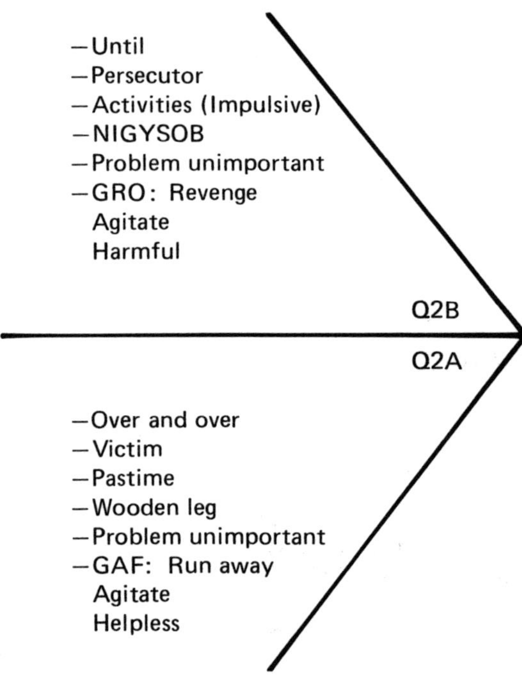

Diagram 9.2
DISTRESS DRAMA Q2
Adventure Story Without Success

KEY

NIGYSOB = Now I've Got You, SOB
GRO = Get Rid Of
GAF = Get Away From

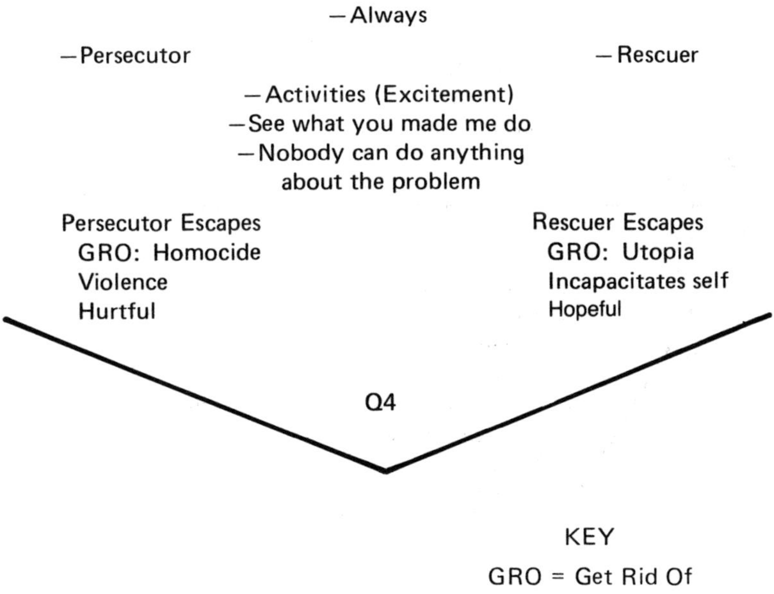
Diagram 9.3
DISTRESS DRAMA Q4
Melodrama Without Laughter

—Always

—Persecutor
—Rescuer

—Activities (Excitement)
—See what you made me do
—Nobody can do anything
about the problem

Persecutor Escapes
GRO: Homocide
Violence
Hurtful

Rescuer Escapes
GRO: Utopia
Incapacitates self
Hopeful

Q4

KEY
GRO = Get Rid Of

Diagram 9.4
DISTRESS DRAMA Q3
Psychological Case-Study Without Resolution

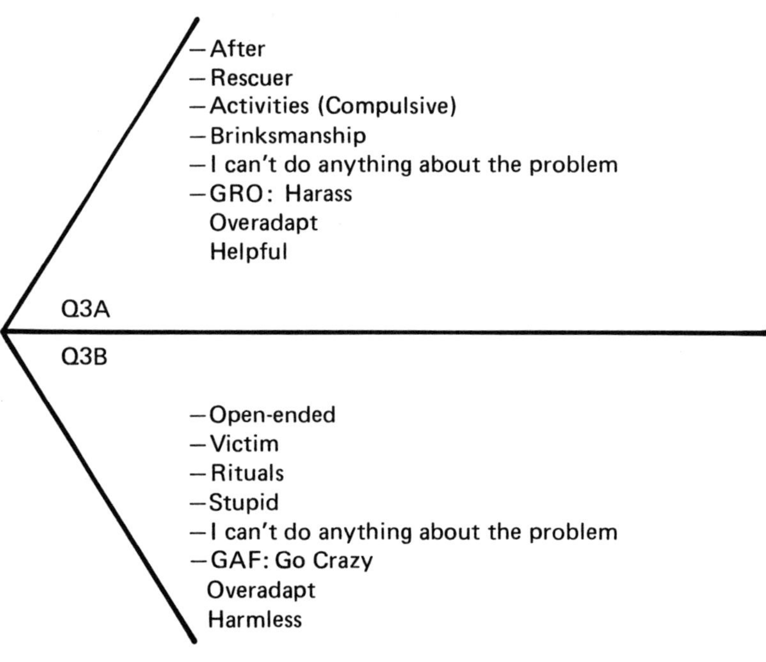

KEY

GRO = Get Rid Of
GAF = Get Away From

In diagrams 9.5–9.8 are listed the options in the Eustress Life-Drama.

Note your favorite Distress Quadrant when you are under pressure. Note the locked-in characteristics which trouble you most. Then go to the center toward the source of your life energies and note the corresponding well-being option in the Eustress Ellipse.

You can follow this same procedure for as many of the locked-in characteristics as you want. In addition, you may follow this same procedure to review all the other locked-in characteristics discussed in earlier parts of the book.

EUSTRESS LIFE DRAMA OPTIONS

Diagram 9.5
Q1 EUSTRESS LIFE DRAMA OPTIONS
A Personal Story

—I acknowledge "That I Am"
—I become aware of the possible
—I maintain my self-esteem when I exercise a small "v" contract
—I learn to say "yes"
—I decide when to be alone
—I build my energy
—I acknowledge problems that exist
—I accept my genetic limitations and my life-energy opportunities

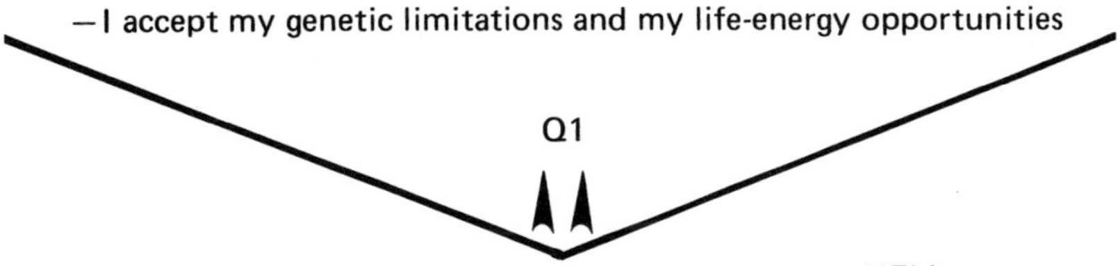

Q1

KEY

v = victim

Diagram 9.6
Q2 EUSTRESS LIFE DRAMA OPTIONS
An Adventure Story

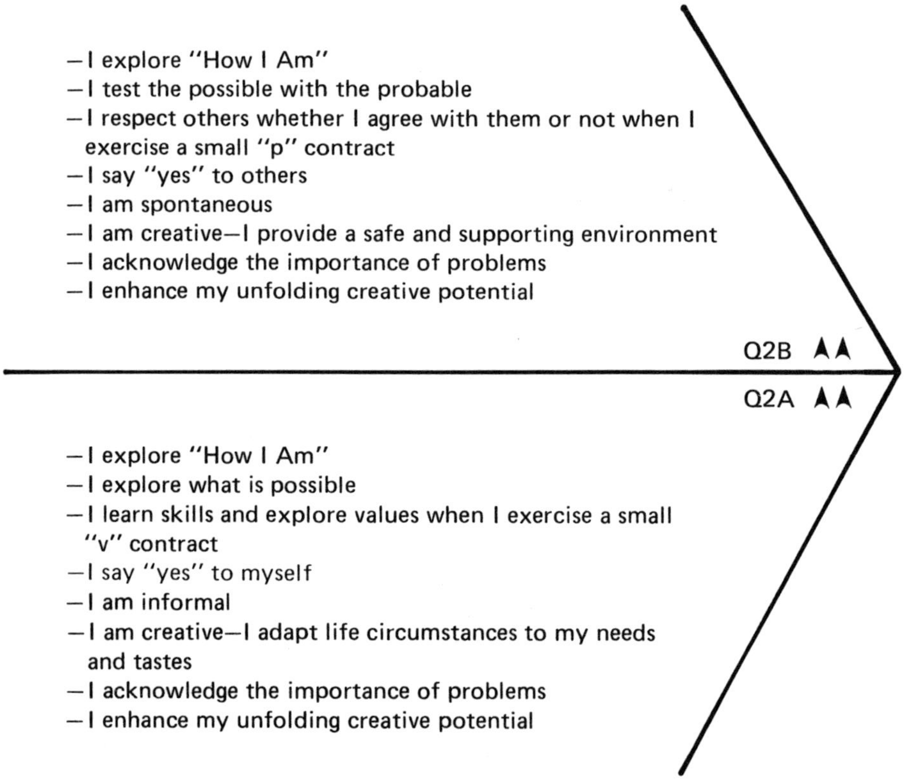

—I explore "How I Am"
—I test the possible with the probable
—I respect others whether I agree with them or not when I
  exercise a small "p" contract
—I say "yes" to others
—I am spontaneous
—I am creative—I provide a safe and supporting environment
—I acknowledge the importance of problems
—I enhance my unfolding creative potential

Q2B ▲▲

Q2A ▲▲

—I explore "How I Am"
—I explore what is possible
—I learn skills and explore values when I exercise a small
  "v" contract
—I say "yes" to myself
—I am informal
—I am creative—I adapt life circumstances to my needs
  and tastes
—I acknowledge the importance of problems
—I enhance my unfolding creative potential

KEY

p = persecutor
v = victim

Diagram 9.7
Q4 EUSTRESS LIFE DRAMA OPTIONS
An Identity Story

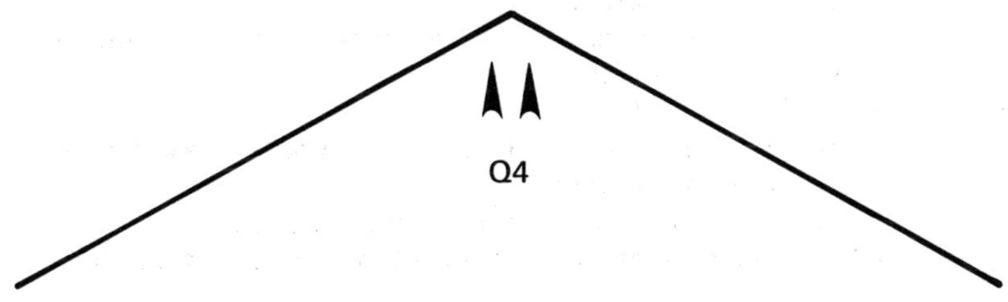

—I establish "Who I Am"
—I choose the probable
—I offer enlightened friendship when I exercise
  a small "p" and a small "r" contract
—I learn to say "no"
—I plan
—I am competitive—I match—not overwhelm
  my opponent
—I believe something can be done about a problem
—I integrate meaningful skills and values—I choose
  my identity

KEY

p = persecutor
r = rescuer

Diagram 9.8
Q3 EUSTRESS LIFE DRAMA OPTIONS
A History Story

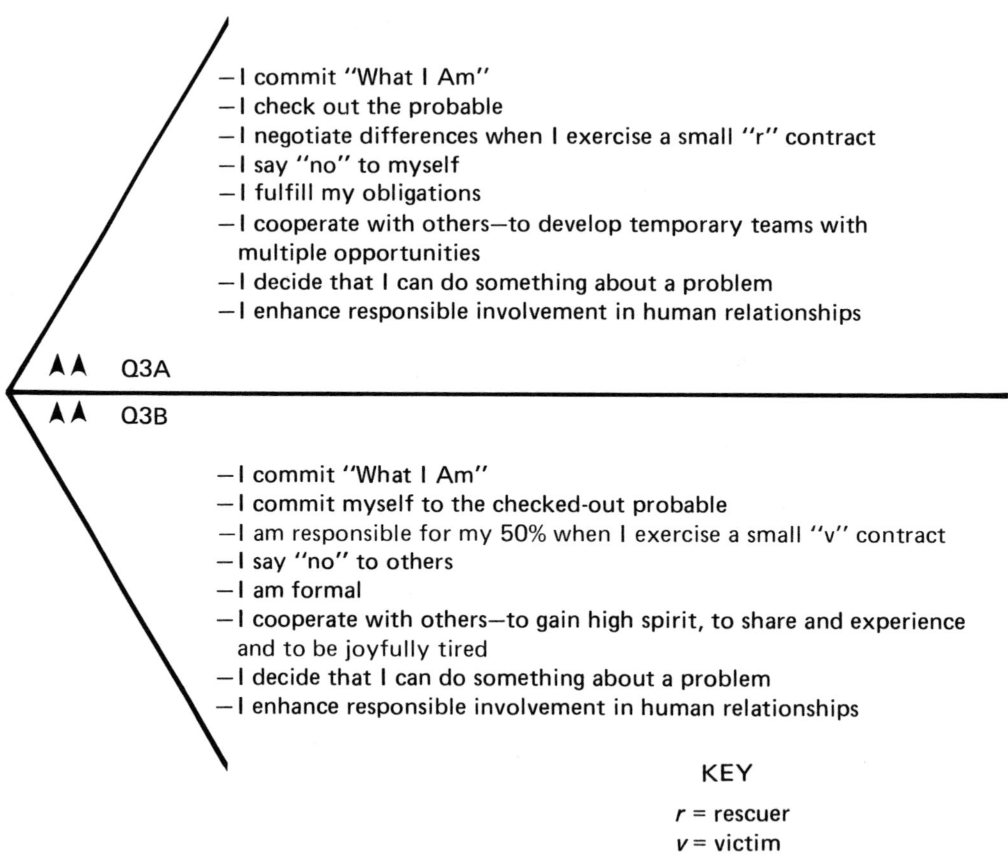

SUMMARY

"Q" is an integrative model. We have brought together in non-technical language information from four intellectual disciplines to aid us in our endeavor—THE EFFECTIVE MANAGEMENT OF PERSONAL STRESS. We have utilized information from three of them—Sociology, Psychology and the branch of Philosophy called Epistemology (the study of how we know we know). We have concentrated, for example, on the Button Pushers who structured our social environment when we were little and on those Button Pushers who continue to dominate our adult lives. We have been concerned equally with the psychological impact on those of us whose buttons were pushed when we were little and continue to be pushed now that we are chronologically grown. We also have brought information about how we think and how we solve everyday problems.

We have touched on a fourth discipline and essential source of information, namely, physiology. There is a growing abundance of information that a direct link exists between sociological, psychological and epistemological Distress and physical disease—and between sociological, psychological and epistemological Eustress and physical health.

It is not our intention at this point to do more than to mention this correlation, because to do so would be to write a second book. We would be remiss, however, if we were not to bring to the attention of the reader three aspects of physical well-being that deserve attention: relaxation, exercise and nutrition. These, too, are pathways in the never-ending quest for a comprehensive description of the "Proverbial Elephant."

EPILOGUE

We conclude this book with an epilogue, relating 18 ways to Eustress yourself. You may want to copy the "18 Wasy to Eustress Yourself" and carry the list with you so that from time to time you can refresh your memory. You may decide, for example, to set aside a few moments each day—perhaps each morning before you lock yourself into your favorite Distress pattern for the entire day—to review each of the 18 Eustress ways. You may emphasize one way one day and another way the next day, or you may rightly pride yourself by emphasizing two or three or even more of the 18 Eustress ways all in the same day.

Soon you will discover that your repertoire of Eustress options has multiplied a hundred fold. You will be more aware, tuned into the wonders of your very being. Each day will be an adventure in the here and now, discovering opportunities, developing skills and exploring values. Equally important, you will discover yourself, and undaunted by obstacles fraught with frustration and disappointments and undaunted even by occasional failures, you will plan anew, because your identity will be secure and you will know who you are. And more. You will reach out meaningfully to others and bring alive a world of committed relationships.

18 WAYS TO EUSTRESS YOURSELF

1. You are a *both/and* Personality.
2. You are aware of, you explore, you integrate and you commit your life energies.
3. You choose your Decision-responses appropriately.
4. You are *up* with yourself, and others are *up* with you, too.
5. You make feelings, both pleasurable and painful, important in your life and in the lives of others.
6. You distinguish between Usefulness and Truthfulness in your thoughts and in the thoughts of others.
7. You are Assertive in your behavior, and you invite others to be Assertive with you, too.
8. You recognize both the Opportunities and the Limitations in a situation.
9. You are Self-Accepting, Self-Reliant, Self-Competent, Self-Approving, Self-Confident and Self-Responsible.
10. You give yourself Affection and Appreciation, and you give others Affection and Appreciation, too.
11. You cope by providing yourself with Permission and Protection and by using your Power in the here and now.
12. You include in your life drama a Personal Story (That You Are), an

Adventure Story (How You Are), an Identity Story (Who You Are) and a History Story (What You Are).

13. You make Contracts with others when you give and when you receive.

14. You finish your Unfinished Business with the appropriate people in your life.

15. You are congruent, sending the same messages both verbally and non-verbally.

16. You make your *yes* a *yes* and your *no* a *no*, and you negotiate your differences with others.

17. You are a Winner, participating in the shaping of your destiny: you use your time creatively, you involve yourself intimately and you resolve your problems realistically.

18. You care for yourself physically, nutritionally, intellectually and emotionally.

REFERENCES

The following is a list, by subject, of resources that have stimulated our imagination and from which we have drawn information for integration into the "Q" Model. (In order not to encumber the text we have not included footnotes.) Many of the resources provided us with what we consider to be Distress Information; others supplied Eustress Information. In some instances we have followed the materials provided by our resources. In other instances we have modified them, because we believe that the "Q" Model enlarges our understanding of the information.

To the authors of each reference we are indebted, and we acknowledge their respective contributions to the "Q" Model. We encourage our readers to examine these references and explore the resources in their original form. Full bibliographic details for each are given in the bibliography.

About the "Q" Model: Ferguson (1979); Saxe (1943); Seeman (1959); Selye (1974, 1975).

"Q"—The Potential for Living: Bohm, D. (1980); Ferguson (1979; 1982); Houston (1982); Satir (1970); Zerin (1980; 1984).

A Bit of Distress Theory: Berne (1972).

Distress Messages from Your Parents: Edwards (1968); Erskine & Zalcman (1979); Kahler (1978); Goulding & Goulding (1978; 1979).

Distress Life Attitudes: Berne (1962a).

Eustress Autonomy: Freud, A. (1966); James, M. (1974); Popper (1963); Zerin (1982).

Eustress Life Attitude: Berne (1962a); Crossman (1966).

Behaviors: Phelps & Austin (1975); Steiner (1971; 1974; 1977).

Six Distress Personality Types That Push Your Stress Buttons: Satir (1978).

Distress Limitations and Eustress Opportunities: Berne (1972); Cousins (1983).

Affection and Appreciation: Berne (1972); Cooper & Kahler (1974); McKenna (1974; 1978); Samuels (1971); Steiner (1971; 1974; 1977).

Permissions and Protections: Clark (1978); Crossman (1966); Erikson (1963); Levin (1982).

Power: Goulding & Goulding (1978).

Distress Dramas: Berne (1972); Karpman (1968); Satir (1978); Steiner (1974).

Distress Themes: Berne (1972).

Distress Players: Karpman (1968); Schiff (1975).

Switching Distress Roles: English (1976).

Finishing Unfinished Business: Zerin (1983).

Eustress Contracts: Berne (1972); Steiner (1974).

Distress Signals: Kahler (1978); Steere (1982).

A Word About the Nervous System: Hassett (1978); Phillips (1975).

A Word About Human Development: Freud, A. (1966); Erikson (1963).

Distress Scenarios: Berne (1972).

Distress Games: Berne (1972); English (1976).

The Eustress Game: Berne (1962a); Fluegelman (1976).

Distress Make-Believe: Schiff (1975).

Eustress Problem-Solving: Miller, et al. (1981); Gilbert (1971); Holton (1967); Popper (1963); Zerin (1982).

Distress Escapes: Ernst (1971); Holloway (1972); Schiff, et al. (1975); Steiner (1974).

Summary: Brown (1984); Cousins (1983).

BIBLIOGRAPHY AND SUGGESTED READINGS

Berne, E., "Classification of Positions," *Transactional Analysis Bulletin*, 1962a, *1* (3), 23. (Courtesy, International Transactional Analysis Association).

————, "Constructive Games," *Transactional Analysis Bulletin*, 1962b, *1* (1), 3.

————, *Sex in Human Loving*, New York: Simon & Shuster, 1970.

————, *What Do You Say After You Say Hello?* New York: Grove Press, 1973.

Bohm, D., "Quantum Theory as an Indication of a New Order in Physics, Part B." Implicate and Explicate Order in Physical Law, Foundations of Physics 3:139, 1973.

————, *Wholeness and the Implicate Order*. Boston: Routledge & Kegan, 1980.

Brown, B., *Between Health and Illness*, Boston: Houghton Mifflin, 1984.

Clark, J. I., *Self-Esteem: A Family Affair*, Minneapolis: Winston Press, 1978.

Cooper, T., & Kahler, T., "An Eightfold Classification System for Strokes and Discounts," *Transactional Analysis Journal*, 1974, *4* (3), 30–31.

Cousins, N., *The Anatomy of an Illness*. Boston: G. K. Hall, 1979.

————, *The Healing Heart*, New York: Norton, 1983.

Crossman, P., "Permissions and Protections," *Transactional Analysis Bulletin*, 1966, *5* (19), 52.

Dusay, J., *Egograms*. New York: Harper, 1977.

Edwards, M., "The Two Parents," *Transactional Analysis Bulletin*, 1968, *7* (28), 37–38.

English, F., "Rackets and Real Feelings," Part II, *Transactional Analysis Journal*, 1972, *2* (1), 23–25.

————, "The Substitution Factor: Rackets and Real Feelings," Part I, *Transactional Analysis Journal*, 1971, *1* (4), 27.

————, "Rackets as the Basis of Games," pp. 186–188, and "The Fifth Position: I'm OK—You're Not OK for Real," pp. 162–175, in *Selected Articles*. Philadelphia: Philadelphia Institute for Transactional Analysis and Gestalt, 1976.

Erikson, E. H., *Childhood and Society*, New York: Norton, 1963.

Ernst, F. H., Jr., "Psychological Rackets in the OK Corral," *Transactional Analysis Journal*, 1983, *3* (2), 96–97.

————, "The OK Corral: The Grid for Get-On-With," *Transactional Analysis Journal*, 1971, *1* (4), 235–236.

Erskine, R. G., & Zalcman, J. J., "The Racket System: A Model for Racket Analysis," *Transactional Analysis Journal*, 1979, *9* (1), 51–59.

Ferguson, M., "Bohm Sees Hologram as Model for New Description of Reality," *Brain/Mind Bulletin*, 1977, *2* (16), p. 1.

————, "Q-Model Ties Psychological Theories Together," *Brain/Mind Bulletin*, 1982, *7* (17), 3.

————, The Aquarian Conspiracy. Los Angeles: J. P. Tarcher, 1979.

Fluegelman, A., ed., *The New Game Book: Play Hard, Play Fair, Nobody Hurts*. Garden City, N. Y.: Doubleday (Dolphin), 1976.

Freud, A., *Normality and Pathology in Childhood*. New York: IU Press, 1966.

Gilbert, F., "Intellectual History: Its Aims and Methods," *Daedulus*, Winter 1971, p. 91.

Goulding, R. L., & Goulding, M. M., *Changing Lives Through Redecision Therapy*. New York: Brunner/Mazel, 1979, 35–37.

———, *Power Is in the Patient*. San Francisco: TA Press, 1978.

Hassett, J., *A Primer of Psychophysiology*. San Francisco: Freeman, 1978.

Holloway, W. R., "Shut the Escape Hatch," Midwest Institute for Human Understanding: The Series of Monographs IV, 1972, pp. 15–18.

———, "The Intrapsychic and Interpersonal in Personality Development and Script Formation," Midwest Institite for Human Understanding: The Series of Monographs X, 1972, pp. 50–57.

———, "Beyond Permission," *Transactional Analysis Journal*, 1974, *4* (2), 15–17.

Holton, G., *Science and Culture*. Boston: Beacon Press, 1967.

Houston, J., *The Possible Human*. Los Angeles: Tarcher, 1982.

James, M., "Self-Reparenting: Theory and Process," *Transactional Analysis Journal*, 1974, *4* (3), 32–39.

Kahler, T., *Transactional Analysis Revisited*, Little Rock, Ark.: Human Development Publications, 1978, 259–260.

Karpman, S. B., "Fairy Tales and Script Drama Analysis," *Transactional Analysis Bulletin*, 1968, *7* (26), 39–43.

Levin, P., "The Cycle of Development," *Transactional Analysis Journal*, 1982, *12* (2), 129–139.

———, *Becoming the Way We Are: A Transactional Guide to Personal Development*. Berkeley: Transactional Publications, 1974.

McKenna, J., "Stroking Profile: Application to Script Analysis," *Transactional Analysis Journal*, 1974, *4* (4), 20–24.

———, *Us: Married, Living Together, Family, Friends*. St. Louis: Emily, 1978.

Miller, S., Wackman, D., Nunnally, E., & Saline, C., *Straight Talk*. New York: Rawson, Wade, 1981.

Phelps, S. & Austin, N., *The Assertive Woman*, San Luis Obispo, Calif.: Impact Press, 1975.

Phillips, R., *Structural Symbiotic Systems*. Private Printing, 1975.

Popper, K., *Conjectures and Refutations*. New York: Basic Books, 1963.

Prigogine, I., *From Being to Becoming*. San Francisco: Freeman, 1980.

Samuels, S., "Stroke Strategy," *Transactional Analysis Journal*, 1971, *1* (3), 23–24.

Satir, V., *Conjoint Family Therapy*, Rev. ed. Palo Alto, Calif.: Science and Behavior Books, 1967.

———, *People Making*. Palo Alto, Calif.: Science and Behavior Books, 1972.

———, *Self Esteem*. Millbrae, Calif.: Celestial Arts, 1970.

———, *Your Many Faces*, Millbrae, Calif.: Celestial Arts, 1978.

Saxe, J. G., "The Blind Men and the Elephant." In B. E. Stevenson, *The Home Book of Verse for Young Folks* (Rev. ed.), New York: Holt, 1943.

Schiff, A., & Schiff, J., "Passivity," *Transactional Analysis Journal*, 1971, *1* (1), 71–78.

Schiff, J. L., in collaboration with A. W. Schiff, K. Mellor, E. Schiff, S. Schiff, D. Richman, J. Fishman, L. Wolz, C. Fishman & D. Momb, *The Chathexis Reader: Transactional Analysis Treatment of Psychosis*. New York: Harper, 1975.

Seeman, M., "Alienation and Engagement," *The Meaning of Social Change*. In A. Campbell & P. E. Converse (eds.), New York: Russell Sage, 1972, pp. 467–527.

———, "On The Meaning of Alienation," *American Sociological Review*,

1959, (*24*), 7831–91.

Selye, H., *Stress Without Distress*. New York: New American Library, 1974.

———, *The Stress of Life* (rev.). New York: McGraw-Hill, 1975.

Sheldrake, R., *A New Science of Life*. Los Angeles: Tarcher, 1981.

Steere, D. A., *Bodily Expressions in Psychotherapy*, New York: Brunner/Mazel, 1982.

Steiner, C., *Scripts People Live*. New York: Grove Press, 1974.

———, *The Original Warm Fuzzy Tale: A Fairytale*. Sacramento, Calif.: Jalmar Press, 1977.

———, "The Stroke Economy," *Transactional Analysis Journal*, 1971, *1* (3), 9–15.

Zerin, E., "Authority and Autonomy," *Journal of Reform Judaism*, Winter 1982, pp. 25–30.

———, "Finishing Unfinished Business: Applications of the Drama Triangle to Marital Therapy," *Transactional Analysis Journal*, 1983, *13* (3), 155–57.

———, "The Four Racket Quadrants," *Transactional Analysis Journal*, 1980, *10* (1), 56–60.

———, "The "Q" Model," *Transactional Analysis Journal*, 1984, *14* (1), 48–62.

Zerin, E., & Zerin, M., "The Rabbi as Counselor," *Journal of Reform Judaism*, 1985 (Winter), 21–29.

THE "Q" MODEL COURSES OF INSTRUCTION

The "Q" Model courses are designed to meet multiple needs and are offered in a variety of formats and hours of instruction. Mental Health and Health Care Professionals, Business Executives and Middle Management Personnel, Educators and Clergy, Individuals, Couples and Families as well as those without psychological sophistication will find different courses and levels of instruction appropriate to their requirements. Many "Q" Model courses are also designed to meet the Family Advocacy, Social Actions, and Military Police needs of the Armed Forces.

In addition to providing useful Wellness, Prevention, and Education courses for the Management of Stress, there are special courses for Mental Health and Health Care Professionals that integrate into original diagnostic and treatment programs disparate Psychological Systems (Freud, Erikson, Mahler, Piaget among others), Family System Theories (Satir, Minuchin, Whitaker, Beavers among others) and Categories of the DSMIII.

The "Q" Model courses are available in three locations: 1) Westlake Village, California (within one hour of the Los Angeles International Airport), 2) at your location by invitation, and 3) Study Tours for Continuing Education.

For a catalogue of The "Q" Model courses and other courses of instruction, contact:

Zerin & Zerin
951 Westlake Boulevard, Suite #206
Westlake Village, California 91361
Telephone: (818) 889-3731